The South Asian Americans

The South Asian Americans

Karen Isaksen Leonard

THE NEW AMERICANS
Ronald H. Bayor, Series Editor

GREENWOOD PRESS
Westport, Connecticut • London

Library of Congress Cataloging-in-Publication Data

Leonard, Karen Isaksen, 1939–
The South Asian Americans / Karen Isaksen Leonard.
p. cm.—(The new Americans, ISSN 1092–6364)
Includes bibliographical references and index.
ISBN 0–313–29788–6 (alk. paper)
1. South Asian Americans. 2. Immigrants—United States.
I. Title. II. Series.
E184.S69L36 1997
305.891'4073—dc21 97–2219

British Library Cataloguing in Publication Data is available.

Library of Congress Catalog Card Number: 97–2219
ISBN: 0–313–29788–6
ISSN: 1092–6364

First published in 1997

Greenwood Press, 88 Post Road West, Westport, CT 06881
An imprint of Greenwood Publishing Group, Inc.

Printed in the United States of America

The paper used in this book complies with the Permanent Paper Standard issued by the National Information Standards Organization (Z39.48–1984).

10 9 8 7 6 5 4 3 2 1

Contents

Illustrations

MAPS

TABLES AND FIGURES

PHOTOS

Series Foreword

Oscar Handlin, a prominent historian, once wrote, "I thought to write a history of the immigrants in America. Then I discovered that the immigrants were American history." The United States has always been a nation of nations where people from every region of the world have come to begin a new life. Other countries such as Canada, Argentina, and Australia also have had substantial immigration, but the United States is still unique in the diversity of nationalities and the great numbers of migrating people who have come to its shores.

Who are these immigrants? Why did they decide to come? How well have they adjusted to this new land? What has been the reaction to them? These are some of the questions the books in this "New Americans" series seek to answer. There have been many studies about earlier waves of immigrants—e.g., the English, Irish, Germans, Jews, Italians, and Poles—but relatively little has been written about the newer groups—those arriving in the last thirty years, since the passage of a new immigration law in 1965. This series is designed to correct that situation and to introduce these groups to the rest of America.

Each book in the series discusses one of these groups, and each is written by an expert on those immigrants. The volumes cover the new migration from primarily Asia, Latin America, and the Caribbean, including: the Koreans, Cambodians, Filipinos, Vietnamese, South Asians such as Indians and Pakistanis, Chinese from both China and Taiwan, Haitians, Jamaicans, Cubans, Dominicans, Mexicans, Puerto Ricans (even though they are already U.S. citizens), and Jews from the former Soviet Union. Although some of these people, such as Jews, have been in America since colonial times, this series concentrates on their recent migrations, and thereby offers its unique contribution.

These volumes are designed for high school and general readers who want to learn more about their new neighbors. Each author has provided information about the land of origin, its history and culture, the reasons for migrating, and the ethnic culture as it began to adjust to American life. Readers will find fascinating details on religion, politics, foods, festivals, gender roles, employment trends, and general community life. They will learn how Vietnamese immigrants differ from Cuban immigrants and, yet, how they are also alike in many ways. Each book is arranged to offer an in-depth look at the particular immigrant group but also to enable readers to compare one group with the other. The volumes also contain brief biographical profiles of notable individuals, tables noting each group's immigration, and a short bibliography of readily available books and articles for further reading. Most contain a glossary of foreign words and phrases.

Students and others who read these volumes will secure a better understanding of the age-old questions of "who is an American" and "how does the assimilation process work?" Similar to their nineteenth- and early twentieth-century forebears, many Americans today doubt the value of immigration and fear the influx of individuals who look and sound different from those who had come earlier. If comparable books had been written one hundred years ago they would have done much to help dispel readers' unwarranted fears of the newcomers. Nobody today would question, for example, the role of those of Irish or Italian ancestry as Americans; yet, this was a serious issue in our history and a source of great conflict. It is time to look at our recent arrivals, to understand their history and culture, their skills, their place in the United States, and their hopes and dreams as Americans.

The United States is a vastly different country than it was at the beginning of the twentieth century. The economy has shifted away from industrial jobs; the civil rights movement has changed minority-majority relations and, along with the women's movement, brought more people into the economic mainstream. Yet one aspect of American life remains strikingly similar—we are still the world's main immigrant receiving nation and as in every period of American history, we are still a nation of immigrants. It is essential that we attempt to learn about and understand this long-term process of migration and assimilation.

Ronald H. Bayor
Georgia Institute of Technology

Preface

Contemporary immigrants can best be understood by learning about their social, political, and cultural history, from which they construct their individual histories, memories, and identities. Thus, chapter 1 of this book offers an introduction to South Asian history, culture, and politics. An overview of such a large area; so many diverse peoples, religions, and languages; and so many centuries of history can only be an exercise in selectivity and interpretation. Furthermore, almost every aspect of South Asian history—political, economic, social, and cultural—is fraught with controversy. Expanding the scope of this volume beyond immigrants from India to include all South Asian immigrants to the United States presents difficulties of inclusion and presentation. Although the first chapter is quite detailed, the rest of the book draws on it to demonstrate the continuing relevance of South Asian civilization to South Asians who have settled in the United States.

Many issues relating to South Asian migration and immigrants in the United States are controversial. Does the American political economy welcome or exploit South Asian immigrants? How do these immigrants perceive the American social, religious, and cultural landscape, and what contributions do they make to it? Do South Asian immigrant experiences and perceptions vary by national origin, by generation, and by gender? If so, how? Although I present my own point of view in exploring these issues, I have tried to give a fair idea of other views as well. I have drawn illustrative information more from West Coast sources than from elsewhere, owing to my location and the newspapers to which I subscribe, but I believe that the general trends apply across the United States. Moreover, there is a paucity of published materials on the smaller South Asian groups, which required me to do original field research in my own region on Afghans, Bangladeshis, Nepalese, and Sri Lankans.

I have tried to reach two audiences: non–South Asians who want to better understand South Asian immigrants in the United States, and South Asian immigrants and their descendants who want to better understand their ancestors and themselves. Materials that seem to me exciting, relevant, and necessary to those understandings are mentioned in the text, and readings that are likely to be readily available are recommended as well. I have followed popular usage in spelling non-English names and words; the latter are italicized and defined. Readers can also refer to the glossary.

ACKNOWLEDGMENTS

Many people helped me by providing information and encouragement—in particular, Rhonda Higdon-Loving, Ghaffar Mughal, Amelia Singh Netervala, and Dr. M. Padmini. Dr. Ram Mohan Roy directed me to some excellent sources. Those who read parts of the manuscript, and whose advice was usually followed, include Dr. Ausaf Ali, Veda Joshi, Mushir Khan, Dr. Pauline Kolenda, Dr. Bruce La Brack, Deeptha Leelarathna, Dr. Johanna Lessinger, Dr. Shampa Mazumdar, the Venerable Dr. Havanpola Ratanasara, I. K. Shukla, Dr. Hakam Singh, Inder Singh, Dr. Supriya Singh, L. B. Tilakaratne, Dr. Sylvia Vatuk, and Major Syed Zaidi. In addition, many editors and readers of Indian, Pakistani, Sri Lankan, Nepali, and Bangladeshi ethnic newspapers and newsletters submitted nominations for the section of Noted South Asian Americans. The embassies and consulates of Sri Lanka, Nepal, and Bangladesh provided helpful references. Cheryl Larsson at the University of California, Irvine, prepared the maps. Special thanks are extended to Deeptha Leelarathna of the *Sri Lanka Express*, M. Faiz Rehman of the *Pakistan Link*, Maheen Anderson, Wilma Chand, Isabel Singh Garcia, Veda Joshi, Dr. Hameed Khan, Dr. Shampa Mazumdar, Amelia Singh Netervala, Atiya Niazi, the Venerable Abbot Walpola Piyananda, Dr. Hakam Singh, and Rasheed Ul Haq for their photographs.

Finally I thank my son, Samuel, who endured piles of paper around the house for months, and my daughter, Sarah, whose writing skills helped polish some of the final manuscript.

1

South Asian Civilizations

DEFINITION, GEOGRAPHY, EARLY HISTORY

South Asia has a long and fascinating history. The geographic term generally includes the contemporary countries of India, Pakistan, Bangladesh, Sri Lanka, Nepal, and Bhutan. Afghanistan has some strong connections to South Asia but is often considered as part of the Middle East because of its equally strong connections to Iran and Central Asia. Some scholars include Burma because it once was part of Great Britain's colonial empire in South Asia, and others include Tibet because of its historical links with India over the centuries. In this book we exclude Burma and Tibet and barely mention Afghanistan and the Himalayan rim kingdoms of Nepal and Bhutan; we pay most attention to India, Pakistan, and Bangladesh (which together constituted India before 1947), and to Sri Lanka. Furthermore, most of our discussion pertains to India and Pakistan, because those countries have sent by far the largest numbers of immigrants to the United States and most of the available statistical material relates to them.

South Asia extends southward from the "Roof of the World": the great mountain ranges of the Hindu Kush, the Karakoram, and the Himalayas, which separate the Indian subcontinent from Central Asia and China. These mountains present a formidable natural barrier to the north, and the great Brahmaputra River and the mountains beyond it provide a natural frontier to the east. Important trade and travel routes crossed these frontiers (in particular, the Silk Road from China to Europe), but most newcomers entered India from the sea or through Afghanistan and the Khyber and Bolan passes.

Map 1
South Asian Nations, Rivers, and Mountains

Most often called Hindustan or India over the centuries, the subcontinent becomes a peninsula whose southern tip ends in the Indian Ocean, with the Bay of Bengal to its east and the Arabian Sea to its west. Just twenty miles southeast of India is Sri Lanka, the island formerly known as Ceylon. It has a fairly autonomous history but has had connections to the subcontinent through Buddhism, trade, and periods of South Indian and European colonial rule. The sparsely populated mountainous kingdoms of Nepal and Bhutan also have had intermittently significant connections with the rest of South Asia.

Within India, the broad river plain of the Ganges and its tributaries was the historic center of settlement in the north, and the Tamilnadu coastal plains were the earliest center in the south. The high Vindhya Mountains divide north from south India, and few kingdoms have reached across them. The languages fall into two major families: those in the north, probably of Central Asian origin, are termed Indo-Aryan (a branch of Indo-European); those in the south, of indigenous origin, are termed Dravidian. There are clusters of tribal peoples and languages as well, located within the rainy jungles of Assam in the far northeast and extending down through the central Indian hills and forests. The modern states within India and Pakistan have been formed along linguistic lines.

The earliest civilization in South Asia, the Indus Valley civilization, is in many ways still a mystery. Generally dated from 3000 to 1700 B.C.E., its extensive series of urban centers and villages was based on the five rivers (*panch ab*, or five waters: the Indus and its tributaries). The territory is now divided between Pakistan's Punjab state and India's Punjab and Haryana states. This civilization had so declined and faded from memory that until its rediscovery in the 1920s it was thought that Indian civilization began with the Aryan (speakers of Indo-Iranian languages) invasions into northwestern India from Central Asia and eastern Europe. The Aryans brought the Sanskrit language and the earliest sacred texts of Hinduism (the Vedas), giving an apparently North Indian Sanskritic and Vedic foundation for all subsequent religious developments.

However, when the archaeological remains of the Indus Valley cities of Mohenjodaro and Harappa were discovered in 1921, and then the hundreds of towns and villages of their hinterland, scholars realized that this civilization not only predated the Aryans in South Asia but had reached a level the Aryans did not attain until at least 600 B.C.E. This stable, highly centralized society had a broad agricultural base and trade reaching to Mesopotamia, and it persisted for over a thousand years. It was a literate society, but the pictographic script has not yet been deciphered. In fact, the script, most often

Map 2
Languages and Administrative Divisions

found on clay seals whose exact use is not known, cannot be assigned conclusively to any major language family. Some scholars argue for a Dravidian origin of the Indus Valley language, thus linking that civilization with an indigenous (now South Indian) population in the subcontinent, but their argument is not widely accepted. The origin of the Indus Valley script has important implications for modern Indian politics, given current questions about the origin and dates of the Aryans (Ratnagar 1996), the South Indian non-Brahman movements against Brahmans, and the imposition of Hindi (a northern vernacular) as India's offical national language.

Whatever the origin of the early Indus Valley people, there is no denying the sophistication of their civilization. The cities were carefully laid out on a rectangular plan and had excellent sewage and sanitation systems. The housing, with its regular gradations in size and number of rooms, suggests that there were different socioeonomic classes. The bigger cities had large water tanks with small cubicles attached to them. We do not know whether the cubicles were changing rooms for bathing or dwelling rooms for priests who presided over purification rituals at the tanks—perhaps analogous to those at Hindu temple tanks centuries later. Similarly, images on some of the clay seals suggest gods, goddesses, and practices that are typical of later Hinduism. The favorite example is that of a horned god with erect penis surrounded by animals. Is this a proto-Shiva, Lord of the Beasts in later centuries? Until the script is deciphered, such interpretations remain highly speculative.

The ending of the Indus Valley civilization is as mysterious as its origin, because scholars can point to no obvious cause for its decline. Major climactic changes may have undercut the agricultural base, or floods or epidemics may have decimated the population. There is some continuity in the potteries typical of the area, although by the time the Aryans arrived the earlier civilization was only a shadow of its former self. There is no good evidence of direct contact with the Aryan incursions (e.g., Aryan conquest of the Indus Valley cities) in archaeological remains or in early Vedic texts.

However, there is no doubt about the next stage of historical development: the incursion of the Aryans and the preeminence of the Brahman caste in religious developments in South Asia from about 1500 B.C.E. on. South Asian history used to start with these nomadic horsemen, who spoke an Indo-Aryan language and brought a priestly elite that recited from the Vedas at sacrificial rituals. The sacred Sanskrit texts of early Brahmanism were preserved by oral recitation for a thousand years and were finally written down around the sixth century B.C.E., when the Aryans began building cities in northern India. Kingdoms can then be traced from various archaeological remains and the coins struck by kings, and to some extent from the great Hindu epic tales, the Mahabharata and the Ramayana. However, these epics and other Sanskrit texts are poor historical sources. There are no individual authors or dated portions of the voluminous texts, and the early standardization of Sanskrit grammar means that chronology cannot be determined from internal comparisons. The content, also, is largely mythological and difficult to relate to figures and events for which historical material exists.

RELIGION AND SOCIETY

Three great religions of South Asia—Hinduism, Jainism, and Buddhism—arose in the Ganges Valley during the sixth century B.C.E., a time of urbanization, political conflict, and social instability. Teachers and seekers after truth developed the grand ideas of classical Hinduism, Buddhism, and Jainism. Hinduism had no single historical founder, not even a series of designated founding figures, and there have always been many points of view within the Hindu tradition. The recitation of Vedic hymns accompanied and sanctified ritual sacrifices, but the Vedas included little speculation about the origins of the universe or of humans and the purpose of human life. By the sixth century B.C.E., however, Hindu philosophers and teachers were developing powerful new concepts to address these mysteries. Among their central ideas were that men sought knowledge of the Brahman (the Supreme Being and ultimate reality) and that the individual self and the universal soul (*atman* and Brahman) were identical, were one. They wrote about *samsara*, the cycle of life, death, and rebirth; about the transmigration of the soul from one life to another; and about *karma*, or actions, which determined one's present status and which could impede or help one's progress toward salvation or liberation. Liberation (*moksha, mukti*, or *nirvana*, release from the cycle of reincarnations) could be won by carefully adhering to one's *dharma*, or duty according to one's station in life. One's station in life varied according to one's age, gender, and marital status—and, in Hinduism, one's caste.

Jainism and Buddhism did have historical founders: Mahavira and Buddha, who were born in 599 and 563 B.C.E., respectively. Both were Kshatriyas (i.e., they were from the king or warrior caste category) and both became ascetics, or renouncers of worldly life. Mahavira was the twenty-fourth and last in the line of Jain teachers. Siddhartha Gautama, the Buddha (the Awakened One), was a royal prince who left his palace to seek experience and understanding of the world. Although their ideas flourished in interaction with those elaborated in Brahmanical texts, they probably represented a reaction to Brahmanical orthodoxy of the time. Jainism and Buddhism also had concepts of *samsara* and *karma*, of disciplines to enhance meditation, and of ascetic renunciation of worldly commitments. Both developed monastic orders, but Buddhist monks lived in retreats or monasteries, and Jain monks more often stayed with lay families.

Jain and Buddhist beliefs differed from Hindu beliefs in important ways. First, they denied the authority of the Vedas, producing instead their own sacred texts (the Buddhist canon in the Pali language was almost immediately established in Sri Lanka). Second, they opposed the caste system, emphasizing the possibility of salvation for all men and women through disciplined acts and meditation. Third, both relied to some extent on Brahman priests for the performance of domestic life cycle rituals, but Buddhism emphatically rejected sacrificial rituals. Jainism stressed nonviolence (*ahimsa*) to all living beings (a category that extended to include trees, stones, soil, and the like), and Jains went to great lengths to avoid harming any living being. Buddhists sought to understand the causes of suffering in the world and worked toward release from the cycle of reincarnations, seeking understanding and progress through their own experiences and avoiding extreme mortification of the body (fasting, painful postures and practices). The Buddha, in early teachings not a divine being but a guide to fellow humans, stressed moderation and right actions, "turning the wheel of *dharma*" to achieve *nirvana*.

In the many strands of Hinduism, *dharma* (religious duty) was related to a caste system based on ranked categories, the *varnas*. *Varna* can be translated as category, order, or color; and the traditional four *varnas* provide a model of the caste system. They reflect broad occupational groupings: the Brahmans, or priests and scholars; the Kshatriyas, or warriors and rulers; the Vaisyas, or merchants; and the Sudras, or artisans, peasants, and workers. One was born into a *varna*—or more accurately into one of the literally thousands of *jatis*, birth-groups or functioning castes (which theoretically could be sorted out into *varnas*)—and marriages were arranged within caste. A fifth *varna*, that of the Untouchables, was very much part of the conceptual and practical system but seldom found a place in Vedic writings. In fact both the Sudras and Untouchables, along with the women of all castes, were barred from hearing or studying the Vedas. For the males of the three upper *varnas*, there was a four-stage life cycle in which boys first became celibate students of the Vedas, then married and became householders, then retired partially from family life to meditate and study, and finally became religious mendicants or *sanyasis*, leaving the constraints of family and caste roles to follow their individual paths to salvation.

The prohibition on women, Sudras, and Untouchables studying the Vedas reminds us that the caste hierarchy was also based on concepts of relative purity and pollution. Thus, the Brahmans were at the top because they were purest, pure enough to intercede with the gods on behalf of others. They knew Sanskrit, avoided intoxicating foods such as meat and liquor, and neither took food from nor ate with members of lower castes; they arranged their children's marriages at an early age to guard against mixed-caste progeny and prohibited divorce and the remarriage of widows. The Untouchables were at the bottom because they worked with and ate polluting substances. Untouchable jobs included disposing of human excrement, washing dirty clothing (even menstrual cloths), cutting off and disposing of body hairs, delivering babies and cleaning up the blood of childbirth, disposing of dead human and animal bodies, and making leather products from animal skins. Women ranked below men in all castes because they could not prevent the bodily production of polluting substances, such as blood from menstruation and childbirth.

Whether one's explanation of caste stressed occupational complementarity or concerns of purity and pollution, it had a coherence and logic for those within the system. One's place depended on performance of *dharma*, and one could achieve salvation through a series of increasingly higher births and rebirths. Thus, socioeconomic inequality in the world was explained and justified, and individuals could look to the future with hope.

This fundamental assumption of inequality by birth also underlies Hinduism's openness to many ways of achieving salvation. In early Hinduism or Brahmanism, the emphasis was on knowledge (*jnana*) and ritual actions (*karma*), paths to salvation best followed by higher-caste men who could study the Sanskrit texts and carry out rituals and actions in the world. But over the centuries a third path, that of devotion or faith, was made accessible to all people, even to women and those of low caste. This *bhakti* path recognized the differential capacities of persons of various castes, genders, and stages of life as they sought liberation. *Bhakti* first appears in the Bhagavad Gita, a poem written between 200 B.C.E. and 200 C.E. and part of the Mahabharata epic. Great southern Indian teachers and poets in Tamil and Telugu from the sixth century C.E. initiated major devotional movements that swept throughout India for the next several centuries, incorporating women and members of all castes into new kinds of devotional worship in temples and other new settings.

These *bhakti* movements did have founding figures and focused on one or another form of the divine. As worship practices shifted from sacrificial rituals mediated by Brahmans to personal devotions focusing on a particular form and name of the Brahman, certain all-India gods and goddesses assumed great prominence. Most sectarian movements can be classified as Vaishnava (focused on an *avatar*, or form of the god Vishnu), or Shaiva (focused on a form of the god Shiva), or Shakta (focused on a form of the goddess Devi). Visual contact with the divine, the receiving of *darshan* (sacred sight or blessing) from an image or a living *guru* or saint, became a crucial part of devotional worship (and did not require literacy); poetry and music were often used to explore and enhance experiences of divinity. All images or idols are viewed as representations of the abstract concept of Brahman, made more accessible and comprehensible by multiple forms and names. In *bhakti* worship the images are installed, cared for, and worshipped not only in homes but in temples and other settings, yet Hindu worship remains primarily an individual rather than a congregational experience, a one-to-one relationship with a personal deity.

The Hindu openness to multiple paths and forms of the divine has been one of the religion's greatest strengths, aiding its expansion throughout the subcontinent. In a process of interaction and synthesis, local gods, goddesses, and ritual practices were incorporated into the expanding Aryan religion. The incarnation of Sanskritic divinities in many forms (gods, like people, could be reborn again and again) legitimized regional gods or goddesses as forms of the great all-India divinities, bringing new devotees to the growing body of beliefs and practices now called Hinduism. Thus, the regional Tamil goddess of the southern Indian town of Madurai could take the name of Minakshi, wife of Shiva and sister of Vishnu, and become part of an all-India pantheon of great gods and goddesses.

It would be a mistake to think of Hinduism as an organized religion, brought into the subcontinent and spread systematically by priestly Brahmans who controlled and benefited from its expansion. The idea that Hinduism is a single structured religion arose quite recently, in the nineteenth century. "The Hindus" used to mean those people living on or beyond the Sindhu or Indus River, a designation given by the Greeks and Persians. The Persians called India "Hindustan" (land of the Hindus), so there were Hindus before there was Hinduism, in a sense.

The numerous and diverse religious beliefs and practices in South Asia now grouped together as Hinduism have not been governed by any centralized authority over time. There was no certifying body to declare one belief or practice orthodox and another heretical. Texts and teachers debated points of view but rarely stated that theirs was the only way. One was a Hindu if one was born into a Hindu family and caste; as long as one recognized the authority of the Vedas as revelation, the choices of personal deity and particular practices were an individual matter. Even the social control of the caste system could be escaped by becoming a *sanyasi* (a person entering the fourth stage of life beyond caste and family control to pursue salvation by teaching, meditating, and living on the charity of others). Women, Sudras, and Untouchables could become *sanyasis* too, because the only requirement was acceptance and initiation by an existing *sanyasi.*

The Brahmans may have ranked at the top of the religious and ritual hierarchy, but those who controlled the land had power over others in all of South Asia, and non-Brahmans were more often the landowners in the countryside. Brahmans traditionally worked as family priests, temple servants, or custodians of smaller shrines and pilgrimage sites—they were essentially dependent on others for their employment. Members of the dominant castes (a term given by anthropologists to those who controlled the land and its produce) employed members of other castes as field laborers, carpenters, goldsmiths, oilpressers, barbers, leatherworkers, and so on, building political alignments among villages, towns, and regions. Tension between religious and secular power has long characterized South Asian society, but it was ultimately the king who enforced *dharma* in society. Kings employed and patronized Brahmans in political systems all over South Asia, and Jain and Buddhist as well as Hindu rulers fulfilled this role.

The dynamic interplay between religion and society—between the principles governing state, caste, gender, and family roles as cross-cutting determinants of social action—can be seen in the playful *Tales of Ancient India* (Van Buitenen 1959). These Sanskrit stories demonstrate the spread of South Asian cultural values throughout the subcontinent, from Kashmir in the far north to the extreme south and beyond to Sri Lanka and southeast Asia.

Buddhism and Jainism lost importance in India as the *bhakti* sectarian movements revitalized Hinduism. Many of these focused on Krishna, probably the most popular among Vishnu's forms, or Rama, another of Vishnu's forms and the hero of the Ramayana epic. Stories linked the gods and goddesses to natural sites such as rivers and mountains, elaborating a sacred geography of ritual and pilgrimage sites throughout India. Another major impetus for the expansion and consolidation of Hinduism came with Sankara's definitive formulation and popularization of the Advaita (nondualistic) Vedanta philosophy, one of six major "schools" or philosophical views. Sankara probably lived in southern India in the eighth century C.E., and he traveled widely in India, institutionalizing his teachings by founding four (or five) regional monasteries. By the eleventh and twelfth centuries A.D. Buddhism was vanishing from its Indian homeland, developing three distinct strands (Mahayana, Hinayana or Theravada, and Tantric or Thunderbolt). Sri Lanka became the home of Theravada Buddhism, the version closest to the austere original teachings of the Buddha, and Sinhalese Buddhism became closely linked to political rule there. Other reasons for Buddhism's decline in India were the socioeconomic strength of the caste system in peasant life and a widespread belief that the Buddha was an *avatar* of Vishnu. (Islam and Christianity in India also have been unable to escape the pervasive influence of caste.) In contrast to Buddhism, Jainism continued to be professed by small numbers of merchants and traders who married within their castes and followed a strictly vegetarian diet, functioning rather like a caste in the broader context of Hindu society.

Whether early kingdoms were ruled by Hindus, Buddhists, or Jains, South Asian rulers traditionally tolerated or encouraged all forms of religion within their territories. Individual kings might have personal preferences, and occasionally a state might briefly favor Shaiva or Vaishnava temples and religious specialists over others, but the royal role was that of patron and mediator rather than promoter of one dominant religion. The legendary King Asoka of the Mauryan dynasty, who reigned in the third century B.C.E., is best remembered among the early kings. Known as the cruel conqueror of Orissa on the eastern frontier, the king whose armies killed thousands of people, Asoka converted to Buddhism and turned against war. He extended peace and patronage to all within his empire, and it is his lion-headed capital (i.e., pillar) that appears as India's national seal today.

Even Asoka's rule, however, barely extended to southern India, where the developing regional cultures differed markedly from those in the north. The next great all-India empire, that of the Mughals over a thousand years later, also failed to reach much of the south. Temples that are stylistically distinctive from those in the north towered over the southern cities and towns, and it has been argued that greater stability and a resulting greater Brahmanical orthodoxy have characterized southern India. The caste composition shows a striking lack of indigenous Kshatriyas and Vaisyas, with Brahmans, Sudras, and Untouchables making up the bulk of the population. Also demonstrating historical Brahman dominance of religious and literary culture, the Dravidian languages show marked differences between the classical written languages (which were heavily influenced by Sanskrit) and the spoken, modern vernaculars of today.

Differential cultivation, caste, and kinship practices in north and south mean that even today, gender relationships also are somewhat different. Northern agriculture is based on the cultivation of wheat by men with draft animals and ploughs, whereas in the more tropical south the irrigation-based cultivation of rice involves women more actively in the agrarian economy. Northern diets rely on wheat and more meat is eaten, whereas southern diets rely on rice and meat-eaters are fewer. Marriage within caste had maintained the hierarchical caste system in both north and south until quite recently, and kinship systems in both north and south are generally patrilineal and patriarchial (except for certain matrilineal groups in Kerala); but in the south, marriage within a circle of close relatives (such as uncle-neice marriage) is encouraged, so that marriage within one's own village is common. Thus, young women can marry men whom they already know and need not be sent out of their home villages. Kinship systems in northern India generally prohibit marriage within several degrees of relationship, and village exogamy (i.e., marriage outside one's own village) prevails. Thus, young women in the north generally marry strangers and reside with their husband's family, away from their parents and acquaintances.

The sex ratio in the south is more favorable to women, with equal numbers of women and men or slightly more women (the demographic norm). In the north there is a system of arranged marriages with nonrelatives in other villages; there is also a higher incidence and amount of dowry (i.e., payment of goods and money when a daughter gets married). These customs have made daughters an economic liability and have led to a higher proportion of males than females in India's northern populations. This has been achieved less by female infanticide (i.e., the killing of baby girls) than by differential health care for daughters and selective abortion. Afghanistan and Pakistan have even less favorable sex ratios for women. There, the adverse effects of economies based on plough agriculture and/or the seclusion of women have been worsened by low female literacy and lack of population planning (resulting in high female mortality in childbirth and greater female child and infant mortality). Nepal and Bhutan, with marriage systems featuring both polyandry and polygyny (i.e., multiple husbands and wives) based on land shortages and shifting cultivation, and Bangladesh and Sri Lanka, with more tropical rice cultivation systems involving women's labor and better literacy, show more balanced sex ratios.

MUSLIM RULE AND MUGHLAI CULTURE

The next great rulers in South Asia firmly established a major new religion and civilizational tradition in the subcontinent. The expansion of Islam beyond Saudi Arabia after the death of the prophet Muhammad in the seventh century C.E. sent traders, soldiers, and missionaries to many lands, including India. The growing diversity within the young religion was reflected in its spread abroad, as Sunnis, Shias, and Sufis all became part of South Asian civilization. Sunni Muslims—winners of the battle for succession to the leadership of the community at Karbala, Iraq, in 682 C.E.—are the majority in India as well as in the Muslim world generally. Shias—the followers of Muhammad's grandson Husain, who was killed at Karbala—constitute a substantial minority of South Asian Muslims. The Sufi orders—brotherhoods within Sunni Islam following a distinctively mystical path—also are well represented in India. Charismatic missionaries whose beliefs and practices were similar to those of devotional Hinduism, Sufis brought many Indian peasants to Islam or to some mixture of Hindu and Islamic elements in the Indian countryside, particularly in Bengal and Sind.

Muslim traders were the first to come. Arab traders had been establishing depots and contacts up and down India's western coast since the eighth century C.E. Entire Hindu trading castes became Muslim in Sind and along the Malabar (Kerala) coast. (Zoroastrian or Parsi traders and refugees, worshippers of the sacredness of fire, also came to western India around the seventh and eighth centuries C.E., fleeing persecution in newly Muslim kingdoms in Central Asia and Iran.) After 1000 C.E., Turkish and Afghan warriors came through the Khyber Pass and ruled parts of northern India, establishing administrative systems tested by Mongol rule in Central Asia and elsewhere. In the southern or Deccan plateau, Shia Muslim rulers of Iranian ancestry established several sultanates that incorporated indigenous non-Muslims at all levels.

In the sixteenth century C.E., Babur, a young warrior from Central Asia who was descended from two world conquerors, the Turk Timur (Tamerlane) and the Mongol Genghis Khan, swept down into the northern Indian plains and founded the Mughal empire in 1526 A.D. Babur, his son Humayun, and (after a brief Afghan interlude) his grandson Akbar conquered Indian rulers or made alliances with them to establish a powerful new state. Akbar's rule began in 1556. He was followed by his son Jehangir, his grandson Shah Jahan, and his great-grandson Aurangzeb, whose rule ended in 1707. The Mughals employed many Muslim immigrants from Iran, Turkey, and Central Asia and also recruited heavily from the indigenous population. Persian, the courtly language most esteemed in the Muslim world, became India's new central administrative language, and all aspiring officials learned it. Mongol and Turkish royal rituals instituted in Delhi were copied all over India. Numerous Hindu rulers became titled nobles at the Mughal court, commanders of military forces, collectors of the land revenue in designated territories, and sometimes givers of daughters in matrimonial alliances.

For some two hundred to three hundred years, Mughlai or Indo-Muslim civilization reigned supreme at courtly and urban centers in much of India, incorporating elements of the earlier civilizational patterns. In the northwest and the Indus Valley, Islam swept over formerly Buddhist and Hindu regions, pushing Buddhism eastward into Tibet, China, and other Asian countries. Impressive mosques, forts, palaces, gardens, and tombs combined Hindu and Mughal architectural elements to dominate the cities and towns of north India. Preceding Mughal rule in central India, the Deccani sultanates had begun patronizing a new vernacular language, Dakhni or Urdu, the language of the military camp. Most often written in the Arabic or Persian script, Urdu's grammar was based on that of the Indo-Aryan vernaculars, but much of its vocabulary came from Persian. Developing further in northern India,

Urdu became the common language throughout the Mughal empire, although the court language, the official language of administration, remained Persian until well into British days. Other arts—painting, music, dancing, jewelery, metalwork, cooking, and so on—flourished in combination with indigenous styles and practices.

The expansion of Mughal power and the growing number of Muslims in South Asia brought even greater diversity to the population and introduced lasting controversies into South Asian history. Mughal rulers, like other rulers, established themselves primarily through military conquest, but Islam was not forced on Indians at the point of the sword, nor did most South Asian Muslims originally come from elsewhere. Only a small proportion of South Asian Muslims—in 1947 about a third of the subcontinental population was Muslim—actually came from outside South Asia; most are descended from indigenous ancestors who converted to Islam. No doubt some converted because of the impressive military victories of the new rulers and for opportunistic reasons. But Islam offered much to Hindus in low-caste positions, for it proclaimed (and to a large extent practiced) the equality of all believers. The new religion emphasized literacy and learning for all its adherents, and the Sufi saints and preachers roamed the countryside, establishing centers close to the peasantry and using music and poetry to enhance emotional commitment to the new faith. In Bengal and perhaps elsewhere, the extension of settled agriculture proceeded under Muslim rulers, so that Islam was readily adopted as the religion of an advancing civilization (Eaton 1993).

Muslim and particularly Mughal policy toward non-Muslims varied by ruler and time period but was generally benign. The population was overwhelmingly non-Muslim, but the emperor and many in the ruling class were Muslim. Yet there was no sustained or systematic attempt to convert the non-Muslim population or subject it to the *jizya* (a tax to be collected from nonbelievers), perhaps because the empire relied heavily on non-Muslim officials. There were certainly episodes of persecution—for example, the raids of the Afghan, Mahmud of Ghazni, who looted temples and destroyed the Somnath temple in Kathiawar, Gujarat, in 1025 A.D. The most notorious episodes involve the last great Mughal emperor, Aurangzeb, who turned against Hindus, Sikhs, and Shia and Sufi Muslims, destroyed some Hindu temples, and attempted to enforce collection of the *jizya* on non-Muslims late in his reign.

Sometimes an emperor acted against or in favor of certain high-caste Hindu practices. Akbar and Aurangzeb both tried to outlaw the (rare) Hindu practice of *sati*, which involved the burning of a widow on her husband's funeral pyre; and Akbar discouraged dowries, the arrangement of marriages at an early age, and the prohibition of remarriages for widows. Akbar favored Hinduism by abolishing the taxes on religious pilgrims that the state traditionally collected at all pilgrimage sites; and he banned the slaughter of cows, honoring the Hindu reverence for the cow that had replaced the early Aryan practice of beef-eating.

The Mughals functioned like earlier and later South Asian rulers, collecting the land revenue and recruiting allies, military commanders, and nobles and officials at all levels from the population they found in India. Conflicts at the Mughal court reflected Sunni-Shia (or Turkish-Irani) and Sunni-Sufi rivalries more than Muslim-Hindu ones. The Mughals continued many essentially Hindu traditions, using sacred Ganges water for their drinking water, giving *darshan* to their subjects. Hindu rituals were observed in the emperor's harem by his Hindu wives and mistresses. Many sons and grandsons of Akbar—including his successors Jehangir, Shah Jahan, and Aurangzeb—were descended from Hindu wives, Rajputs from the great ruling families of Rajasthan who were allies in empire. The great emperors patronized religious and artistic specialists and diverse institutions (although Aurangzeb turned against music and musicians in 1668, in an anti-Sufi move). The emperor Akbar and other Muslim nobles and scholars took an active interest in Hinduism, having Sanskrit texts translated into Persian and consulting Brahmans about their meanings. Akbar himself initiated a new religion at his court combining beliefs and practices from the religions known to him, including Christianity. Akbar's great-grandson Dara Shikoh (who lost the throne to his brother Aurangzeb in 1658) was even more appreciative of Hindu philosophies.

Islam and Hinduism contrasted in many ways. Islam tried to control and enforce among Muslims the central core of beliefs and practices set out in Allah's revelation to Muhammad (i.e., the holy Quran), whereas the boundaries of Hindu belief and practice were extremely flexible and often unmarked, much less policed. The early practice of Aryan animal sacrifices had waned and vegetarianism was highly esteemed by Hindus, whereas Muslims practiced animal sacrifices and ate meat (but not pork). Hindus sought knowledge and experience of the one all-pervasive divine force that had many forms, names, and images, whereas Muslims sought to obey an all-powerful Allah who did not take other forms and could not be represented in images.

Islam, like Brahmanism earlier in India and all religions everywhere, inevitably both influenced and was influenced by its societal context. Some Muslim practices in South Asia have strong Hindu overtones of concern with purity and pollution, and some life-cycle observances, such as weddings, are like those of the surrounding Hindu society. Previous caste practices survive in many endogamous Muslim groups, despite their reorientation to Mecca as the direction of prayers and the goal of pilgrimage. Indian Muslims adopted many kinds of South Asian dress and food, sometimes even avoiding beef out of deference to their Hindu neighbors.

On the other hand, the uncompromising monotheism and passionate egalitarianism of Islam spurred new religious developments in India. Great poets such as Kabir and Nanak in fifteenth- and sixteenth-century northern India spoke out against religious distinctions, against caste, and against images, rituals, and the outward markings of religious faiths. The latter, Guru Nanak, laid the basis of the Sikh faith in the Punjab; and the nine gurus who followed him deepened the Sikh sense of themselves as a community separate from both Muslims and Hindus. The Sikhs contested later Mughal political authority in the Punjab and then fought the British as well, staking territorial claims and developing their own sacred sites, notably the Golden Temple in Amritsar. But other religious sites continued to be shared. The shrines of Sufi teachers and saints are visited by Muslims and Hindus alike, and Muslim musicians hold hereditary positions in some of India's greatest Hindu temples (i.e., the shrine of Lord Viswanath in Benares, the most sacred of Hindu cities on the Ganges).

Another controversial topic is that of the position of women in Hindu and Muslim societies. Adherents of each major religion tend to blame the other for the South Asian pattern of seclusion of high-status women and their subordination to men. Muslims point to the influence of Hindu purity and pollution practices that constrain high-caste women, restricting their movement or employment outside the household, prohibiting divorce and remarriage, and encouraging *sati* (the word means "virtuous woman"). Some Hindus maintain that the seclusion of women, perhaps even the practice of *sati*, developed under Muslim rule to protect Hindu women from the conquerors. But historical developments within Hinduism and Islam (and in other world religions, for that matter) adequately explain women's subordination. In both religions, early examples of strong, learned, independent women gave way over time to patriarchal and patrilineal societies based on economic systems that restricted women of high caste and class to domestic production, the bearing of children, and work within households. In both, religious law (the Brahmanical Dharmasastras and the Islamic Sharia) reinforced the dependence of women on men and their legal subordination to men in various ways. In both, the male monopoly of religious scholarship and leadership helped institutionalize beliefs and practices based on different and complementary roles for women and men. (And in both religions, gendered beliefs and practices have been subsequently changed by men and women in accordance with changing societal conditions.)

COLONIALISM AND ITS IMPACT

Mughal rule was followed by British rule in much of South Asia. By the early eighteenth century, the power of the Mughals in Delhi declined and that of the western Indian Maratha rulers increased, and regional Mughal governors such as those in Hyderabad, Bengal, and Oudh became independent of Delhi. External powers also began to impinge on South Asia. The expansion of European seaborne trade brought private companies to India's coasts and to Ceylon. The Portuguese landed in Goa on India's western coast in 1498 and in Ceylon in 1505; they began ruling coastal Ceylon in 1594, coexisting with the central Buddhist kingdom of Kandy and the northern Tamil kingdom of Jaffna. In 1658 the Portuguese lost Ceylon to the Dutch; and in India, too, the Dutch, French, Danish, and British private companies were being drawn into South Asian politics. When battles for succession to Mughal appointments took place, the French and British companies took opposite sides. European-trained Indian troops (*sepoys*) and European-made military weapons revolutionized military conflicts, making the Europeans desirable as mercenaries or allies. All over the subcontinent, political and financial actors took note of the rising power of the British. In 1757, when the East India Company's Robert Clive captured Calcutta, his allies were Hindu bankers and a Mughal general. Confirmed by the Mughal emperor in Delhi as revenue minister of Bengal, Clive "stood forth as Diwan [revenue minister]," and a new era began in South Asian history.

But the full impact of British colonialism was not felt until the nineteenth century, as British rule crept over much of the subcontinent (and took Ceylon from the Dutch in 1795). At first, the continuities between Mughal and British rule were striking. East India Company officials learned the Mughal system and continued its administrative and judicial practices for many decades, retaining Persian as the language of administration until 1830. Company officials initially accepted Mughal titles and attended the Mughal court. A school was set up in Calcutta to teach indigneous languages, and Company officials learned about Hinduism and Indian Islam.

As the British struggled to implement the land revenue and judicial systems, they began to change them, with momentous consequences for Indian society. The Permanent Settlement of Bengal in 1793 fixed land revenues in perpetuity and was meant to create clear titleholders to land and make land a saleable commodity (thereby bringing India closer to Britain's developing capitalist economy). One result was that those given titles could not pay the high and nonnegotiable land revenue (the Mughals had taken less and negotiated more). Thus, the control of agrarian production shifted to new castes and classes. British rule empowered new people in the countryside and cities alike, as ambitious Indians reoriented themselves to the new rulers. In Calcutta, Madras, and Bombay a new political culture arose.

In some respects comparable to the earlier extension of Mughal rule and Mughlai culture, this new political and literary culture eventually extended throughout the subcontinent. But British migration to India was minuscule compared to earlier Muslim migrations, and the Christian religion made little headway there compared to Islam. In fact, the East India Company prevented Christian missionaries from entering its territories for as long as it could. There were already small numbers of Christians in India (and Jews, in Travancore and Bombay). St. Thomas may have died near the tip of southern India in the first century C.E.; there were Nestorian or Syrian Christians on the Kerala coast by the third century C.E.; and there were small Christian enclaves in Portuguese Goa (south of Bombay) and French Pondicherry (south of Madras). But officials believed that missionary activity would disrupt the Company's trade (as well as the private fortunes many of them were making on the side), and only in 1813 did the British government force the Company to open its territories to missionaries, as a condition of renewal of its charter to trade in the east. Missionaries had campaigned vigorously for this. They argued that the Company represented a Christian nation, yet it profited from a cruel and pagan religion by collecting a pilgrim tax at the temple to the great Jagannath (Lord of the World, an *avatar* of Vishnu) in Puri, where some pilgrims were crushed to death under the huge wheels of the god's processional chariot. Their campaign brought the word *juggernaut* into the English language.

Another charter provision forced on the Company by the British government concerned education, a benefit the Company was expected to confer on India's "natives." The consequences of the establishment of educational facilities were far greater than those of the admission of missionaries—although the two were related, because the main achievement of Christian missions turned out to be the development of Western-style educational institutions in India. In fact, here we confront most directly the issue of "Orientalism," of Western and colonial stereotyping of South Asian civilizations, and indeed of the impact of Orientalism on South Asians themselves. The shaping of Indian minds by the English language and Western education still lingers, and its enslaving or liberating effects are vigorously discussed and debated (Nandy 1983; Chatterjee 1986, 1993).

Britain's perceptions of India and its relationship to India were changing

(Suleri 1992). Early officials might have adapted themselves to Mughlai administration and culture or become fascinated with the orderly Brahmanical model of society revealed by Sanskrit texts, but as European commerce and industry fed imperialist ventures abroad, the "otherness" of the East loomed larger. By the time Company officials seriously took up their obligation to provide education to India's indigenous people, admiration for India's earlier Brahmanical and Mughlai civilizations had turned to ignorant contempt. In 1830, English displaced Persian as the language of administration, and this was followed by decisions about the provision of education to Indians. Thomas Babbington MacCaulay's "Minute on Education" of 1833 to the East India Company argued that Western literature was far superior to that of the East, and the Orientalists who had favored the promotion of Indian learning lost to those who favored Western learning. Even so, the content of Western education could have been taught in indigenous languages, but the decision was to teach in English, to achieve MacCaulay's goal of producing "a class of persons, Indian in blood and colour, but English in taste, in opinion, in morals and intellect" who could usefully serve the Company.

Forced to allow missionary activity and promote education, the Company still tried not to interfere with indigenous religions. It resisted setting policies against *sati* or in favor of widows' remarriage or minimum ages for marriage or sexual intercourse ("the age of consent" issue), despite educated Indians' requests to act on these issues. Finally, pushed by Bengali social reformers, the Company outlawed the performance of *sati* in 1829, and Indian social reformers pushed for action on related issues. But in mid-century the Company's apprehensions proved well founded, for Indian perceptions of interference with religion did contribute to a major rebellion against the East India Company.

This first great movement against British rule, known as the Sepoy Mutiny or the First War of Independence, came in 1857. Unrest had become widespread as English control tightened throughout India. Rumors of Christian missionary activity swept through the newly recruited Indian military units, and the immediate cause of their rebellion was the issuing of new cartridges for the Enfield rifles that allegedly were greased with both beef and pork fat, thereby requiring both Hindus and Muslims to pollute themselves as they bit off the cartridge caps for firing. The uprising drew in feudal rulers because the Company was taking "native states" under direct rule, refusing to recognize heirs according to Hindu inheritance law. The Nawab of Oudh in Lucknow, northern India, and the Rani of Jhansi, in central India, became leaders of the uprising; and as it spread, the aged Mughal emperor in Delhi was persuaded to become its nominal leader.

By 1858, however, a strong British counterattack was under way, aided by the recently established telegraph service and newly opened Suez Canal. Delhi fell to the Company in 1858, with terrible consequences for the city and its inhabitants. Both Indians and British committed such atrocities in 1857 and 1858 that memories of them disturb relations between Indians and British to this day. The last Mughal emperor, Bahadur Shah, was exiled to Burma, where he died many years later, far from his beloved city of Delhi.

After 1857, the British Crown stepped in and India became a colony of Great Britain. The remaining princely or native states were left unannexed, so the subcontinent was a patchwork of British direct rule (by British officials) and princely rule (by Indian rulers). In the third of the subcontinent that never came under direct British rule, British Residents (agents appointed to advise Indian rulers) controlled external relations, ensuring that British hegemony filtered into the princely states. Because of the Mughal emperor's assumption of leadership in 1857, anti-Muslim prejudices led to some British favoring of Hindus, and the final setting aside of the Mughals also produced some Muslim resistance to British systems of education and employment.

Right after the 1857 uprising, three institutions of higher education were initiated in India—in Delhi, Calcutta, and Bombay—capping a system of English education beginning with primary schools. The effects of this were far-reaching, because Indians, often multilingual, proved excellent students. Moreover, they worked for the British Raj (colonial government in India) at its lower levels and pushed for advancement into the Indian Civil Service (ICS), which was set up after 1857 by the British government of India. But unlike earlier Mughal recruitment, British recruitment only recognized merit up to certain levels, and then Indians met a thinly disguised racial barrier. Indians could only be "subalterns," or subordinates—in the British army, subaltern was the rank below that of captain. An influential school of historical interpretation spearheaded by Indians has taken its name (the Subaltern School) and its mission (to uncover or reconstruct the history of those denied voices, power, and self-definition) from this fact and from current theoretical work (Guha 1994).

Entrance to the higher level of the ICS (or "steel frame") of British Indian administration was very competitive. One had to pass an examination administered only in England itself, a requirement that was difficult for most Indians to meet. The exam had to be passed before the age of 22; and because Indians generally counted age from conception, they were "older" and had less time to qualify than the Englishmen. Also, the exam included horseback riding and other skills learned by the British but not necessarily by the Indian upper classes at the time. The few Indians who did join the ICS could not always withstand the isolation and prejudice they experienced on the job. In

1900, of the 900 top positions filled by recruitment in Britain, only 12 were held by Indians. The situation was not much better at the end of the colonial period, when there were some 2,000 such positions.

Even after India was annexed by the Crown and came directly under Parliament and a secretary of state for India—in 1858 the governor-generals of Company days gave way to the viceroys of the Raj, and in 1876 Queen Victoria was proclaimed Empress of India—there was little investment in India's economic infrastructure, and little concern with its industrialization or the welfare of its population. The government invested when the cost was low and the returns were immediate (e.g., in the building of roads, railroads, and irrigation canals) but did not invest much in sanitation systems or public works, which would have benefited the public at large. Technological advances such as the postal and telegraph system aided the maintenance of law and order and the flow of commerce. Schools directly supported by government were far fewer than those given small grants-in-aid and run by missionaries and Indian educators.

Finally, British colonial administration, particularly the judicial system and the taking of the census, emphasized certain British understandings of Indian society and contributed to new Indian understandings of their own society. To administer justice, the Mughal practice of applying religious and caste customary laws to members of the various communities was followed, but the British codified and standardized Hindu law on an unprecedented scale. They sought the advice and interpretation of Brahmans in this task, thereby orienting all Hindu inheritance, marriage, and family law toward Brahmanical norms. Not only was the model a high-caste one, but multiplicity was reduced in the drive for uniformity, and emphasis was given to the larger religious categories of Muslim and Hindu instead of to the many smaller categories within and across those labels.

Similar results came from the decadal (once every ten years) taking of a census from 1871 (undertaken in India before Britain). The caste system had struck early British administrators and missionaries as highly unusual and significant, and when the census was inaugurated caste was an important question on the schedule. The administrators used the census to elicit details of language, religion, caste, and family and household composition. Because the census volumes listed castes under *varna* headings and often in hierarchical order, castes that were placed "incorrectly" began to organize and petition British officials to reorder the listings. Caste associations were formed, often reflecting new leadership by members of the educated elite and covering larger areas than those under traditional headmen or elders.

Such activities emphasized caste ranking and competiton among castes, as well as among religions groups. The descriptions compiled for some communities' beliefs and practices showed that they could be listed as Muslim or Hindu or Sikh, and there was pressure to conform to one or another. Moreover, census numerical totals by religions led to the designation of "majority" and "minority" communities. The British mapping and publication of the caste and religious composition of India, region by region, heightened awareness of these collectivities and encouraged organization and competition on the basis of those memberships in new ways. Whether or not this was deliberate "divide and rule" tactics or simply the result of new undertakings and technologies, the effect was a consciousness not only of difference but of demographic advantage or disadvantage.

All over South Asia, the end of the nineteenth century saw the initiation of voluntary associations in cities and towns by Western-educated young men. Some of them sought to represent caste interests to the government, and others sought to carry out religious or social reforms within their communities. Among the Muslims, Sir Sayyid Ahmad Khan was an Islamic modernizer and the founder (in 1875) of Aligarh Muslim University. Religious and social reform efforts often focused on the position of women, because missionaries and colonial officials frequently used the "status of women" as a measure of social progress and ranked South Asian values and behaviors concerning women below those of the West. Some reform associations promoted the education of women, or, in high-caste communities that prohibited it, the remarriage of widows. Because men and women tended to be segregated within the higher castes and classes, women students needed women teachers; and because women were considered to perform complementary but different roles in society, girls' schools needed a domestic science curriculum. Despite these limitations, education for girls became socially acceptable and steadily increased.

In Bengal, the British colonial culture valued Western rationality and discounted indigenous knowledge and practices, producing the first of many reform movements. The brilliant scholar Raja Ram Mohan Roy founded a religious and social reform movement, the Brahmo Samaj. This "rational" Hinduism without images or castes exerted powerful influences in Bengal and elsewhere, but in the end it became an endogamous community, almost a caste itself. The Arja Samaj in western India (also anti-caste but a revivalist movement, turning back to Vedic beliefs and practices) had more of a mass impact. Both movements enhanced the position of women through education and participation in rituals. But despite considerable rhetoric about the remarriage of widows, this reform remained a largely abstract ideal—even for most Hindu reformers who advocated it at the end of the nineteenth century. Exceptions were Mahadev Govind Ranade, a Maharashtrian Brahman who married a widow, and Viresalingam Pantulu, a Telugu Brahman college teacher who recruited some of his students to marry young virgin widows and performed the marriages himself.

Educated Indians sought greater opportunities in government, seeking positions in the ICS and participation in municipal, district, and provincial government. The British response was slow, reflecting the attitude that Indians must first prove themselves "qualified." In the 1860s some Indians were nominated to various boards and councils, then some were indirectly elected, and finally in the early twentieth century some were directly elected to municipal councils and provincial legislative councils. Only educated and middle-class Indian men were allowed to vote, and certain areas of government were reserved for British officials.

At the beginning of the political reform movement, educated Indians politely requested greater inclusion in government, sending small delegations and petitions to British officials. The Indian National Congress, founded in 1885 by an Englishman and an elite group of Indians, followed this model for many years, holding an annual conference to pass resolutions. The annual dues were high, the membership was small, and the language of meetings and communications was English. In 1907 a small group of educated Indian Muslims, convinced that its community had special interests, formed the Muslim League, which proceeded in much the same way. In 1909, when direct elections to municipal, district, and provincial bodies were conceded, the British provided separate electorates for Muslims—a proportion of the seats was reserved for Muslim candidates and voters. Because of this decision the British have been accused of trying to "divide and rule," and certainly it helped produce the partition of 1947, the splitting of British India into independent India and Pakistan.

The political scene changed dramatically with the return of the lawyer Mohandas Karamchand Gandhi from South Africa, where he had begun not only a legal practice but a political career. Born in Gujarat in 1869, Gandhi had been schooled in England and then worked in South Africa, where his opinion of British colonial rule shifted radically. There he led ordinary Indian merchants and workers in civil disobedience movements for political goals. When he returned to India in 1915, he brought new ideas and tactics to the Indian National Congress movement. Gandhi argued against the hegemony of Western rationalism and the English language, asking that Hindustani be used and drawing on indigenous concepts and issues to mobilize mass support. Gandhi talked about *satyagraha* (an insistence on truth, or "truth force"), *ahimsa* (nonviolence), and *swaraj* (self-rule), ideas that resonated with ordinary Indians. He dressed simply in handwoven cotton and asked his fellow Indians to give up imported clothing that had been manufactured in English factories; he talked about reviving handicrafts, and he gave out spinning wheels so that people could spin their own cotton. He drew Muslims and Hindus together, making support of the Islamic Caliphate in Turkey an Indian National Congress party issue during World War I (thus supporting Turkey against Britain).

Above all, Gandhi was a brilliant political strategist. He reorganized the Congress party in 1920, setting very low membership dues and devising a many-layered structure based on linguistic provinces (anticipating the linguistic states of independent India). This transformed the Congress party from a gentleman's club into a nationalist movement with a mass base. Gandhi's campaigns focused on issues of exploitation or unfair taxation of Indians, such as the plight of indigo plantation workers or the British tax on salt. When Gandhi led the Salt March in 1930, simply walking to the sea to gather salt, the British arrested and jailed 60,000 people. Gandhi drew women into the nationalist movement, as leaders and in the front lines of nonviolent demonstrations. He renamed Untouchables *Harijans*, or children of god, and worked to abolish most forms of Untouchability. (However, in 1932, when the great Untouchable lawyer Bhimrao Ramji Ambedkar pressed for separate electorates for Untouchables, Gandhi fasted to prevent it, saying that as Hindus they would be lovingly included in the larger community.) His unexpected and highly successful ideas and tactics won over other leaders of the Congress, including Motilal Nehru and his son Jawaharlal Nehru, and Gandhi became known as Mahatma, the Great Soul. Always, he assumed and appealed to a British sense of justice and fair play, confounding British administrators in India and politicians in Britain as well.

Successive British government commissions and conferences moved toward a devolution of power, and all parties began to debate the details of the future government. In 1928 the Congress party committed itself to the abolition of Untouchability, providing votes for women, and advocating Hindustani (the script unspecified) as the national language—but not to providing separate electorates for Muslims. The Muslim lawyer Mohamed Ali Jinnah, a long-time worker for Hindu-Muslim unity, left the Congress and went to England at this time because of the latter two decisions; he also disliked Gandhi and his insistence on nonviolence.

Jinnah returned to India in 1935 but not to the Congress. He became a leader of the Muslim League, which was beginning to put forward the idea that Hindus and Muslims were two nations, not one. When Britain's Government of India Act in 1935 offered a federal structure and elections in

1937, Jinnah became permanent president of the Muslim League and campaigned hard. However, the League lost heavily in the elections, doing well only in the Muslim-minority areas and not in the Muslim-majority provinces of the Punjab, Bengal, Sind, and the Northwest Frontier.

Jinnah then reorganized the League along the lines of Gandhi's 1920 Congress reorganization, fashioning a mass-based party and mounting vigorous campaigns in Muslim areas. Himself a markedly secular person with a Parsi wife, Jinnah called for an Islamic homeland to be based in the areas where Muslims were a majority. Playing on Muslim fears of living under a majority Hindu government, he called for a *Pakistan* (i.e., a land of the pure), a concept proposed in 1930 by the great Urdu poet and modern Muslim philosopher Dr. Muhammad Iqbal (the name "Pakistan" was coined somewhat later by a student at Cambridge). In the 1945 elections the League won decisively, capturing all seats set aside for Muslims but failing to form ministries in the Punjab and the Northwest Frontier, key Muslim-majority areas whose support was needed to form Pakistan. A frustrated Jinnah failed to convince the British cabinet mission of 1946 that Britain should "divide and quit"; the mission recommended instead a union of provincial and princely units and specified an interim government based on political party representatives. When the Indian National Congress failed to act decisively on this plan, Jinnah and the League went back to their demand for Pakistan and called for a "direct action" day on August 16. The unspecified "action" was to be a departure from constitutional means; when the event took place, there were bloody killings in Calcutta and beyond, with Hindus and Muslims both involved in rioting. Persuaded by the impressive Muslim League victories of 1945 and the August 16 militance, the British moved to partition India and grant independence quickly. Also contributing to this move were the facts that (1) an exhausted Britain was emerging from World War II under a new Labor government, which favored independence for India, and (2) a little-publicized but violent mutiny took place in the Indian navy in 1946. Recalling the 1857 uprising (the Sepoy Mutiny mentioned earlier in this chapter), the British government realized that it was not willing to hold even the Crown Jewel of British colonies at any cost.

INDEPENDENCE AND NATION-BUILDING

In 1997 and 1998, most of the South Asian nations will commemorate fifty years of independence from British colonial rule. On August 14 and 15, 1947, with very little advance planning and preparation, Pakistan and India gained independence. In 1971, Pakistan split into Pakistan and Bangladesh.

Sri Lanka became independent of Great Britain in 1948. Nepal, Bhutan, and Afghanistan were always independent nations, although Afghanistan fought off a Russian intervention from 1979 to 1989 and is still in a state of civil war. The last fifty years have seen significant changes in South Asia, some of which prompted immigration to the United States. Table 1.1 summarizes current conditions in these South Asian countries, and the following discussion highlights issues of concern to South Asian immigrants in the United States.

Pakistan, Bangladesh, and India

The partition of India into India and Pakistan in 1947 took place amid rioting and large-scale violence. Despite valiant efforts by the departing Viceroy Lord Louis Mountbatten, Governor-General Mohamed Ali Jinnah in Pakistan, and Prime Minister Jawaharlal Nehru (and citizen Mahatma Gandhi) in India, the transfer of power was far from peaceful. More than half a million lives were lost and at least 13 million people became refugees, as Muslims left India for Pakistan and Hindus and Sikhs left Pakistan for India. Prior to independence, inadequate provision was made for the accession of many of the 562 princely states to India or Pakistan (only 11 fell within Pakistan's new boundaries). This oversight was particularly unfortunate for the two largest of these states, Hyderabad and Kashmir. Hyderabad, a Hindu-majority state with a Muslim ruler located in the middle of India, was taken into India in 1948 by Indian military action. Kashmir, a Muslim-majority state with a Hindu ruler located in the mountainous regions to the north of both Pakistan and India, was ceded to India by its maharajah in October 1947. Confusion, controversy, and violence marked both transfers, and in both cases appeals to the United Nations were subsequently dropped or resulted in unimplemented resolutions. The Kashmir issue has sparked two wars between India and Pakistan and may still be unresolved.

Pakistan has had the more difficult time. Its two halves were geographically separated by 1,500 miles of Indian territory, and the difficulties of integrating the western and eastern populations could not be overcome by a common religion. Tensions focused on languages and the settlement of the incoming refugee population. The Bengali speakers in the east and the Punjabi, Sindhi, Baluchi, and Pushtu speakers in the west agreed reluctantly that Urdu (Hindustani in Urdu script, which was the language of most refugees coming from India to Pakistan) should be the national language. The refugees from India, called *muhajirs* (refugees or exiles), played major roles in the early decades of Pakistan's formation: they brought money and considerable ex-

Table 1.1
Socioeconomic Measures: South Asian Nations, 1994

	Square Kilometers	Population	Life Expectancy (years)	Percentage Literate: Male & Female	National Product Per Capita ($)	Total Fertility Rate	Percentage of Population, Age 0–14
Afghanistan	647,500	21,251,821	45	29: 44 & 14	NA	6.21	42
Bangladesh	144,000	128,094,948	55	35: 47 & 22	1,040	4.39	40
Bhutan	47,000	1,780,638	51	NA	700	5.39	40
India	3,287,590	936,545,814	59	52: 64 & 39	1,360	3.40	35
Nepal	140,800	21,560,869	53	26: 38 & 13	1,060	5.15	43
Pakistan	803,940	131,541,920	58	35: 47 & 21	1,930	6.35	44
Sri Lanka	65,610	18,342,660	72	88: 93 & 84	3,190	2.08	29

Source: Central Intelligence Agency, *The World Factbook 1995* (Washington, D.C., 1995).

pertise in administrative, military, educational, and business arenas. The city of Karachi on the southern coast developed rapidly into the new nation's financial and administrative capital under *muhajir* leadership, but later a new city, Islamabad, was developed in the center of the country as the national capital.

Early efforts at democracy were followed by long periods of military rule. Jinnah died suddenly in 1948 before giving a clear idea of the proposed parliamentary democracy or its Islamic dimensions, and the constitution produced in 1956 was set aside by martial law from 1958 to 1962. At that time a new constitution and presidential government was tried, until martial law was imposed again from 1969 to 1971. Political power rested with those in western Pakistan, and most development occurred there. Pakistan aligned itself with the United States against the Soviet Union, accepting economic and military aid. Even though elite families grew rich and the country's per capita income rose, economic gains were not distributed throughout the population. The more populous eastern half functioned like a colony of the west, and its educational and industrial development was neglected. Elections were held again in 1970 but produced a victory for the East Pakistan Awami League, a victory the western politicians and the Pakistani army refused to honor. Instead, the army was sent to East Pakistan. The liberation war of 1971, with India's help, produced the new nation of Bangladesh.

Bangladesh is 83 percent Muslim and 16 percent Hindu. Bengali is its national language. Under a secular, democratic, and socialist constitution at first, the impoverished young People's Republic succumbed to military rule in 1975, and secularism and socialism have given way to an emphasis on Muslim identity and integration into the world capitalist system. Elections in 1996 brought some stability, but the annual flooding of the rivers (which usually brings prosperity) can be unpredictable and sometimes threatening. The level of poverty has been lifting slowly, and Bangladesh remains heavily dependent on foreign aid. Bangladesh has a good educational infrastructure; in fact, education, public health, and the general status of women are now better there than in the former West Pakistan. But per capita income is low, unemployment is high, and the astounding population density (over 2,300 people per square mile, according to Harris 1996) causes many young men to seek work in the Middle East, Malaysia, Japan, South Korea, Singapore, and elsewhere. Bangladeshi migration to the United States consists largely of educated (intermediate or college, 12 or 14 years of schooling), unmarried young men between 20 and 30 years of age, although there is also a component of highly educated professionals.

After 1971, the Islamic Republic of Pakistan experienced five years of

"Islamic socialism" under Zulfiqar Ali Bhutto and the Pakistan People's Party (PPP), winners of the 1970 election in the west. Then General Zia ul-Haq reimposed martial law in 1977, and Mr. Bhutto was arrested and executed. Under Zia, the influence of Islamic parties and Islamic law increased. Just as he was proclaiming elections to return Pakistan to civilian rule, Zia was killed in a plane crash in 1988. Bhutto's daughter Benazir and the PPP, the largest but not the majority winner in the 1988 elections, formed a government and remained in power until 1990. The first woman elected to head a Muslim country, Benazir Bhutto was returned to power again from 1993 to 1996. The military remains a powerful player in politics, although at present from behind the scenes.

Vigorous political competition has not helped solve Pakistan's problems. Corruption is widespread, the rural areas and lower classes have benefited little from development, and literacy may actually be declining as the population rapidly increases. These problems undermine the nation's earlier economic progress, as does the need to support many thousands of Afghan refugees who fled to neighboring Pakistan when the Soviets entered Afghanistan in 1979. International relief agencies help with this burden, but the Afghans have brought an escalating culture of guns and drugs into Pakistan, adding to the ethnic and linguistic antagonisms already active in the country. (Small kingdoms and chiefdoms in northern and western Pakistan have only recently been incorporated into the country, and they are not always under central government control.) In Karachi, for example, intermittent problems of law and order are so severe that military control must be imposed, as Sindhis indigenous to the region compete for control of the city with the *muhajirs*, incoming Pathans, and other internal migrants. The general deterioration of socioeconomic prospects in Pakistan is producing several streams of emigrants. Many professionals and workers go temporarily to the Middle East; many young people who are sent abroad for education, as well as educated professionals taking job opportunities in the United States, Canada, and Australia, often end up emigrating permanently.

India has remained a secular parliamentary democracy, the largest democracy in the world. The introduction of a constitution (written by Ambedkar) in 1951 and the long historical development of the Congress party have helped maintain stability—in fact, the party stayed in power for almost all of India's first fifty years. The problems of poverty and population growth are being steadily overcome through industrial and agricultural modernization and through the expansion of literacy and public health measures. The early years of courageous nonalignment and neutrality have made India a leader of the Third World, but it has always maintained a strong military establishment (and has fought three wars with Pakistan). More recently, border tensions with China and the collapse of the Soviet Union in 1991 have pushed the country more toward trade and political agreements with the West. India made major changes in its economic policy in 1991, and development measures show that these changes have been positive in many ways. Also, literacy is steadily rising and fertility is falling. But the results of the free market reorientation are controversial, and income differentials may be increasing.

India has faced potentially divisive problems posed by religious, linguistic, and caste differences. The partition did not solve what South Asia calls a "communal" problem, a problem between religious communities (in India, chiefly between Hindus and Muslims). An early victim was Mahatma Gandhi, assassinated in 1948 by a Hindu who thought Gandhi was favoring the Muslims. Many Muslims left India for Pakistan, but about 13 percent of India's population today is Muslim; and on the whole the Muslims are poorer and less educated. A major cause of prejudice against them is the retention of Muslim personal (customary family and community) law. The Constitution of 1951 guarantees freedom of religion, but it also sets the goal of a uniform civil code for all citizens. India did undertake sweeping reforms of Hindu personal law in the 1950s (including Sikhs, Buddhists, and Jains as Hindus), but Muslim personal law remains politically untouchable, although many argue that it is unjust to women and outmoded in other respects. The Urdu language is another problem, now seen as a Muslim language and the vehicle of Muslim identity. Because Muslim Urdu-speakers are scattered throughout India, Urdu does not have a state of its own (as do India's other major vernaculars) and its survival is harder to ensure.

The more immediate problems center on Kashmir and on rising Hindu communalism. The possibility that renewed militancy in Kashmir could cause yet another war between India and Pakistan puts pressure on all Muslims within India. Kashmir is important to both India and Pakistan, for winning it seems necessary to validate each nationalist movement—India needs to keep it to justify its claim to be a secular state, and Pakistan needs to get it to fulfill its claim to Islamic statehood. Many of India's Muslims have relatives in Pakistan and are suspected (unfairly) of being sympathetic to the idea of a separatist or pro-Pakistan Kashmir. To all these issues must be added the surge of neo-Hinduism or Hindu communalism that occurred during the 1990s. The Hindu communalism promoted by the Bharatiya Janata Party (BJP) led to the illegal and violent demolition of a sixteenth-century mosque in northern India in 1992; the BJP wants to "rebuild" an alleged earlier temple there, on what is said to be the birthplace of the Hindu god Rama. This incident has been a rallying point for Hindu nationalists and represents a powerful threat to India's secular goals. The neo-Hindu movement gathers funds and support from Hindus overseas, including many who find new value in their religion as a basis of identity in the United States.

Language has also been a divisive force. Hindi (Hindustani in Sanskrit-derived script) was declared India's official national language, but its imposition was resisted and delayed by Dravidian-speakers in the south to whom it is just as foreign as English. English has remained an associate language at many levels, and under a "three-language formula" students are required to learn Hindi, their mother tongue (usually the state language, or another vernacular if Hindi is their mother tongue), and English. The States Reorganization Commission of 1956 redrew colonial administrative boundaries along linguistic lines, recognizing the importance of mass education in the mother tongues for participation in a democracy. However, India's elites and others still value an English education. (Among Asian immigrants to the United States, the South Asians stand out for their excellent English language skills.) Only now, in the 1980s and 1990s, are India's universities gradually switching over to vernacular mediums of instruction, and only now are Indians who do not speak English well becoming politically dominant in state and federal legislative bodies. The United Front government of Prime Minister Deve Gowda, which took office in 1996 (a broad coalition against the BJP), marks the first real departure from control by the Western-educated elites from the higher castes and classes.

The third divisive force is caste. Indeed, India has attacked its inheritance of societal inequalities quite directly. On the one hand, the Constitution rules out discrimination on the basis of caste; but on the other, it provides for a quota system of compensation for past injustice. Lists or schedules of Untouchables and Other Backward Classes (the Scheduled Castes and Tribes, and OBCs) have been drawn up, and qualified members of these groups are allocated land, scholarships, places in schools, and places in government service. At least 30 percent of the Indian population falls into these categories, with considerable regional variation. Untouchables are diffused throughout every village and town in India, always lowest in social status and almost always lowest in economic status as well. Their numbers and integral roles in local society make them important voting blocs. Tribals generally form small clusters in remote areas, and they are being pulled into the expanding societies around them. Because the census no longer records their previous religious category (animist), they have become officially Hindu. The numerous tribal languages, spoken by over 12 million people, are becoming extinct. Only in areas of the northeast such as Assam—where they are numerous, well educated, often Christianized (therefore with international allies), and mounting armed insurgencies—are they considered politically important.

Despite India's official stance against caste, the system of compensatory discrimination and reserved seats has acquired a dynamic of its own. (Reserved seats are not separate electorates, but seats for which parties are required to put up certain types of candidates for whom the general electorate will vote—for example, the 1996 coalition government is proposing 33% reserved seats for women.) Conversion among Untouchables to Buddhism, Islam, or Christianity means loss of access to quotas, and this has strengthened the Untouchable movement. Particularly in South India, the Brahman dominance of education and government service has been reduced, causing an emigration of Brahmans. The Mandal Commission's 1990 recommendations to raise minority quotas to over 40 percent led a few higher-caste students to commit suicide, and the recommendations remain unimplemented by the Centre. But certainly as an increasing share of resources being directed away from the higher, traditionally literate castes, the emigration of well-educated professionals from India is bound to increase.

Caste is no longer a census category in India, so changes in caste composition cannot be measured, but it remains a significant force in Indian life. Caste still regulates many economic relationships in rural India (fully 75% of India is rural), and caste is important in modern politics because of appeals to "vote blocs" and the selection of candidates on that basis. The erosion of high-caste power has been slow but steady. Even on the domestic front, where arranged marriages within caste reinforce the old system, intercaste and intercommunity marriages of all kinds are no longer unusual in urban areas.

In the 1990s, religious conflicts are more threatening to Indian national integration than is casteism. A militant Sikh separatist movement based in the Punjab has been overcome, but the neo-Hindu movement is potentially very explosive. Some Hindus (who constitute 80% of the population) seem to see Muslims, a poorer and less-educated minority, as a privileged group to be resented and even feared. It is ironic that Muslims who rejected the two-nation theory and remained within secular India are now regarded as a nation within India by members of the majority population who originally opposed the two-nation theory.

Afghanistan, Sri Lanka, Nepal, and Bhutan

The other four nations in South Asia have had diverse political trajectories in the last fifty years. Nepal and Bhutan have remained isolated but dependent on good relations with India. Afghanistan and Sri Lanka have interacted significantly with Pakistan and India, respectively. Afghanistan's border with Pakistan stretches for almost 1,000 miles. Its majority Pushto- or Pakhtun-speaking population extends into Pakistan's northwestern frontier areas, but traditional enmities persist between the two countries. Afghanistan's rulers fought off British Indian invasions in the middle and late nineteenth century and again in the early twentieth century, as Britain engaged in a "Great Game" with Russia in Central Asia. More recently, the Soviet Union and the United States competed to supply aid to the Afghans, and the Soviet Union invaded Afghanistan in 1979 but was forced out in 1989. Outside interest in Afghan politics (on the part of the Soviet Union, the United States, Pakistan, and India) has intensified the jockeying for political power within Afghanistan, and the situation remains unstable almost a decade after the Soviet departure. Refugees (perhaps one-third of the Afghan population has fled, mostly to Pakistan) are one result of the continuing instability.

Sri Lanka, too, has lasting historical legacies, particularly from its ties to British colonial India. Home to both Tamil- and Sinhala-speakers, the island has most often been united under Sinhalese Buddhist rulers since a Sinhalese king defeated a Tamil king in 101 B.C.E. In later centuries, parts of Sri Lanka were ruled by the Portuguese, Dutch, and finally the British. Ultimately becoming independent of Britain in 1948, Sri Lanka has moved rapidly from a plantation economy to a socialist welfare state and, after 1977, to a free market economy, achieving growth despite escalating disparities and serious internal conflicts.

Ethnic antagonisms have complicated the sharing of power in the island. The dominant group is Sinhalese Buddhist, with Tamil Hindus and Christians making up almost 20 percent of the population. There are also smaller groups of Muslims (Tamil-speakers), Burghers, and Malays. Soon after independence, most descendants of the Tamils brought from India in the mid-nineteenth century by the British as plantation laborers were unable to become citizens (legislation required three generations of paternal ancestry in Ceylon and proof of income or property). The 1956 declaration of Sinhala as the national and official language also provoked conflict, and Tamil was subsequently recognized as a national language in the northeast. In the 1960s, some 400,000 stateless Tamils were repatriated to India and others were given citizenship, but many were left in legal limbo and became refugees. The Tamils have sought greater autonomy within Sri Lanka, and after terrible rioting in Columbo in 1983 the escalating violence has sent Tamil refugees to India and elsewhere. An Indo–Sri Lankan accord in 1987 brought Indian peace-keeping forces to the island, but conditions have worsened since their departure in 1990.

Sri Lanka was the first country in Asia to implement universal suffrage (in

1930, even before gaining independence), and it has conducted nine elections since 1948. Majority rule through a parliament was replaced in 1978 by a presidential system that concentrates power in the hands of an executive president. There have been political assassinations and major insurrections by leftists and by Tamils. Although similar actions have occurred in the rest of South Asia, perhaps because Sri Lanka is such a small country they have obscured the considerable achievements of this young nation. It has been a generous and successful welfare state. Literacy rates are about 90 percent, life expectancy is 72 years, there is free medical care, and the birth rate has dropped significantly. Education has been free since the 1940s, resulting in a large number of educators and professionals. However, per capita income is low, the gap between rich and poor is widening, and unemployment and underemployment are high. Many Sri Lankans are leaving the country to seek better or safer opportunities elsewhere. Sri Lankan workers and housemaids are numerous in the Middle East, and the United States has gained outstanding scientists and educators who were fully trained in Sri Lanka.

Nepal is located on the northern fringes of South Asia between India and China. It was the only Hindu monarchy in the modern world until 1990, when the royal family inaugurated multiparty constitutional government. A pillar erected by the emperor Asoka over two thousand years ago marks Buddha's birthplace in southern Nepal. Most Nepalese are Hindus, many are Buddhists, and many are both. Linguistically, Indo-Aryan languages and Tibeto-Burman languages mingle, and the people are diverse. Independent kingdoms in the Kathmandu Valley were unified under the Shah dynasty in the late eighteenth century. After losing a war with the British in 1817, Nepal regained some territory for supporting the British in 1857, but its kings lost control to hereditary prime ministers (the Ranas) in the 1840s and only regained supremacy with India's help in 1951 (relations with India remain highly important). The reigning king, Birendra, has long welcomed international development aid and advisors. Experiments with limited forms of democracy began in 1958; now the king is head of state, but a prime minister and a largely elected bicameral legislature hold executive power. Because internal communications and transport are hindered by difficult terrain (ranging from a lowland almost at sea level to the highest mountain in the world, Mt. Everest), Nepal depends heavily on tourism, but this has brought serious environmental problems. Members of the elite and the royal family continue to be educated in India and abroad, but there are few emigrants.

To the east of Nepal across a small slice of India, the Buddhist kingdom of Bhutan remains relatively isolated. The country is culturally close to Tibet (and therefore China) but politically close to India. Bhutan was a British protectorate from 1911 and after 1949 became an Indian protectorate. Roads to India were built in 1960; there are none to China. The official language is Dzongka and the majority of the population are Bhotias, both Tibetan in origin. Since King Jigme Singye Wangchuk came to the throne in 1972, the subsistence agricultural economy has been supplemented by limited and highly priced tourism. Internal political conflict has caused a large number of refugees of Nepalese origin to leave Bhutan for Nepal, but very few Bhutanese migrate to the United States.

Of Special Note

Some general points should be made about common American perceptions of the South Asian nations that send immigrants to the United States today. The first concerns the prominence of women political leaders in South Asia. Among the explanations for this are the traditions of female power, or *shakti*, and the great goddesses—important elements among the many beliefs that constitute Hinduism. But there are other, more familiar, explanations. Sri Lanka had the first woman head of state in modern times: Prime Minister Mrs. Sirimavo Bandaranaike, from 1960 to 1965 (after her husband, Prime Minister S.W.R.D. Bandaranaike, was assassinated) and also from 1970 to 1977. Mrs. Bandaranaike became prime minister again in 1996, and the president (now the more powerful position) is her daughter Chandrika Kumaratunge. India, Pakistan, and Bangladesh have also had women heads of state. Indira Gandhi (the daughter of India's first prime minister, Jawaharlal Nehru) was herself prime minister from 1966 to 1977 and again in 1980, but she was assassinated in 1984 to avenge her sending of the Indian army into the Golden Temple of the Sikhs in Amritsar. (She was trying to put down the militants agitating for a separate Sikh Khalistan, or "land of the pure.") In Pakistan, Benazir Bhutto (daughter of the executed former prime minister, Zulfiqar Ali Bhutto) has twice been prime minister, from 1988 to 1990 and again from 1993 to 1996. (Before her, Mohamed Ali Jinnah's sister Fatima had run unsuccessfully for the presidency in 1964.) In Bangladesh, Sheikh Hasina (daughter of the independence leader Sheikh Mujibur Rahman, who was assassinated in 1975) took over in 1996 from the widow Khaleda Zia, prime minister of Bangladesh from 1991 to 1996. (Zia's husband, Captain Ziaur Rahman, had been president of Bangladesh for a time prior to 1990, when Bangladesh changed from a presidential to a prime ministerial system.)

All these women were closely related to leading male politicians, and until quite recently this could be said of women political officeholders in the United States as well. The involvement of more ordinary women in politics owes much to the notion that political parties should nominate certain proportions of women to increase their representation in public life. In fact, the prevailing ideologies in both South Asia and the United States have been strongly patriarchial. Both India and the United States have established compensatory discrimination programs for women as well as minorities, and their records with respect to women's suffrage and the participation of women in politics have been astonishingly similar (Katzenstein 1978). However, South Asian nations are clearly ahead of the United States in terms of women holding top political positions.

Another conspicuous feature of South Asian migration to the United States is the bringing of relatively new religions to America: Hinduism, Buddhism, and Islam. Islam is about to become the second largest religion in the United States, after Christianity. These religions have long histories in South Asia, and their interrelationships were generally characterized by peaceful interaction and tolerance of religious diversity. In fact, Western religious history has been marked by far more violence. But long political traditions of even-handed rule have been forgotten as more recent religious conflicts have taken center stage in some South Asian countries. Headlines in the U.S. press often emphasize these conflicts or the "exotic" aspects of religion in South Asia, but South Asian religions have already contributed much to the United States. The nonviolent politics grounded in Jainism, Hinduism, and Buddhism and pioneered by Mahatma Gandhi has not always prevailed within India or Sri Lanka, but its moral, religious, and political relevance has been obvious to African Americans and other people throughout the world. The equality of all believers within the Muslim world community also attracts many in America.

Finally, there are fundamental commonalities between U.S. and South Asian nation-building efforts. The problems "back home" in South Asia are not so different from those the immigrants encounter in the United States. Nationalist movements against colonial rule have led to post-independence struggles to institute varying forms of democracy in India, Pakistan, Bangladesh, and Sri Lanka. Like those in the United States, these struggles try to bring about unity in diversity. With its far longer sweep of history, the diversity has been even greater in South Asia, and the new national boundaries reflect some attempts to deal with that issue. In fifty short years the South Asian nations have become different from each other, but their people are still dealing with problems from the past.

As at home, South Asians find poverty, unemployment, and prejudice in the United States. Here, too, the government is concerned with the rights of minorities and programs of compensatory discrimination, educational standards, the role of language (the national language and the mother tongues), and other issues related to race, class, ethnicity, and gender. The intervention of world powers in South Asia continues today, somewhat less overtly than in the past, through the workings of the global economy. People within South Asia work for companies based outside their borders, and South Asian workers and professionals alike have become international and transnational migrants, working and settling abroad. We turn now to their histories in the United States.

REFERENCES

Chatterjee, Partha. 1986. *Nationalist Thought and the Colonial World: A Derivative Discourse.* London: Zed Books.

———. 1993. *The Nation and Its Fragments: Colonial and Post Colonial Histories.* Princeton: Princeton University Press.

Eaton, Richard Maxwell. 1993. *The Rise of Islam and the Bengal Frontier, 1204–1760.* Berkeley: University of California Press.

Guha Ranajit, ed. 1994. *Subaltern Studies I: Writings on South Asian History and Society.* Delhi: Oxford University Press.

Harris, Michael. 1996. "Bangladeshis." In *Encyclopedia of American Immigrant Cultures,* ed. David Levinson. New York: Macmillan.

Katzenstein, Mary. 1978. "Towards Equality? Cause and Consequence of the Political Prominence of Women in India." *Asian Survey* 18: 473–86.

Nandy, Ashis. 1983. *The Intimate Enemy: Loss and Recovery of Self under Colonialism.* Delhi: Oxford University Press.

Ratnagar, Shereen. 1996. "Revisionist at Work: A Chauvinistic Inversion of the Aryan Invasion Theory." *Frontline,* Feb. 9, 74–80.

Suleri, Sara. 1992. *The Rhetoric of English India.* Chicago: University of Chicago Press.

Van Buitenen, J. A. B. 1959. *Tales of Ancient India.* Chicago: University of Chicago Press.

2

Early South Asian Immigrants, 1900–1947

EARLY ASIAN IMMIGRANTS

Immigration from South Asia to the United States occurred during two contrasting periods of U.S. history, and it must also be placed in the broader context of Asian migration to the United States. The early phase of South Asian immigration, consisted largely of men from the British Indian province of the Punjab. They came from predominantly farming backgrounds and worked in agriculture in California. These Punjabi men came at the end of a series of Asian migrations to the West Coast, which started in the mid-nineteenth century; a series that ended because U.S. immigration laws were changed to discriminate against Asians in 1917 and 1924. The second phase of South Asian immigration began after 1965, when the new Immigration and Naturalization Act reversed the historic patterns to give preference to Asian immigrants with needed skills (Chan 1991: 145–65). Thus, the American context was significantly different for the first and second waves of South Asian immigration.

The immigrants themselves were also very different. In the first case they were drawn primarily from one province in India, whereas in the second they were drawn from all over India and from Pakistan, Bangladesh, Sri Lanka, Afghanistan, and Nepal. In the first case they were men from rural soldiering and farming backgrounds, whereas in the second most were families from urban, highly educated backgrounds. Understanding the early immigrant experience points up its sharp contrasts with the experiences of later South Asian immigrants (i.e., those who came after 1947 and 1965).

Conditions in both California and India's Punjab province explain why the Punjabi men emigrated, how they fit into the California political economy, and the resources they brought with them to the American West. By the time the Indian Punjabis began arriving around 1900 on the West Coast of the United States, public opinion and federal and state policies were turning against Asian immigrants. Other immigrants from Asia—Chinese, Japanese, and Koreans—had already been working in California. In fact, ethnic diversity has characterized California from its early days (Chinese gold miners accounted for approximately one-fifth of all gold miners shortly after the Gold Rush began in 1848), and Asians played major roles in the historical development of agriculture in California.

Before the discovery of gold in the mid-nineteenth century, California was a pastoral, semi-isolated region, with cattle hides and tallow as its most profitable products. After the discovery of gold it became one of the world's centers of mining, and subsequently it experienced the gradual development of a corporate, capital-intensive form of agriculture—in contrast to the small family farm tradition in the East and Midwest. By the late 1870s, large-scale irrigation systems in California's valleys allowed fruit and vegetables to be cultivated commercially. As improved and irrigated acreage grew, crops rose in value and more farm laborers were needed (Daniel 1982).

The role of Asian immigrants in California agriculture, at first thought to be one of cheap labor that both initiated and perpetuated the development of large-scale agribusiness (Taylor and Vasey 1936; McWilliams 1978), has been shown to be far more varied (Chan 1986). But early misconceptions that agribusiness was built on the backs of a series of migrant labor populations, starting with the Chinese and ending with the Mexicans, still color California history. According to this older version, after the Chinese Exclusion Act of 1882, Japanese immigrants came to work in agriculture; and after the Gentlemen's Agreement between the United States and Japan in 1907 barred Japanese laborers, Korean and Asian Indian (Punjabi) immigrants came to work in the fields. Then the "Barred Zone" Immigration Act of 1917 stopped almost all Asian immigration. However, Filipinos, with their peculiar status as U.S. "nationals" (a result of U.S. possession of the Philippines after the Spanish-American War of 1898), and Mexicans could still enter the United States, and many worked in agriculture.

In this erroneous "history" that treated the various Asian groups as functionally equivalent to each other, the Punjabis were portrayed as just another group of Asian agricultural laborers. However, people within the various Asian immigrant groups functioned quite differently in the evolving agricultural economy. The Chinese built levees, reclaimed peat soil, and leased large acreages in the Sacramento delta to grow potatoes and other extensive crops. Elsewhere, they went into truck gardening and orcharding at every level: as owners, tenants, laborers, fruit and vegetable peddlers, commission merchants, and farm cooks. The Japanese worked first as contract laborers but many soon became tenants, growing rice in northern California and oranges and lemons in southern California from about 1900 onward. The Japanese soon specialized in intensive cultivation of certain crops, such as strawberries. They did so well, in fact, that a reactionary wave of discrimination inspired passage of California's Alien Land Law in 1913 and follow-up amendments to it in 1920 and 1921. These laws relied upon the restriction of U.S. citizenship to those of "white" or African American race to discriminate against the Japanese, who like the Chinese before them were declared "Orientals." The laws barred aliens who were ineligible for citizenship from leasing or owning agricultural land. They were applied as well to the Koreans and Asian Indians who came during the first and second decades of the twentieth century.

Punjabis, too, fit into California's regional economies at many levels. They helped initiate rice cultivation in northern California, grew grapes and other crops in central California, and moved to the southern Imperial Valley to help establish cotton growing. Many Punjabis began to move up the agricultural ladder despite legal discrimination and prejudice based on ethnic stereotyping.

Asians working in California agriculture could do well by relying on their own skill and energy; sometimes they were helped by non-Asian neighbors and business partners. After 1920, however, two decades of adverse economic conditions changed the situation for all U.S. farmers, and even the renewed demand for agricultural products and the price surge during World War II did not offset the effect of technological advances. Fertilizer, tractors, and other machinery required more capital and narrowed the range of opportunities for individuals trying to enter agriculture. The increasing scale of farming also required more capital to buy or lease land, making inheritance the key element in ascending the agricultural ladder. From the 1940s onward, the surest way to obtain a farm was to inherit it from a father or grandfather, so newcomers had a much harder time becoming landowners.

Thus, established family life became a necessary and significant condition of landholding in rural California after World War II. In this context the Asians were at a disadvantage. All the Asian immigrant groups had a low proportion of women, some more than others; for Asian Indians there were 1,572 men per 100 women in 1930 (Leonard 1992: 23). The disproportionate sex ratios, combined with California's laws against marriage across

racial lines, made it difficult for Asian immigrants to establish families. Few were able to bring wives from their own countries or to marry women in California. The Chinese "sojourners" had come intending to return to their wives and families back home, and most remained bachelors in America. The Japanese, with their powerful government at home, were able to bring wives from Japan through the "picture bride" system (i.e., marrying a woman without returning to Japan and recognizing her by her picture when she arrived in America). The Koreans fell under Japanese rule after 1910 and were treated similarly by the U.S. immigration officials, but they brought few women. The Indians, under British colonial rule, had no assistance from a home government (actually, most of the early Punjabi immigrants were involved in political movements against British rule in India).

Like the Chinese before them, most of the Punjabis were married but had come without their families. When the Punjabis decided not to return to India but to settle down in the United States, they sought local women whom they could legally marry—and they found them among the Mexicans and Mexican Americans. Their wives and children became known as "Mexican Hindus," and they became part of the rural California farming scene. These biethnic families retained a strong sense of connection to India and an identity as "Hindus," as we shall see.

THE PUNJABI PIONEERS

The six or seven thousand Indians who came to the western United States between 1899 and 1914 were chiefly peasants from India's Punjab province, men from martial castes and landowning families. Perceived as illiterate and backward, they often encountered hostility in America. The man in charge of the 1909 Federal Immigration Commission's investigation of East Indian laborers along the Pacific Coast said that "the Hindus are regarded as the least desirable, or, better, the most undesirable, of all the eastern Asiatic races which have come to share our soil . . . between one-half and three-fifths of them are unable to read and write" (Millis 1912: 381). In this and other literature of the time, all those coming from India were termed "Hindu," and "Hindu" was opposed to "American," suggesting that association between the two, much less assimilation of one to the other, was unlikely and undesirable.

Despite their unfriendly reception, within a decade of their arrival the Punjabi peasants were vigorously contesting their placement at the bottom of the rural hierarchy. They dealt with their new circumstances with skill and confidence. Almost immediately they established relationships with bankers and lawyers, getting loans and filing court cases, in their new settings. Their success was partly because of their hard-working Punjabi background and perhaps also because of their previous experiences with British colonial rule. More important, the British colonial background helps explain why Asian Indians were immigrating to California and the United States at this time.

At the turn of the century, the Punjab remained something of a frontier area along India's northwestern border, marked by centuries of invading conquerors from Alexander the Great to Babur, the founder of the Mughal empire. British rule had come relatively late to the Punjab compared to other regions of India, with the hard-fought Sikh wars of 1846–1848 annexing most of the Punjab to the British Empire. The flat plains of the Punjab, already watered by the five rivers that give the region its name (*panch ab*) and by a network of canals dating from Mughal times, began to prosper as railway and road links and new irrigation canals were developed there from the 1860s onward.

The peasants of the Punjab valued their land and worked it themselves. This, and their military ability, earned them a special place in the eyes of the British. Moreover, despite its relatively recent subjugation, the Punjab "held for the Queen [Victoria]" when British rule in India was challenged in 1857. This earned imperial gratitude and preferential recruitment for Punjab's martial castes into the British Indian military service, particularly for members of the Sikh faith. (Although the people of the Punjab shared a common language, Punjabi, they belonged to three major religions: Islam, Hinduism, and Sikhism.)

Approximately 85 percent of the early immigrants to the United States were Sikhs, and another 10 or 12 percent were Muslims. The Sikh faith developed from a fifteenth-century religious reform movement that drew important elements from both Hinduism and Islam. It is monotheistic, stresses the equality of all men, and has a long history as a brotherhood of fighting men (sometimes against each other, sometimes against the Mughals or the British). Today Sikhism claims an identity distinct from Islam and Hinduism, but at the turn of the century religious distinctions were far less important in the Punjab—caste, kinship, and locality were more important elements of identity than religion (Oberoi 1988). The significant numbers of Muslims and Sikhs in the Punjab meant that India's caste system (the religiously justified social system based on principles of inequality) was largely overridden there by the principle of equality. As a result, there was much competition between many types of people. Punjabi culture stressed landownership, courage, willingness to take risks, and some justification of violence to avoid defeat and submission. Punjabi society was patrilineal and patriarchial (i.e., inheritance was through the male line, and authority rested with men), and men valued family honor, prestige, independence, and equality (Pettigrew 1975).

By the early twentieth century, Punjabi peasant proprietors were being incorporated into the world economy. At this time overseas emigration, initially thought of as a temporary move, became a common strategy. The primary forces behind migration were population pressure, subdivision of land, and rural debt—and probably a quest for status and adventure. The central agricultural region of the Punjab became the chief source of immigrants to the American Pacific Coast. Land fragmentation in the Punjab increased as mortality decreased and more sons survived to inherit equal shares of the patrimony; thus, the sons of cultivators took up military service or wage labor abroad. (At the outbreak of World War I, more than 65% of Indian combat troops came from the Punjab; by 1917, Punjabi enlistments accounted for almost 50% of the men recruited in India: Ellinwood 1976). A 1916 source reported that a man who earned 16 cents a day in India could earn 2 dollars a day in the United States; and an emigrant from the Punjab who had returned to his village asserted in the late 1920s that in America a man could do as he pleased. In the United States, he said, there was plenty of land and plenty of money, whereas in India one could not borrow, as no one would advance him money (Darling 1930: 28–29).

Most of the men who migrated to Canada and the United States from the central Punjab were from the so-called martial races and from landowning castes. Although to other Americans these men were known collectively as "Hindus," most of them were actually Sikhs and Muslims, members of monotheistic religions committed to the equality of all believers. Real Hindus, representatives of India's dominant religion with its many gods and caste system, were very few. Within these religious groupings, there were further divisions according to caste or region of origin. Almost all the Sikhs were Jats (warrior/farmers), although there were also a few Chuhras (untouchables). Among Muslims there were Rajputs (warrior/farmers), Arains (gardeners), and even some Pathans (Pushto- or Pakhtun-speakers from the northwestern frontier and Afghanistan). The Hindus were Brahmans and Khatris (merchants) from urban areas of the Punjab.

A significant proportion of the pre-1914 immigrants had served in the British military and police and had seen service overseas, from China to East Africa and Lebanon. Punjabis fought in China's Boxer Rebellion in 1900 and served even before that in the treaty ports. Sikhs stationed in Hong Kong built a *gurdwara* (temple or church) there in 1910 (Dhillon 1981: 166).

Punjabis serving overseas learned about the opportunities in the western United States. Steamships linked Hong Kong to the Philippine Islands, Canada, California, and Mexico. Men sailed from Calcutta to Hong Kong, a trip of about twelve days, and then boarded another ship to Canada or the United States, a journey of eighteen or nineteen days. One estimate put the cost of the entire trip from India to Canada at 300 rupees, which could be obtained by borrowing from relatives, pawning ornaments, or mortgaging land. Passengers got rations and did their own cooking, usually forming large groups to do so.

Most men proceeded on their own to Canada (which was a British Empire dominion) and to the United States. Typical stories show the imperial genealogy. A Sikh immigrant to Canada, one Sergeant Singh, produced a book of references from British army officers in India, merchants in Australia, and bankers in Hong Kong. Another man, interviewed in Venice, California, in 1924, said: "I was born in the Punjab district of India and served on the police force in Hong Kong, China, for some years. While I was in China several Hindus returned and reported on the ease with which they could make money in America and so I decided to go" (Leonard 1992: 31).

The United States attracted the Punjabi men as Canada began tightening admission requirements. But as Punjabi immigration to the United States increased, growing prejudice made it more difficult to gain admittance. There was a rising rejection rate of Asian Indian applicants by the Bureau of Immigration and Naturalization. Before 1907, fewer than 10 percent of applicants for admission were rejected; but in 1909, 1911, and 1913, 50 percent or more were rejected (Jacoby 1982: 37). The Immigration Act of 1917 was the final blow, with its "barred Asiatic zone" and literacy provisions; and the National Origins Quota Act of 1924 confirmed the earlier exclusionary principles.

In their first years in California, most of the Punjabis moved around the state in small groups, working on railroads, in lumbering, and in agriculture. A small group of Muslims sold tamales and popcorn in San Francisco, but most moved in large groups, with a "boss man" who spoke English best and contracted for farming jobs on their behalf. They first found work in the orchards, vineyards, and sugarbeet fields of northern California; then in the vineyards and citrus groves of central California; and finally, following the annual sequence of harvests, in the cantaloupe and cotton fields of the southern Imperial Valley. The Punjabis in California kept in touch with those settling in Canada and the state of Washington, and with those moving on to Texas, Arizona, New Mexico, Utah, and Colorado.

Like other Asians, Punjabis experienced racial and ethnic discrimination and were usually segregated in the "foreign sections" of California's cities and towns. Japanese, Chinese, and Hindus shared rooming houses and restaurants. Mexicans and blacks, and later Filipinos, also settled in the foreign sections. A few "Hindu store men" owned groceries, bars, and boarding houses in these sections and served as contacts for the newcomers. In Los Angeles, Punjabi pioneers owned land in the city as early as 1913; most Punjabi men in Los Angeles resided in the vicinity of Little Tokyo and worked at a variety of occupations, as peddlers, interpreters, elevator operators, butlers, and "photoplayers" (i.e., actors).

Fragmentary sources give some insight into how the South Asian immigrants saw themselves in the new land. The Punjabis imposed familiar landscapes on the California countryside, according to accounts from two time periods. One written account by an early Punjabi immigrant comments on the California landscape. Puna Singh, who moved to northern California from Utah in 1924, gave his first impressions:

> On arriving in the Sacramento Valley, one could not help but be reminded of the Punjab. Fertile fields stretched across the flat valley to the foothills lying far in the distance. Most of the jobs available were agricultural and I found many Punjabis already working throughout the area. (Singh 1972: 109)

The same emphasis on similarities appears in fuller accounts from later Punjabi immigrants. One man who joined the older immigrant community in the Yuba City/Marysville region in northern California wrote about the "Land of Five Rivers" in an elaborate evocation of the Sacramento Valley as the Punjabi homeland, explicitly bestowing the old name on the new environment (Leonard 1992: 34–35). The framing of the new landscape in familiar images appears to be a significant adaptive strategy for immigrants, and we will see it again as the more recent South Asians relocate themselves. Perhaps this is a way for immigrants to empower themselves in new contexts, a way of taking charge of the physical landscape and emphasizing continuities with the past.

FORMATION OF A BIETHNIC COMMUNITY

Most of the early immigrants from India experienced family life in the United States as members of a biethnic community, by marrying women of Mexican ancestry. The fact that this happened at all, and that it happened on a relatively large scale, has been difficult for some of the newer South Asian immigrants to understand. But in the early twentieth century, pervasive racism and the ways in which California agriculture was developing presented many challenges to the Punjabi pioneers. A close look at their lives shows important continuities and even more significant discontinuities in the South Asian immigrant experience.

The origins of the Punjabi-Mexican community lie in the Imperial Valley along California's southern border. Men from the Punjab were among the farmers who flocked there to work the newly irrigated land in the first decade of the twentieth century. The Punjabis came as laborers but soon began to lease and buy land; at first some obtained American citizenship, but later they lost that right. Then not only the physical landscape but the political landscape and their place in it struck the Punjabi men as decidedly similar to what they had left behind in British India. They fought hard for their rightful place in society, and particularly for a place on the land. Legal constraints and social stereotypes based on race and national origin determined the conditions the Punjabis encountered in America; and even in the area of family life, their experience was shaped by legal constraints as strongly as by personal choices. Unable to bring their wives and families from India because of the restrictive immigration laws, those who wanted a stable family life in the United States married predominantly Spanish-speaking women, producing families known locally as "Mexican-Hindus."

The Punjabi men entered a rapidly developing, highly competitive agricultural economy, which would become a major (if not the major) producing region in California. Asians were among the first to arrive in the Imperial Valley: in 1901, the first and only house in the new town of Imperial was a tent hotel run by "a Chinaman." Imperial was the headquarters of the Imperial Irrigation District, and later El Centro, with its railroad station, became the Imperial County seat. The county courthouse, recorder's office, sheriff's office, and jail were located there, along with banks, dealerships in cars and farming equipment, and stores selling farm supplies, groceries, and clothing. Most of the Punjabi farmers began by leasing land, but tenancy meant insecurity; most large companies leased for only three years at a time. The Punjabis worked hard to cultivate good relationships with both absentee and local Anglo growers, bankers, and shippers.

Local society did not welcome the Punjabis as they took up farming; they encountered both social and legal constraints. In 1910 the Imperial Valley *Holtville Tribune* printed a critical article on "the Hindu and his habits and why he should be prohibited at once from landing in California." Noting that a few Hindus had appeared on the street of Holtville, the writer commented that "Cotton picking time is attracting a doubtful looking bunch of all shades and kinds," people who threatened the "college-bred population, its culture and refinement" (*Holtville Tribune*, Sept. 16, 1910). This local prejudice reflected nationwide discriminatory trends in the United States.

After 1913, South Asian admission to the United States through legal channels was difficult, and the Immigration Act of 1917 barred almost all Asians. Earlier restrictions had been forthrightly based on race (the 1882 Chinese Exclusion Act) or national origin (the 1907 Gentlemen's Agreement with Japan), but the 1917 bill correlated physical with cultural distance and expressly denied entry to immigrants from areas west of the 110th and east of the 50th meridian (Asia). Literacy tests were required, but it was the Asiatic exclusion provisions that would "especially bar Hindus," according to the local Imperial Valley press. Nonetheless, men from India continued to arrive in the Imperial Valley. By 1918, the press worried that the Hindus were becoming "a menace" because they were no longer content to be day laborers—they were interested only in farming for themselves. Initially enumerated in the 1910 census as laborers, the Punjabis soon began sending sizeable money orders from the local post offices as remittances to India. Many became successful farmers, and leases recorded in the county courthouse show many Punjabi farmers and partnerships, some of them linking the more numerous Sikhs with Muslims or Hindus.

In other parts of California the Punjabi men stayed in labor camps or rooming houses, but in the Imperial Valley they began to settle into local society more permanently. They lived in wooden shacks on the land they were farming along the country roads and canals. There were economic setbacks (after World War I many cotton farmers went bankrupt), but the 1923 Supreme Court *Thind* decision barring them from U.S. citizenship was a more catastrophic blow (Jacoby 1958). That decision pronounced people from India to be Caucasian but not "white persons" in the popular meaning of the term, a ruling that made them "aliens ineligible to citizenship" (like other Asians) and subjected them to California's Alien Land Laws. The Alien Land Laws, devised to halt the Japanese immigrants' rapid progress in agriculture, prohibited the leasing and owning of agricultural land by aliens who were ineligible for citizenship. The Supreme Court decision thus struck directly at the men's ability to earn a living as farmers.

Despite these setbacks, many Punjabi men decided to stay and establish families. Their search for local brides was hampered by California's laws that prohibited marriage between people of different races. (These laws were not repealed until 1948 in California.) Punjabis were generally classified as nonwhite and were not given marriage licenses to marry white women in California. ("Hindu Weds White Girl by Stealing Away to Arizona," a 1918 headline blared.) But women of Mexican ancestry raised no objections, and Punjabi men and Hispanic women soon secured marriage licenses routinely, although the marriages caused some conflicts between Punjabis and Mexican men. Punjabi farmers turned to women or girls who were picking cotton in their fields. Just at this time, Mexican families displaced by the Mexican Revolution were moving across the border, finding work in cotton fields from Texas to southern California. Thus, the labor markets and the Punjabi-Mexican marriage networks developed in tandem, from El Paso, Texas, to California's Imperial Valley. One marriage to a Punjabi led to others as the Mexican women called relatives and friends and helped arrange more matches.

The Punjabi-Mexican marriages began in 1916 in southern California, when Sher Singh and Antonia Alvarez married; in 1917, Sher's partner, Gopal Singh, married Antonia's sister Anna Anita. The women had been picking cotton on the Punjabis' land, having moved from Mexico with their mother to El Paso and then to the Imperial Valley. The brides were 18 and 21 years old; the men were age 36 and 37. By 1919, two more Alvarez sisters and a neice of Antonia and Anna Anita had married Punjabis also. These and almost all Punjabi-Mexican marriages were civil ceremonies, and no attempts were made to carry out Punjabi religious or secular marriage customs. One wife remembers that when she married, "another Hindu offered me money, but my husband did not accept, saying 'we are not in our country.' "

The sister-partner marriage patterns were reproduced in household arrangements as well, with partners commonly residing in joint households with their brides. The hot climate—summer temperatures could reach 120°—was hard on the newcomers, and families lived in tents or dirt-floored wooden shacks, often without ice, electricity, or running water. The deep irrigation ditches had to be forded at a dash by horse and buggy. The hardships of the early years included cultural adjustments within the marriages. The Sikh men took off their turbans but kept on their iron wrist bangles. Husbands or bachelor partners taught the Hispanic wives how to prepare Punjabi-style vegetables, pickles, chicken curry, and *roti* (bread). Some bachelor householders stayed on as helpful "uncles" when children were born to the couples.

Table 2.1 shows the distribution of marriages made by the Punjabis in California from 1913 to 1949 by type of spouse and region, placing couples in the region where they first settled and where their first children were born. These married men represented between one-fifth and one-third of the Indian population, so it is possible to say that Punjabi-Mexican family life

Wedding photo of an early Punjabi-Mexican couple, Valentina Alvarez and Rullia Singh, El Centro, California, 1917. Courtesy of Wilma Chand, Yuba City, California.

Table 2.1
Spouses of Asian Indians in California, 1913–1949

Counties	Types of Spouses											
	Hispanic		Anglo		Black		Indian		American Indian		TOTALS	
	No.	*%*	*No.*	*%*	*No.*	*%*	*No.*	*%*	*No.*	*%*	*No.*	*%*
Yuba Sutter Sacramento San Joaquin	45	50.6	25	28.1	9	10.1	8	9.0	2	2.3	89	23.6*
Fresno Tulare Kings	38	76.0	11	22.0	0	0	1	2.0	0	0	50	13.2*
Imperial Los Angeles San Diego	221	92.5	12	5.0	6	2.5	0	0	0	0	239	63.2*
TOTALS	304	80.0*	48	12.7*	15	4.0*	9	2.4*	2	0.5*	378	100.0

*Percentage totals should be read horizontally, save for the final right hand totals column, which tallies vertically.

Source: Karen Leonard, family reconstitution from county records (vital statistics, civil and criminal records, and interviews with informants).

reflected the basic pattern of Indian family life in America in these early decades.

Some marriages were based on love and some were based on economic need. One woman told of her husband-to-be cavorting on his horse in the row ahead of her as she picked cotton, while his partner courted her sister by dropping a gaily colored handkerchief over her hair. Another woman, whose uncle was weighmaster to Punjabi cotton growers, fell in love with the boss at first sight. And a daughter told how her mother met her father: "She worked for my father, although not very hard—she was a very beautiful woman!" Marriage to a Punjabi was often a good option for these women, especially when the groom was one's boss or another man of the farmer class. One man said of his parents' marriage: "Pakistanis were growing cotton. . . . When they hired workers, my mother was among them. Tom whistled at her and she liked him. Lupe's parents were happy, she had married a boss."

Later allegations of narrow economic motivations for the marriages are not correct, although many new immigrants from India, anxious to explain the marriages out of caste and community, think that the wives could hold land for the men and often did so. In fact, the men were not barred from owning and leasing land until 1923 (when the *Thind* decision denied them access to citizenship and they came under the jurisdiction of the Alien Land Laws), and the biethnic marriage pattern was well established before that date. In any case, it was the wives who acquired the status of their husbands upon marriage, and not the reverse. Thus, a woman marrying an ineligible alien became ineligible for citizenship herself or lost her citizenship, according to the Cable Act (a federal act in effect from 1922 through 1931 that applied to women but not to men).

Furthermore, the allegation is not valid that the men married to produce children who would be American citizens by birth and therefore would be able to own land. Most Punjabis in the Imperial Valley did not begin putting land in the names of their children until 1934, well after most marriages and many childbirths had occurred. Even when the Punjabis began using this strategy, they were not only copying the Japanese (who had begun doing this to get around the Alien Land Laws many years earlier) but were responding to a specific court case of 1933 that challenged the practice of Hindu farmers holding land in corporations with Anglos (Leonard 1985). Indeed, the Punjabis' marriages were not opportunistic attempts to secure land, but commitments to permanent residence in the United States; they simply reflected the men's decisions not to return to India and the families they may have had there.

PUNJABI-MEXICAN FAMILY LIFE

The Punjabi-Mexican couples had many children. County fertility and mortality records, though starkly quantitative, tell much about the lives of these pioneer families. Most births occurred at home with a midwife in attendance, very rarely a doctor. Birth certificate entries show the mothers moving about for successive births, in accordance with their husbands' leasing arrangements. The names of the children and parents on the certificates usually were misspelled because the parents were illiterate in English and others filled out the blanks for them. Often the ages given for the father and mother were also incorrect (with wildly varying ages given for the man and woman in successive years). My own computation of maternal fertility shows an average of 6.4 children each, but most couples lost one of every six or seven children born to them. The large numbers of children included some stepchildren from the women's previous marriages. Court records and other evidence show family disruption due to divorce, desertion, high maternal and infant mortality, and even a few murders (Leonard 1992: 73–78).

These demographic indicators of Punjabi family life reveal important dimensions of the early immigrant experience—notably the denial of medical expertise and institutions to those with darker skins and less money, and the presence of problems within the marriages themselves.

But tensions were balanced by accommodations as the Punjabi-Mexican families formed a distinctive new community. Outsiders viewed the men, women, and children as a community, calling them "Hindus" or "Mexican-Hindus," and there were collective activities—weddings, dinners and dances, holiday outings—in which both men and women participated. For the men, networks based on kinship, so fundamental to Punjabi society, were weak in California because only one or two members of a family had migrated. They relied on new friends, shipmates from the long journey, and workmates in California agriculture. For the women, places of origin in Mexico were relatively unimportant; kinship was the most obvious basis of their networks. That was supplemented by the *compadrazgo* (i.e., godparent) system: fictive kinship or sponsorship promoted by the Catholic Church that linked Punjabi-Mexican couples through their children. Non-Catholic Punjabi men were accepted as godfathers by Catholic churches throughout the American Southwest, but they might be given Hispanized names on official documents (e.g., "Arturo Gangara" for "Ganga Ram"). Because the godparents were almost entirely drawn from within the Punjabi-Mexican community, the *compadrazgo* system strengthened relationships between the Punjabi-Mexican couples rather than integrating the Punjabi men into local Mexican-American communities.

Most wives of the Punjabis learned little about the religions, castes, and regional cultures of India. They knew some basic names and practices but sometimes got them wrong. Comments from wives included the following: "My husband was a member of the Singh religion . . . he was twenty, twenty-one years older than me [sic] but this race does not look old. . . . My husband's partner told me that if a Muslim came to the door, the Hindu would not let him in but would talk to him outside." "Oh, yes, we ate beef, but there was another kind of Hindu, called Mohammedan, and they didn't eat pork." "Her three husbands were all Mohameds, though I'm not sure, one couldn't eat beef and another pork." "My husband told me the Hindus and the Pakistanis do not like each other in India, but here they are all united."

The Punjabi men maintained strong connections with each other and even built a Sikh temple in Stockton, in northern California, which was the only Indian religious center in the state from 1912 until the late 1940s. The Stockton temple drew not only Sikhs but all the Punjabi men and their families for political and social activities. The Ghadar Party, an Indian nationalist party supporting India's freedom from Great Britain, was founded in northern California in 1913 and rallied Punjabi men and money for the cause. Similarly, Indian immigrant leaders organized to gain American citizenship and carried out drives that also mobilized Punjabi men and money. These activities, as well as the networks of Hindu bosses and crews, Hindu labor camps, and Hindu stores and storemen in the towns, kept the men in touch.

The Punjabi-Mexican marriages involved some very real adaptations and discomforts for the Punjabi men as they learned new relationships among love, marriage, and divorce. Above all, the men learned about women's rights to divorce. A farmer in Selma eloquently testified about his experiences:

> In this country, it's a different class of people. You can't force love here, women go where they want to, even if they're married, even with three or four kids. In India, you could only get a divorce after India got freedom. Here, women go away, here it's different. The woman is the boss in this country. A woman can have four husbands, a man can have two or three women. What you gonna do, that's the way with love. . . .
>
> Sometimes I feel like I'm suffering here, you know, trouble at home. Here, when you marry, you have woman trouble, kid trouble, not like in India. When I got here, I saw, you have liberty, women have liberty, you know. The way it is here, I've been separated, divorced. In India, you stay together all

> your life. In this country, you have love. When you love a person, you stay with her, with her kids and everything.
>
> I divorced Carmen, when she went away to Mexico. I couldn't do anything, so I filed for divorce. She had two more kids by then. My wife in India, she'd died already by that time. Yes, I knew about divorce. In this country, I no sleep. Everybody was divorced, I could see what they were doing. It's only normal, you see the customs of the country, and so you have to do that.
>
> In this country, when she wants to go, my wife, she says, "All right, sonny honey, I'm going," and I say, "I can't stop you." It's because of love, therefore I couldn't stop her. (Singh 1982)

The themes of Singh's narrative are romantic love as the basis of marriage, men's inability to exercise effective control over women, and the ever-present possibility of divorce.

There were many stable, happy marriages among these couples as well. The long-lasting couples successfully negotiated certain immediate obstacles, such as a husband's expectation that his wife would cook and clean for his partners as well as for him. The fact that some men also had wives and children back in India was not a major source of marital instability in California. The relatives in India were distanced by law as well as geography, far from the minds of the Punjabi-Mexican families. Some women did know their husbands had been married in India; others found out later or preferred not to know. One man arranged for his brother back in the Punjab to take over responsibility for his wife and daughter there. Some husbands simply stopped writing, and some lost their Indian wives in the 1918 influenza epidemic but sent money to surviving children through relatives. Many men did tell their California wives about their Indian wives and families and sent remittances to India for years.

The successful marriages were characterized by some degree of bilingualism, although few of the men were rated excellent speakers of Spanish and no wife ever really learned to speak Punjabi well (many understood it adequately). But real mastery of a common language seemed relatively unimportant; in any case, many people argued that there were similarities between Punjabi and Spanish. "Spanish is just like Punjabi, really," they said, illustrating the point by citing similar words and grammatical constructions. Not only language, but other aspects of Punjabi and Mexican culture were viewed as essentially similar. Rather than emphasize or even mention the restrictive marriage laws that played a major role in determining their choice of spouses, the men and their descendants talked about the similar physical appearance of the Punjabi men and Mexican women. Further, they argued that Mexicans and Punjabis shared the same material culture. Unable to visit the Punjab in the early decades of their marriages, the women found it harder to learn about Punjabi culture, but they accepted the men's reports of similarities, and some of the long-time wives viewed themselves as "Hindu." By this statement, they meant that they cooked Indian food and conducted their households in a "Hindu" fashion to suit their husbands.

RELIGION AND POLITICS

Another important characteristic of the happy marriages was respect for the religions of both husband and wife and mutual support of religious observances, despite a certain absence of knowledge. The wives and children learned little about Indian religious beliefs and practices during the men's early decades in California. Many Muslim, Hindu, and Sikh men did not even transmit correct English terms for their religious faiths to their children. Thus, some members of the second generation continue to refer to all the Punjabi men as Hindus without realizing it is usually a misnomer, and a few men are designated by such improbable combinations of first and last names as "Ali Singh" or "Ghulam Singh." Others refer to the "Singhs" or "Mohammeds," knowing the men were not really Hindus but being unsure of the correct religious terms. The fathers were mostly unable to read, teach, or explain their own religious texts, if they had copies. Furthermore, the children did not know the Punjabi language, much less Arabic, so that the beauties of the Granth Sahib or the Quran were inaccessible to them. The Roman Catholic Church was clearly hospitable to these families, allowing the Punjabi men to stand as godfathers in church ceremonies, Hispanizing their names on baptismal certificates, and in some cases allowing them to be married in religious rites without any meaningful evidence of conversion to Catholicism.

The children's religious training did not produce conflict between Punjabi husbands and Mexican wives. The men encouraged their wives to continue their own religious beliefs and practices—after all, it was women who taught religion and culture to children. The men had work to do, every day all day, and they were not themselves prepared to teach their religions. They were willing for their children to become Catholic, and they supported the idea of religion, in the best tradition of Indian tolerance; they did inculcate respect for Sikhism, Hinduism, or Islam.

Markers of religious identity—the external signs differentiating Sikh, Muslim, and Hindu in India—largely disappeared among the pioneers. In outward appearance the Sikhs initially had been marked by the beard, long hair, and turban required by orthodox Sikhism. Retention of these characteristics proved difficult in the face of American prejudice, and in any case, many wives preferred their men to be clean-shaven. Several women explicitly linked the giving up of the turban and beard to their wedding day. "The labor camp men wore turbans and the family men took them off," said one daughter.

Not only the children's religious training, but their names and the language spoken in the home reflected the mothers' authority in the domestic realm. Socialization into an essentially Mexican-American domestic culture marked their early years. "Maria Jesusita Singh," "Jose Akbar Khan," "Armando Chand"—their names seem both strange and beautiful, clearly marking their biethnic identities. A few fathers insisted on recording Indian names for their sons, but these were seldom used. In the home, most children spoke Spanish with their mothers and Spanish or English with their fathers; few learned to speak Punjabi. (Older boys who worked in the fields with "Hindu crews," especially some of the Mexican stepsons, did learn Punjabi appropriate to the work situation.) Aunts and grandmothers, godmothers, and other children reinforced the Spanish-speaking culture of the mothers, and most of the Punjabi-Mexican children attended schools in which Spanish-speaking children predominated. Outsiders usually classified these Punjabi-Mexican children as "Mexicans." To this day, some people in the Imperial Valley think of "Singh" as a Mexican-American surname. But the "Mexican" identification was a contested one for the children, not least by Mexican Americans themselves, and the Punjabi men had such pride in their heritage that the children ultimately drew closer to their "Hindu side."

For all the Punjabi men and their families, being Hindu meant politics more than religion, for the men had a passionate interest in both U.S. and Indian politics. The Punjabi farmers were highly political men, fighting hard for citizenship in the United States and freedom for India. They took their wives and children to political rallies where Syed Hossain, Madame Pandit, and other figures from the Indian independence movement spoke. The children regarded themselves and their families as an integral part of the Indian nationalist movement; and the twin achievements of South Asian access to naturalized U.S. citizenship in 1946 and of independence for India and Pakistan in 1947 marked high points in the lives of both first- and second-generation "Hindus."

SECOND-GENERATION IDENTITIES

Members of the second generation tended to move away from an identification as Mexican toward one as Hindu. The children of the Punjabis worked selectively with what they knew of their biethnic heritage, choosing

The Stockton Sikh Temple and Punjabi-Mexican and Sikh community members welcome Madame Pandit, ca. 1946, from the Indian National Congress party. Courtesy of Isabel Singh Garcia, Yuba City, California.

certain aspects of the strong Punjabi identity presented by their fathers. The daughters generally respected their fathers and Punjabi culture, but they had no Punjabi women to emulate. However, they did represent India and Pakistan as "queens" at county fairs and other events, putting on the unfamiliar sari and other newly acquired South Asian clothing to do so. The sons experienced stronger pressures to "be Punjabi," but it was not always possible to emulate their fathers.

"Being Hindu" meant many things, both positive and negative, to the children growing up in these biethnic families. It meant Indian food. Chicken curry and *roti* were always featured at festive family dinners, along with other Indian foods such as lime pickles and certain vegetables. It meant some religious practices, such as prohibitions on food and drink and particular burial customs. As the old men began to die (most were some ten to twenty years older than their wives in America), the widows and children had the responsibility of carrying out "proper" cremations (for Sikhs and Hindus) or burials (for Muslims, in "Hindu" plots in California's rural cemeteries). De-

Punjabi-Mexican daughters represent India at the Campfire Girls All States Nation Dinner, Marysville, California, about 1964. Courtesy of Isabel Singh Garcia, Yuba City, California.

scendants take great pride in their Indian ancestry; many claim to be both Catholic and Sikh, or Catholic and Muslim.

Indian religious practices that did affect family life in California for members of the second generation centered on two things: dietary prohibitions and death rituals. For Muslims, pork was forbidden, and the meat they did eat was supposed to be ritually slaughtered. Muslims were not supposed to drink intoxicating liquor. Most Muslim Punjabis seem to have observed the prohibition on pork, and some took care to obtain kosher meat from Jewish suppliers. For the Sikhs and Hindus, beef was the meat to be avoided, although many descendants said their fathers ate it, and many Punjabi fathers drank liquor.

The children have vivid memories of funerals, because on those occasions people tried to follow Indian customs. In the early decades most of the Muslim burials were in Sacramento, where a building for a mosque was finally purchased in the 1940s. Other Punjabi Muslims came and prepared the body for burial, stripping it, washing it, and shrouding it in clean white linen. Verses from the Quran were read as the coffin was lowered into the ground, and men jumped down into the grave and filled it in with dirt, paying no heed to the soiling of their best suits. The distribution of fresh fruit to family members and guests ended the burial service.

When a Sikh died, the Punjabi Sikhs were equally strict about the proper disposal of his body. First, a photograph was taken of the body with a turban placed on the man's head, whether or not he had worn one in the United States. (By the early 1940s a researcher remarked that the rarely worn turban marked a "most religious" Sikh in California.) In the photo, the dead man's partner or wife stood behind the coffin, and friends surrounded him. The photo was sent home to the family in India as proof of his death and his orthodoxy, although the bare heads of those in the background may have raised questions. Second, the Sikh's body was cremated, being sent for that purpose to Sacramento, Los Angeles, or Yuma, Arizona; the ashes could be sent back to India or put into the Salton Sea or the Pacific Ocean.

In those days the Catholic women believed cremation was a sin, and many widows wished to bury their husbands where they themselves would be buried: in the Mexican Catholic section of the local cemetery (they rarely succeeded in this). But when it came to infants and children, the Sikh and Hindu men gave in—there are many children's gravestones marked "Singh" in California's rural cemeteries. The Catholic funerals held for most children were attended by Sikhs, Muslims, Hindus, and Hispanic relatives and friends.

Few if any of the Muslim farmers observed the prescribed daily prayers and the annual month-long fast, or *Id*, in their early decades in the United States, according to their children. Copies of the Quran and prayer rugs were scarce. Families did gather to commemorate the annual *Id* (breaking the month-long fast together) even if they had not fasted, and those present who could read and explain the Quran did so. Fathers sometimes promised to "bring someone out from Washington, D.C." to answer their children's questions about Islam; indeed, for at least one Muslim's funeral, men did come from Washington. For a short time an Arabic class was convened for the children being brought up in the Imperial Valley, an endeavor related to the conversion of one Hispanic wife to Islam. She was an enthusiastic and zealous speaker for the religion in the Imperial Valley, but hers does not seem to have been followed by other conversions.

The Sikh temple in Stockton did draw Punjabi-Mexican families to some religious, social, and political functions, and members of the second generation socialized with each other on many occasions. In the Imperial Valley, a building for a Sikh temple was purchased in the 1940s. Like the Stockton temple, it became a community center for all Indians to a considerable extent. Informal visiting on Sunday afternoons at the temple followed the midday religious service, which the women and children might or might not attend. The men sat in a circle on the lawn under the trees while the women cooked and the children observed, listened, and, later, ate. The families visited each others' homes frequently, and there were holiday outings that were enjoyed greatly by the young people.

The Punjabi-Mexican youth were pushed together by discrimination from the larger society, too. Not only the school systems but public facilities such as restaurants, barber shops, movie theaters, swimming pools, and even many churches were segregated well into the 1940s and 1950s. One daughter remembers her mother insisting on sitting in the Anglo part of a certain movie theatre. Others among the oldest children remember being barred from a swimming pool or being denied seats on public transport until after others had been seated (and as a result sometimes not getting a seat at all).

Other important shared experiences for many Punjabi-Mexican teenagers came through their work in agriculture. The sons worked and socialized together all over California, moving for seasonal agricultural work from one Punjabi foreman to another and meeting every year with other Punjabi-Mexicans in labor camps, fields, and orchards. Girls from the poorer families worked just as their brothers did.

DATING AND MARRIAGE

The Punjabi-Mexican children were singled out in the schools, sometimes characterized as unusually handsome or beautiful, and also set apart by parental restraints. Both Punjabi fathers and Mexican mothers were strict about the daughters dating in high school. As the second generation grew up, the fathers began to talk more about the complexities of Punjabi social structure and tried to influence their children's choice of dating and marriage partners. This led to some intergenerational difficulties, which we will explore in some detail because of the comparisons and contrasts to intergenerational difficulties in the newer South Asian immigrant population (since 1965).

Fathers began to talk about religious, regional, and caste distinctions in India. A Muslim father might point out that not only should the children of Muslims not marry those of Sikhs, but there were distinctions within the religious groups. For example, this father would argue, not all Muslims were the same: some families stemmed from low-caste Muslims back in the Punjab, whereas he, and therefore his children, were higher-caste Rajputs. And Sikh fathers delivered similar messages: there were Jat Sikhs and Untouchable Sikhs. The men were from three different regions of the Punjab (Majha, Malwa, and Doaba), and the children of a person from one region should not marry those of another, Sikh fathers insisted.

Sons seem to have presented stronger challenges to paternal authority than did daughters, on a wider range of issues and for a longer time. Although daughters and sons alike clashed with their fathers over dating and marriage partners, fathers had several clear expectations of their sons. They wanted them to work hard, excel at everything they attempted, and earn their inheritance. A son explained how difficult it was to deal with one of the fathers in the Phoenix area, a man so obstinate that "if he fell in the river, you'd have to look for him upstream." The children of Muslim fathers, strictly prohibited from eating pork, were unable to participate in a favorite teenage recreation in the Imperial Valley: weenie roasts in the desert. This prohibition was a source of real regret, and in at least one instance it became a test of adulthood. One son, back home after serving in World War II, tried to demonstrate his independence by ordering a pork dish at a family dinner in a local Chinese restaurant. His father rebuked him angrily, forbidding him to eat it, "not in front of me and not when I pay!"

Daughters were not expected to achieve through work, nor were they seen as waiting for an inheritance. The issue of property transmission bore much harder on the sons also, because almost no Punjabi father actually gave over control of his property before his death. The Punjabi fathers' expectations for a daughter were not nearly so well defined. Although they did center on her marriage, once that occurred she was essentially beyond paternal advice or control.

The daughters and sons of the Punjabis married young, and most of their partners were Hispanic or Anglo. Even though there were enough Punjabi-Mexican children to intermarry in the Imperial Valley, they showed no preference for marriages with each other. Although a few fathers did succeed in persuading their daughters to marry older Punjabis (still available), these marriages did not usually turn out successfully. The mothers usually supported their daughters in making their own choice of spouse. "Dad wanted me to marry a well-established man eighteen, maybe twenty-eight, years older. . . . He tried three times to get me married, but mother said 'no way!' It bothered him a lot that I made my own decision." And a mother arguing on behalf of a daughter who wanted to marry someone of "the wrong caste" burst out with "What is this caste thing, we're all Americans here!"

BEING MEXICAN, "HINDU," AND AMERICAN

If they were wary about spouses from India or Pakistan, many Punjabi-Mexican children were curious about their own Indian relatives, especially if there were half-brothers or half-sisters. One daughter recalled her father telling them stories about "our family that we never met." Many family men, however, were reticent about the families they had left behind. The Punjabi-Mexican children, like many other Americans, thought of Indians and Pakistanis as poor inhabitants of underdeveloped countries. One reason to refuse marriages with people there was to avoid having to send money or sponsor immigrants from there: "They'll all want to come over," one daughter quoted her mother saying as she turned down a "loop of engagement" from India for her.

In all cases, the second generation's perceptions of their Punjabi or "Hindu" ancestral homelands were somewhat unclear. One reason for the children's inability to locate themselves on South Asian maps was their fathers' deliberate de-emphasis of Punjabi language and culture. This was partly due to the demands made on their time by work. One daughter reported revealingly, "My dad talked about India to his grandchildren; he had time then." But another reason was commitment to their new country, a commitment to "being American." They accepted the restrictions on immigration as permanent and considered their children Americans. Another daughter remembers her shock and sense of loss when her father suddenly stopped the evening sessions of Punjabi lessons and stories about the Punjab—he announced that since his children were Americans, they had no need to learn his language and culture. Other fathers gruffly turned back queries about the Punjab and its language, stating that they were in America now and there was no point learning about India.

But if the men and their families had traveled far from India, India came to them, in the form of a massive immigration from South Asia after 1965. The arrival of large numbers of new immigrants from South Asia after 1965 has irrevocably altered the social landscape and the ways in which the Punjabi pioneers and their descendants construct their identities. Members of the second generation who had identified themselves as Hindu or East Indian have found little in common with the new immigrants from India and Pakistan, and the new immigrants bring with them boundaries that had been nonexistent or blurred by the earlier immigrants. The "old Hindus" had all been from one province, all Punjabi-speakers. Furthermore, they were rural people, largely uneducated in any language. They made major adaptations to live and farm in the United States, changing dress and diet, learning new languages, and marrying new wives from different cultural backgrounds. They depended on local people—bankers, farmers, storekeepers, landowners, and county officials—for their very livelihood. Colonial subjects when they came, they fought for India's freedom but also for their political rights in the United States.

The barriers to meaningful relations with the Punjabi homeland made these early immigrants and their families unconcerned with judgments that might be formed about them back in India. They proceeded to become both "Hindu" and "American" in ways ranging from adopting new concepts of marriage based on romantic love to religious practices that treated men and women equally. The "Hindu" category in the United States included all the early immigrants. Personal names lost much of the religious and regional meaning they held back in the Punjab, and religious differences receded in importance, particularly for the children. Most members of the second generation married outside the Punjabi-Mexican community. Despite these changes and the adoption of a strong "American" component of individual identity, most Punjabi-Mexicans have retained an allegiance to an identity as "Hindus." Even the early immigrants' spouses, predominantly Hispanic women, actively contributed to the construction and maintenance of a "Hindu" identity in the United States, an identity necessarily very different from that being constructed now by the more recent immigrants from South Asia.

REFERENCE

Chan, Sucheng. 1986. *This Bittersweet Soil: The Chinese in California Agriculture, 1860–1910.* Berkeley: University of California Press.

———. 1991. *Asian Americans: An Interpretive History.* Boston: Twayne.

Daniel, Cletus E. 1982. *Bitter Harvest: A History of California Farmworkers.* Los Angeles: University of California Press.

Darling, Malcolm Lyall. 1930. *Rusticus Loquitur, or the Old Light and the New in the Punjab Village.* London: Humphrey Milford, Oxford University Press.

Dhillon, Mahinder Singh. 1981. *A History Book of the Sikhs in Canada and California.* Vancouver: Shromani Akali Dal Association of Canada.

Ellinwood, Dewitt C., Jr. 1976. "An Historical Study of the Punjabi Soldier in World War I." In *Punjab Past and Present: Essays in Honour of Dr. Ganda Singh,* eds. N. Gerald Barrier and Harbans Singh, 337–62. Patiala: Punjab University Press.

Holtville Tribune, Sept. 16, 1910.

Jacoby, Harold S. 1958. "More Thind against Than Sinning." *Pacific Historian* 11:1–2, 4, 8.

———. 1982. "Administrative Restriction of Asian Indian Immigration into the United States, 1907–1917." *Population Review* 25: 35–40.

Leonard, Karen. 1985. "Punjabi Farmers and California's Alien Land Law." *Agricultural History* 59: 4, 549–62.

Leonard, Karen Isaksen. 1992. *Making Ethnic Choices: California's Punjabi Mexican Americans.* Philadelphia: Temple University Press.

McWilliams, Carey. 1978. *Factories in the Field: The Story of Migratory Labor in California.* Salt Lake City: Peregrine Smith.

Millis, H. A. 1912. "East Indian Immigration to the Pacific Coast." *Survey* 28:9, 379–86.

Oberoi, Harjot S. 1988. "From Ritual to Counter-Ritual: Rethinking the Hindu-Sikh Question, 1884–1915." In *Sikh History and Religion in the Twentieth Century,* eds. Joseph T. O'Connell, Milton Israel, and Willard G. Oxtoby, 136–58. Toronto: Centre for South Asian Studies, University of Toronto.

Pettigrew, Joyce. 1975. *Robber Noblemen: A Study of the Political System of the Sikh Jats.* Boston: Routledge and Kegan Paul.

Singh, Mola. 1982. Interview with author, Selma, California.

Singh, Sardar Puna, adapted by Jane P. Singh. 1972. "My Early Years in America." *Sikh Sansar* 1:4, 109–10.

Taylor, Paul S., and Tom Vasey. 1936. "Historical Background of California Farm Labor." *Rural Sociology* 1: 281–95.

3

The New South Asian Immigrants

NEW NATIONS, NEW IMMIGRANTS

The twin achievements of access to naturalized U.S. citizenship in 1946 and independence for India and Pakistan in 1947 marked new trends in South Asian immigration. In 1946, as a result of extensive lobbying by Indians in the United States, the Luce-Celler bill allowed citizenship through naturalization and use of the Indian quota of 105 immigrants per year set by the 1924 National Origins Quota Act. (That quota had been used from 1924 to 1946 only for whites born in India due to the 1923 U.S. Supreme Court decision declaring Indians Caucasians but not "white" and therefore ineligible for U.S. citizenship.) Those Indian pioneers who became American citizens could now revisit their places of origin and sponsor relatives to immigrate. In 1947–1948, when Great Britain's Indian empire gave way to the independent nations of India, Pakistan, Sri Lanka, and Burma, each new nation was allowed an annual quota of 105 immigrants.

An even greater spur to new migration came with the 1965 U.S. Immigration and Naturalization Act, which reversed decades of discrimination and initiated preferential admission of Asian immigrants (Chan 1991: 145–65). As these changes in U.S. immigration law took hold in the late 1960s, the totals rose dramatically. In fact, they are still rising (see Appendices I and II for migration and census statistics). Now Asians, not Europeans, constitute the majority of immigrants to the United States.

Under the 1965 Immigration and Naturalization Act, visas are issued by national origin on the basis of preferred skills or family reunification. There are annual quotas of 20,000 for each country, and visas are given in seven preference categories (including occupation, family relatives, and refugees). The first waves of South Asian immigrants came under the occupational preferences; they were urban, highly educated professionals migrating in family units. Newer immigrants, utilizing the preference categories for relatives, have somewhat lower qualifications and are having a harder time in the United States, as we will see.

The United States has the largest foreign-born population in the world (in 1990 it was 19.6 million, 8% of the total U.S. population). The number of Asian Pacific Islander Americans is expected to triple between 1990 and 2020 or 2024, bringing Asian Americans themselves to 8 percent of the total U.S. population. Census projections continue to be adjusted upward as family-based immigration continues to increase, particularly in the over-65 age group. The Census Bureau expects immigration to outstrip births among Asian Americans for the next thirty or so years, so that the Asian American population will continue to be more than half foreign-born. (This is true across all groups except the mostly native-born Japanese.) In 2020, more than four in ten Asian Americans will live in California; New York and Texas will be the only other states with at least one million Asian Americans. Current public debate and legislative activity seems to be heading toward new restrictions on immigration, but barring that, immigration will take the U.S. population to about 383 million by 2050, an increase of 50 percent in six decades (*India-West*, Dec. 18 & 25, 1992; Feb. 26, 1993; June 2, 1995: 35; May 6, 1994).

South Asians coming to the United States are responding not only to changing U.S. immigration policies but to the global political economy. The structuring of international capitalism, wage differences between countries, political instability in South Asia, family reunification—all these and other factors have produced levels of international migration unprecedented in history. The South Asian countries do not restrict emigration, perhaps because of their continuing problems of unemployment (particularly among the educated) or because of the welcome infusion of foreign-currency remittances sent to the homelands by emigrants (Minocha 1987: 359). The "brain drain" issue is of real concern—it is estimated that one-fourth of the graduates of Indian medical colleges come to the United States annually—but has not led to any significant restrictions on the migration of highly skilled professionals to the United States (Weiner 1990: 243, 247–49; Minocha 1987: 364–67).

The "Asian Indian" category, a census category replacing "East Indian" since 1980, is an important group within the broad "Asian American" category. Asian Indians in the 1990s moved from fourth largest of the Asian American groups to third largest (LEAP 1993), and they stand out among the Asian Americans for their balanced gender ratio. They also make heavy use of occupational and investor categories of the 1965 immigration reforms to develop family networks in the United States and then avail themselves of the family reunification provisions (Hing 1993; Minocha 1987: 350). The categories of relatives currently most used are the fifth preference category, siblings of U.S. citizens and their spouses and children, and the second preference category, spouses and unmarried sons and daughters of resident aliens and their children (*India-West*, Apr. 24, 1992).

India sends the largest number of immigrants annually to the United States (see Appendix I). After India come Pakistan, Afghanistan, Bangladesh, and Sri Lanka; Nepal and Bhutan send negligible numbers. In 1990, the Bangladeshis began outnumbering the Afghans. (Refugees are an increasing factor in migrations. The Afghans are just behind the Palestinians in world ranking, although most Afghans migrate to Pakistan.) Indians and Pakistanis together account for about 90 percent of all South Asian immigrants, and India's share of South Asian immigrants is still by far the largest, although an increasingly higher percentage of Pakistan's population is emigrating (Minocha 1987: 350).

The new pattern of South Asian migration and settlement is quite unlike the earlier one in many ways. Table 3.1 illustrates the changes by decade in the Asian Indian population distribution in the United States, particularly the explosion after 1965 and the shift away from the rural base in California. This table, reflecting census data, is based on self-identified ethnicity and may include South Asians other than those from India—even Fijians or Guyanese of Indian ancestry. Sri Lankans, Bangladeshis, Pakistanis, and others are supposed to include themselves as "Other Asians," but "Asian Indian" is often used interchangeably with "South Asian" in everyday situations, due to the overall numerical dominance of immigrants from India.

The new immigrants differ from the earlier ones in their places of origin and socioeconomic characteristics. The recent immigrants come from all over South Asia, with the smaller countries sending increasing numbers in the 1990s. All the languages of the subcontinent are probably represented in the United States, although the relative numbers of speakers are unknown. Around 1980, the most numerous language groups in the New York area were Gujaratis (34%), Hindi-speakers (20%), and Dravidian-speakers (24%, all four languages together) (Leonhard-Spark and Saran 1980), but the concentrations differ elsewhere. An estimate for southern California around 1980 put Punjabis and Gujaratis at 20 percent each, Urdu-speakers at 18 percent,

Table 3.1
Asian Indian Settlement by Decade

Year	United States	California	Percentage in California
1910	2,544	1,948	77
1920	2,544	1,723	69
1930	3,130	1,873	59
1940	2,405	1,476	60
1950	2,398	815	34
1960	8,746	1,586	17
1970	13,149	1,585	16
1980	387,223	57,901	15
1990	815,447	236,078	29

Sources: Brett Melendy, *Asians in America* (New York: Hippocrene Press, 1981), tables VII, VIII, IX; U.S. Bureau of the Census, *Census of Population 1980*, IB, General Population Statistics (Washington, D.C.: Government Printing Office, 1982); U.S. Bureau of the Census, *Census of Population 1990*, IB, General Population Statistics (Washington, D.C.: Government Printing Office, 1992).

Hindi-speakers at 16 percent, speakers of South Indian languages at 12 percent, and Bengalis at 11 percent (Hossain 1982). Now, the complexity and diversity of the community are striking—there are many kinds of Hindus, Muslims, Buddhists, Christians, Sikhs, and Parsis (or Zoroastrians) settled in the United States. "Traditional" caste and community categories still have significance in the lives of the immigrants, particularly for purposes of marriage. People from South Asia can almost always tell a fellow immigrant's background (language, religion, perhaps caste) from his or her name, and some new immigrants change their names to avoid such categorization.

Because they have immigrated recently and so many are employed in industrial and service sectors of the economy as scientists, engineers, and health professionals, Asian Indians are more concentrated in metropolitan areas than the general U.S. population. About 70 percent are concentrated in the eight major industrial-urban states: New York, California, New Jersey, Texas, Pennsylvania, Michigan, Illinois, and Ohio (Bhardwaj and Rao 1990: 206–7). There are preferred urban destinations within the United States, leading to concentrations of Indians and Pakistanis in California, New York, New Jersey, Illinois, and Texas; the preferred cities are New York, Chicago, San Jose, the Los Angeles/Long Beach metropolitan area, the Washington, D.C., metropolitan area, and Houston, Texas. (Immigrants from Bangladesh and Sri Lanka prefer Florida as well.)

Students coming to the United States for higher education constitute a steady stream of immigrants. In 1994, India sent the fourth largest group of foreign students to the United States (16,419), after Japan (65,681), Korea (38,510), and China (36,318) (*India-West*, May 10, 1996: B34). Many who came as students in the 1950s for training or advanced study stayed on; more than half of all Indian immigrants who changed their status in the 1950s and 1960s to that of resident alien had come initially as students (Minocha 1987: 361). Two increasing groups of immigrants are refugees and seekers of political asylum, those in the latter category being chiefly Indian Punjabi or Kashmiri political activists fighting for an independent Khalistan or Kashmir.

Another source of immigration is the Immigrant Visa Lottery, popularly known as the green card (resident alien card) lottery. Under this program, 55,000 persons are selected randomly each year, by computer, for purposes of achieving diversity from countries with low percentages of immigration to the United States. This lottery was part of the 1990 Immigration Act, and it began in 1995. Pakistanis, Sri Lankans, and Bangladeshis can apply but not Indians, and applicants for the lottery must have twelve years or a high school level of education and recent work experience in an occupation requiring two years of training or experience. The popular program has created a new category of "winners." It is a better way to get to the United States than through the recently exposed "Brooklyn brides scam" in which hundreds of Bangladeshis were paying to marry New York women who "vacationed" in Bangladesh and subsequently applied for visas for their husbands (*Pakistan Link*, Dec. 8, 1995: 6).

The annual arrival numbers fluctuate in response to the U.S. economy and to specific immigration legislation and regulations. When the 1986 Immigration Reform and Control Act (IRCA) was passed, the Special Agricultural Worker (SAW) clause was used to legalize Indian, Pakistani, and especially Bangladeshi workers in agriculture. The subsequent phasing out of IRCA contributed to a decrease in immigrant totals in 1994. The 1990 Immigration Act made it easier to get nonimmigrant visas for religious workers, but new federal regulations in 1995 made it harder to hire foreign workers as temporary professionals. Also in 1995, battered spouses of citizens or permanent residents became able to file for permanent residence on their own behalf, whereas it became more difficult to file successful applications for political asylum.

All changes in U.S. immigration law and visa regulations are much discussed in South Asian journals and newspapers in the United States and abroad, and current backlogs are reported for the preference categories. Generally, the relatives of citizens have preference in the family reunification categories. Thus, in 1994 if a U.S. citizen went to Pakistan, married there, and applied for the spouse's entry to the United States, it took only the processing time for the spouse to enter the United States. But the spouse of a permanent resident, or green card holder, had to wait almost three years, and the waiting time was about the same for unmarried sons and daughters of green card holders. The backlog period was more than eleven years if one was a sibling of even a U.S. citizen. Given the long waiting period for siblings, it made more sense to bring one's parents over and have them become permanent residents or citizens so that they could apply for their children—doing this will get one's siblings here sooner.

Organizations of South Asian professionals zealously scrutinize new visa allotments and changing employment regulations of the relevant sectors of the economy. For example, South Asian doctors worried in the mid-1990s about policies that set quotas for foreign-born residents in hospitals and about the impact of proposed changes in the system of medical care. Many permanent residents faced the question of whether or not to become American citizens—a question that is increasingly important because of considerations like those mentioned above, but with international ramifications as well.

MIGRATION AND TRANSNATIONALISM

Questions of citizenship now require careful consideration, because many migrants have family networks, financial interests, and political commitments that span two or more nations. Taking U.S. citizenship is one way of dealing with the complexity and changeability of U.S. immigration law and regulations, but this was not at first seriously considered by most South Asians who came after 1965. They thought of themselves as economic migrants, men and women coming to the United States for education or for work experience. Many planned to take their expertise back to the home countries when employment opportunities there improved. Many had promised their parents that they would return. There was no immediate reason to opt for U.S. citizenship, especially for those from India. India does not allow dual citizenship, so becoming a U.S. citizen means giving up one's Indian citizenship. Aside from the emotional barriers to doing that, there are practical reasons for remaining an Indian citizen. These involve the holding of property and bank accounts in India and the fact that it is not necessary to obtain a visa to visit there. As long as the cost of remaining a noncitizen in the United States was not high, there were strong reasons to retain Indian citizenship. In the first two decades after 1965, Indians and other South Asians, unsure whether they would stay or return, took relatively little interest in American politics.

For Pakistanis, dual citizenship seemed possible, and many obtained U.S. citizenship as others had obtained British citizenship earlier. For one thing, a U.S. passport allows one to travel more easily to India—India and Pakistan punish each other's citizens by delaying and denying visas when relations between the two nations are bad, and that is all too frequent a circumstance. But the United Kingdom and Pakistan have a dual citizenship agreement and the United States and Pakistan do not; however, because one did not physically surrender the Pakistani passport when swearing allegiance to the United States, it could be retained and used to revisit Pakistan without getting a visa. In 1996, Pakistan decided to issue a "residency card" or national identification card for Pakistanis who had become U.S. citizens; the card allows its bearer all rights except voting in Pakistan. Bangladeshis and Sri Lankans can have dual citizenship, but Nepalese cannot.

In the decade since the mid-1980s, however, some of the factors in the above equation have changed, so that the social and political landscape looks rather different in the 1990s. South Asian families are now more strongly rooted in the United States. The first generation has brought up a second generation and realizes that it will not be easy to take the children "back home." Many original immigrants have finally told their parents they will not be returning and are instead bringing their parents to the United States, at least for the annual visits required to maintain their status as permanent residents. And as more and more immigrants bring their siblings and other relatives, whole families are shifting permanently to the United States, so there is less reason to return to South Asia. Citizenship status expedites family reunification, because citizens are preferred over permanent residents in terms of bringing relatives. Finally, there are federal estate tax benefits for citizens with respect to U.S. tax credits for foreign estate taxes and marital deductions (*India-West*, Mar. 11, 1994).

Other factors are less personal but nonetheless have strong impacts on immigrants' decision making. These relate to economic and social discrimination against minorities and/or immigrants and the need for political representation of South Asian interests. Citizens are in a much stronger position than noncitizens to challenge existing laws and practices, mobilize public opinion, and initiate new laws. Moreover, there is a desire to help the homelands by changing U.S. policies toward them, influencing the U.S. government to be more pro-India or pro-Pakistan, and to give more money for development in Bangladesh or for one faction or another in Afghanistan. This kind of influence requires funding and support for one of the major political parties, preferably the one in power. South Asian interests must be protected, and local, state, and federal political representatives are more responsive to voters.

For some years Indians hoped that India would change its policy and allow dual citizenship. In fact, dialogue with each new Indian ambassador to the United States centered on this question. It now seems that India will not make this change, and its official representatives urge Indians who have settled in America to consider it their home. "India may be your *janam bhoomi* [birthland] but America is your *karam bhoomi* [livelihood land]," Ambassador Abid Hussain told an Orange County Indian audience in 1993, echoing phrases not original with him but increasingly voiced; he also urged Indians to become politically active in the United States. The Indian government has extended, instead, invitations to Non Resident Indians (NRIs) to invest money and fund projects that will benefit the homeland, and the other South Asian countries have extended similar opportunities.

Response to such invitations has been good on the individual level, as remittances flow back to relatives in the home countries, but South Asian Americans have also responded collectively to needs in their homelands. Bangladeshis have funded colleges and sent funds for flood relief; Indians have established medical colleges and veterinary schools and have raised funds for earthquake relief; Pakistanis have developed a global organization to invest in the home country; Nepalis have set up university scholarships for disadvantaged women; and Sri Lankans have contributed to their country's cancer hospital. These and many other projects are being undertaken "back home."

To counter rising anti-immigrant feeling in the United States, the Immigration and Naturalization Service began actively encouraging legal immigrants to become U.S. citizens, publicizing the benefits and the process widely. Legal permanent residents can become naturalized U.S. citizens after five years of residence, and they must be able to read, write, and speak English and have a basic knowledge of the history and government of the United States (*India-West*, Dec. 3, 1993).

Indian immigrants who came to the United States from 1970 to 1979 had a naturalization rate of 53.6 percent (*India-West*, Dec. 24 & 31, 1993: 35). That rate has risen: in 1996, Asian Americans as a whole had a naturalization rate of 81 percent, as high as that of immigrants of European ancestry. Of these Asian Americans, a low percentage are actually registered to vote (53%, like Latinos, and lower than African Americans at 61% and whites at 69%), but once they register they vote at a higher rate (76%) than any other ethnic group (*Los Angeles Times*, Mar. 27, 1996: A18). The threats posed by anti-immigration sentiments in the mid-1990s and the cutoffs of some public benefits—Supplemental Security Income (SSI) and disability benefits even to legal immigrants—undoubtedly mean that more South Asians will become U.S. citizens.

Transnational considerations complicate life for the post-1965 first-generation immigrants in their growing tendency to bring their parents to the United States. The migration of elderly people from South Asia has been rising. This results partly from a natural desire to unite the family and care for the elders and partly from a strategic use of the preference categories to shorten the waiting periods. Moreover, it may be easier to bring parents over permanently than to subject them repeatedly to the application process for visitor visas, which have become harder to obtain. Family tragedies often result when legitimate requests for visitor visas are denied by U.S. consulates in Karachi, New Delhi, or Dhaka. Noncitizen seniors continue to be eligible for certain U.S. government benefits. Immigrants take many factors into consideration as they plan how best to care for their elderly parents.

Transnationalism also links more than two nations, as South Asians emigrate not only to the United States but to the United Kingdom, Canada, and Australia. They may also work for periods of time in the Middle East (where it is not possible to settle permanently), so that brothers or sisters may be in Saudi Arabia or the United Arab Emirates for a decade or more. Such dispersion of family members results in complicated journeys as parents and children travel back and forth. Some migrants do not come to the United States directly but reside elsewhere at first. For example, Afghan immigrants have tended to come by way of Germany, and Indians may come through the United Kingdom or Canada. Many Indians, Pakistanis, Sri Lankans, and Bangladeshis come to the United States after working in the Middle East. There has even been a pattern of intermediate or stepwise (moving step by step) migration within the Pacific Rim (Barkan 1992: 98–99, 207).

It is possible to study transglobal migration by examining patterns of labor migration across national borders in response to changes in the world capitalist economy. Certainly, some in the South Asian immigrant communities in the United States do fit the model of the proletariat envisioned by many scholars of transnational migration (Schiller, Basch, and Blanc-Szanton 1992). But more prevalent, particularly in the first decade or so of immigration after 1965, are highly educated professional people. Another way of conceptualizing them is to talk about a *diaspora.*

The term was traditionally used rather narrowly for the Jewish diaspora, but recent usage seems to include almost any segment of a people living outside its homeland. Six characteristics were recently proposed to define diasporic communities (Safran 1991): (1) that members or their ancestors have been dispersed from a center to two or more other regions; (2) that members retain a collective memory of the original homeland; (3) that they believe they are not and perhaps cannot be fully accepted by the host society; (4) that they regard the homeland as the true home to which they or their descendants should eventually return; (5) that they are committed to the maintenance or restoration of the homeland; and (6) that they continue to relate to that homeland and to define their collective consciousness by that relationship.

The South Asians in the United States, however, do not quite fit the definition of diasporic communities. They diverge from the definition in several significant ways. First, the experience of most early and later South Asian immigrants is not one of being "dispersed" from their homelands but of leaving voluntarily. It is true that within each nation there have been pressures that might cause one group to leave more readily than others. After all, most Afghans migrated as political refugees, and perhaps Muslims are leaving India, *muhajirs* leaving Pakistan, and Tamils leaving Sri Lanka disproportionately. It may also be that many South Asians are skeptical of being fully accepted by the U.S. host society, although others feel that this has been achieved. Yet even if these cases could be made, and although the South Asian immigrants retain collective memories of their homelands and often organize themselves in the United States on that basis, many have recognized that the "myth of return" is indeed a myth. South Asian immigrants are settling in the United States and contributing to its public life in many ways.

SOCIOECONOMIC PROFILES

Having looked closely in Chapter 2 at the relatively small, geographically concentrated Punjabi-Mexican pioneer community, we now move to a broader analysis of the very large, diverse, and geographically diffused contemporary South Asian communities. The novelist Raja Rao has said, "What links the overseas Indians is the idea of India" (Assisi 1989), suggesting that diasporic communities retain collective memories of the homeland, continue to relate to the homeland, and may even define themselves primarily with reference to it. But the new South Asian immigrants to the United States have more in common than ideas. They share socioeconomic characteristics, changing occupational and gender roles within the family, and organizational patterns.

The post-1965 immigrants from South Asia have encountered opportunities rather than constraints in the United States, on the whole. They are highly educated, urban, professional people from all over South Asia. They represent many languages, regional cultures, castes, and religions. Legal barriers do not influence their choice of spouses, and they tend to come as family units, with women almost equal in numbers to men. They have the means to import and support many aspects of South Asian culture. Well placed in the American economy and founders of their own networks of new immigrants, they have no compelling reason to recognize the rural, less well-educated, half-Indian descendants of Punjabi peasants as "real Hindus" or South Asians. In fact, they feel threatened by the example of the Punjabi-Mexican descendants. At first glance, these new immigrants appear to be successfully "maintaining" South Asian culture and identity in the United States, albeit an emergent, transnational middle-class culture (Appadurai and Breckenridge 1986).

Yet there are changes even among the first generation of new South Asian Americans. People migrating are "changed by their travel but marked by places of origin" (Clifford 1989: 188). This chapter begins to explore the changes brought by travel and settlement in the United States.

South Asians are doing very well in the United States. Those born in India have the highest median household income, family income, and per capita income of any foreign-born group in the 1990 Census. A study of foreign-born professionals shows foreign-born Indians to be the highest paid, with an annual median income of $40,625 (*India-West*, Oct. 1, 1993; Apr. 22, 1994). A 1991 survey of five Asian American groups showed that Indians held the most IRAs (individual retirement accounts) and stocks and were the most highly educated (*India-West*, Jan. 25, 1991). Immigrants born in India also were the highest percentage with a bachelor's degree or higher and the highest percentage in managerial and professional fields. (Foreign-born Indians numbered 593,423 in the 1990 Census; 450,406 of those were born in India: *India-West*, Apr. 22, 1994.)

Figures 3.1 through 3.4 profile those born in India, the South Asian immigrant population for which statistics are most readily available. The figures show a relatively young working population, a very high level of educational attainment, many in professional occupations, and a very high level of household income. In terms of family stability, immigrants from India lead the foreign-born in percentage of population married and are at the bottom in percentage of those separated and divorced. The most common household size is four (*India-West*, Oct. 1 & 8, 1993).

Among the skilled South Asian professionals, many are doctors. In 1980, of the approximately 400,000 Indians in the United States, 11 percent of the men and 8 percent of the women were physicians and another 7 percent of the women were nurses (and 17% of the men were engineers, architects,

Figure 3.1
India-Born Population of the United States as of 1993 by Age Groups

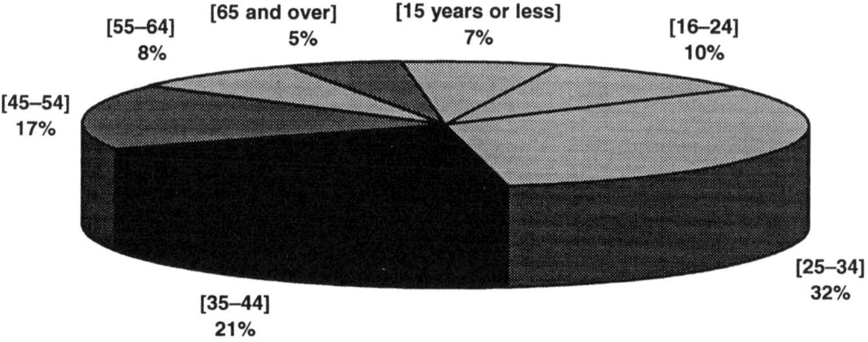

Source: U.S. Bureau of the Census. 1994 Current Population Survey. Washington, DC: U.S. Government Printing Office, 1994. Table prepared courtesy of Ghaffar Mughal. (CPS is the source of the official government statistics on employment and related economic and demographic variables conducted monthly for over 52 years. The March supplement, also known as the annual Demographic File, contains the monthly demographic and labor force data described above, plus additional data on work experience, income, non-cash benefits and migration. Analysts use the March CPS to update information based upon the Census which is repeated every ten years. The last census was done in 1990. 1994 March CPS was based upon a sample suvey of about 57,000 housing units containing records on about 163,000 persons.)

or surveyors: *India-West*, Nov. 27, 1992). One recent estimate puts Indian doctors at more than 20,000, or nearly 4 percent of the nation's medical doctors; in fact, the largest ethnic body of doctors in the United States is the American Association of Physicians from India (*India-West*, Feb. 26, 1993; *India Today*, Aug. 15, 1994: 481). The Association of Pakistani Physicians of North America overlaps somewhat with the Islamic Medical Association of Canada, and there are associations of Indian pharmacists and Indo-American physicians and dentists. Another large group is that of Indian computer professionals working in the United States. Indian engineers are the second largest foreign-born group of engineers, just behind the Chinese (*India-West*, Dec. 1, 1995: A29), and Indian business students outnumber any other international group (Tilak 1996: 48f). Occupational patterns for Asian Indian men and women in the United States suggest that, as in India, many Asian Indian women are working in professional positions (Desbarats 1979). For example, in Bakersfield, California, forty of the ninety doctors from India are married to each other—that is, the ninety doctors include twenty couples (Sethi 1989). Frequently both spouses are working, and savings rates are high (Minocha 1987: 362–63).

Figure 3.2
India-Born Population of the United States as of 1993 by Educational Attainment

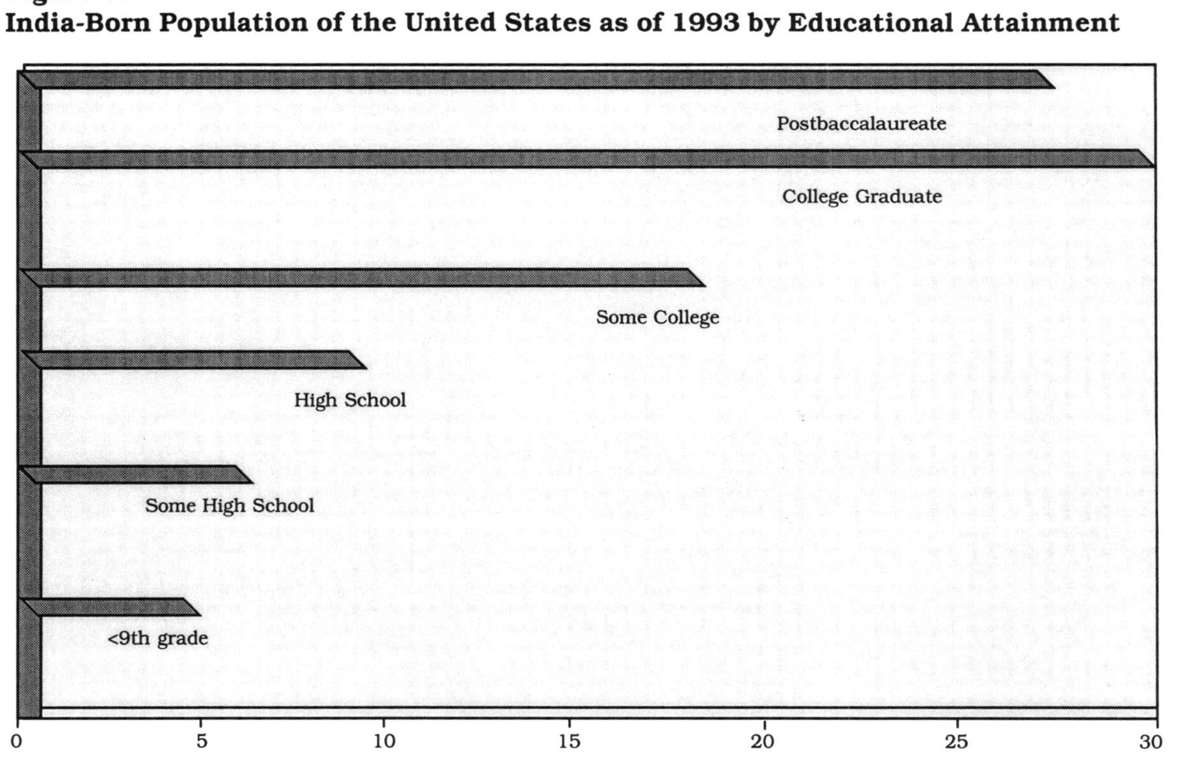

Source: Current Population Survey, March 1994. (see 3.1)

Figure 3.3
India-Born Labor Force in the United States as of 1993 by Sector of Employment

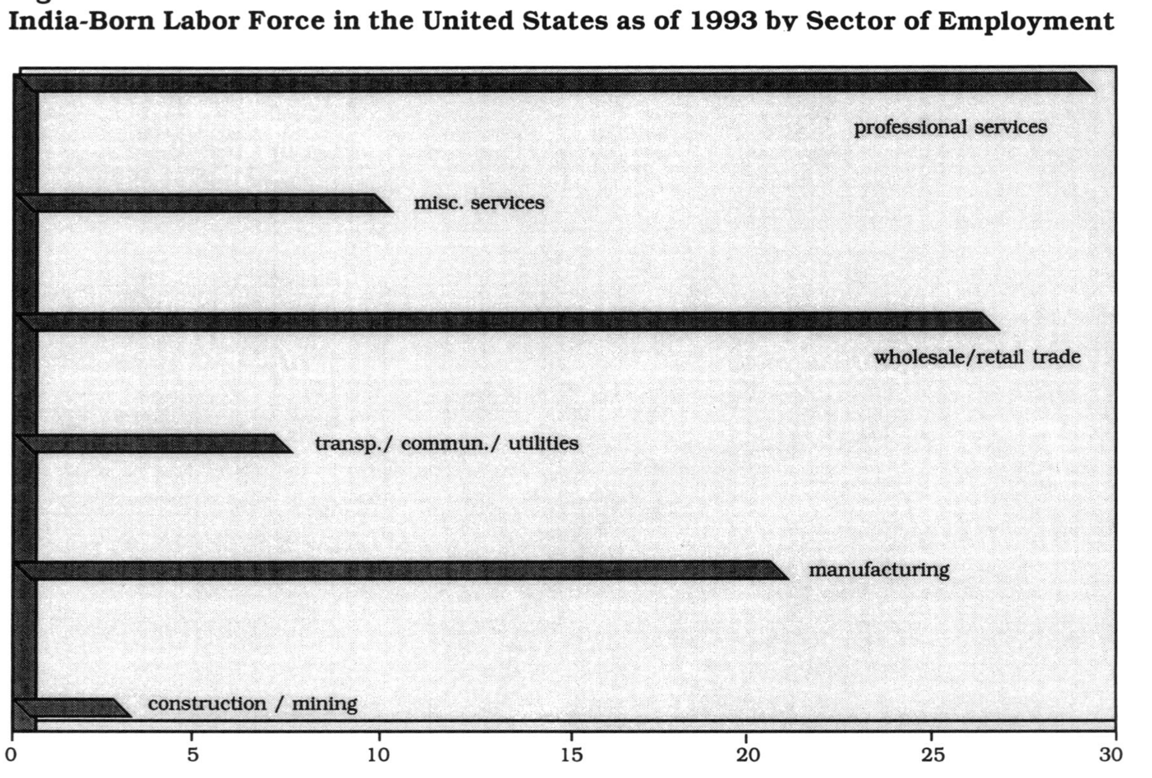

Source: Current Population Survey, March 1994. (see 3.1)

Figure 3.4
India-Born Population of the United States as of 1993 by Household Income Categories

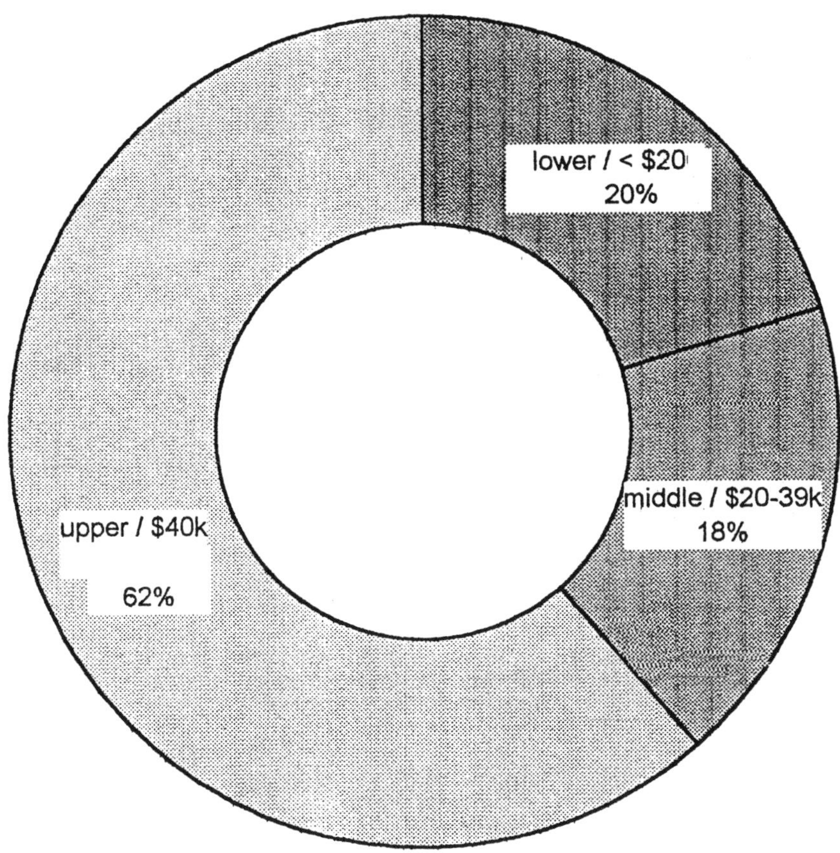

Source: Current Population Survey, March 1994. (see 3.1)

The first wave of post-1965 immigrants accounts for the high socioeconomic standards reflected in Figures 3.1–3.4. In contract, Indian immigrants arriving since 1985 show a much lower percentage in managerial and professional jobs, a much lower median income, and a much higher unemployment rate (Melwani 1994: 60c–f). Many of these later immigrants, who came under the Family Reunification Act, are not so well qualified, and their arrival occurred during a recession in the U.S. economy. Thus, the percentage of South Asian families in poverty is relatively high, putting those born in India 12th on the lists of both families in poverty and individuals in poverty (*India-West,* Oct. 1, 1993). The effects of the U.S. Immigration Act of 1990 should reverse this slight downward trend, because the legislation sharply increased the numbers of highly skilled immigrants from India (and Asia generally) at the expense of nonemployed immigrants (parents and spouses of citizens) and unskilled workers (*India Currents*, May 1993: C74). The 1990 Act also helped spur increases in the Bangladeshi, Pakistani, and Sri Lankan populations.

There are, however, two reasons to expect increasing polarization within the Indian and South Asian immigrant communities—or at least a continuing decline of the socioeconomic measures. First, there are illegal immigrants, about which the census tells us nothing. Some come through Mexico or Canada; others come on tourist or student visas and overstay. Particularly among the Bangladeshis but characteristic of all nationalities, members of this group scramble for jobs as dishwashers, truck-loaders, convenience store clerks, and other casual labor. Their first priority is to secure legal status, and lawyers and ethnic associations advise and work for these immigrants. Some illegal immigrants marry American citizens. In fact, the matrimonial advertisements in the ethnic press often indicate preferences for spouses who have green cards or are U.S. citizens.

Second, there is some evidence that the second generation of Indian Americans (again, that "Asian Indian" census category) may bring down some of the high socioeconomic measures reported above. As of 1988, U.S.-born Asian Indians (along with U.S.-born Filipinos) had much higher levels of unemployment (7.6% for the Indians) than did other Asian Americans or non-Hispanic whites, and only 35 percent of them (compared to 73% of foreign-born Indians) had completed more than sixteen years of schooling (*India-West*, Oct. 14, 1988–1996). A recent study shows that in California, Oregon, and Washington, just over 10 percent of the Indian American population is living below the poverty line, with a serious unemployment problem. An even more detailed state-by-state study found that California had the highest percentage of Indian American children living in poverty (14%, whereas the national average is 9%) (*India-West*, Aug. 18, 1995: C1, C15, C18; Dec. 15, 1995: A1, A31–32).

The initial post-1965 Asian Indian immigration featured professionals and their families, but since the mid-1970s more immigrants have been starting small businesses or investing in such businesses as a part-time sideline (Lessinger 1985: 6). Ethnic self-employment has often been equated with ethnic enclaves or an ethnic economy, and one might argue that ethnic economies have developed in those states of heavy South Asian immigrant concentration, such as New York and California. South Asians do cluster in certain businesses that employ new immigrants and cater to the needs and tastes of South Asians. Examples include Indian, Pakistani, Sri Lankan, and Bangladeshi grocery stores, *sari* and yard goods stores and boutiques, and 220-volt electrical appliance stores (for appliances to be taken to South Asia). South Asian–owned insurance and real estate businesses also rely heavily on co-ethnic networks for their clientele. And major American companies are also utilizing ethnic networks: New York Life recently established an Asian Indian marketing division (*India-West*, Feb. 9, 1996: A33). Restaurants, motels, and travel agencies typically attract mixed clienteles, but ethnic networks are also important for them. Certainly, the owners of restaurants and travel agencies are key community figures: restaurants cater for South Asian community events, and travel agents compete to obtain inexpensive tickets for U.S. residents and their visitors.

There has been less research on South Asian entrepreneurs than on Chinese, Japanese, or Korean immigrant entrepreneurs (but see Leonard and Tibrewal 1993). The large numbers of highly educated professionals who came as immigrants immediately after 1965 were seemingly poor candidates for "middleman minority" status, (i.e., the sociological concept that immigrants cluster in ethnic enclaves to maximize ethnic resources and succeed in an alien culture and economy). But as socioeconomic disadvantage looms larger in the South Asian population, self-employment and occupational clustering are becoming visible.

The move into self-employment and small businesses is partly a result of the earlier immigrants' sponsorship of relatives who are less qualified than themselves, but there may also be new barriers to entry into the U.S. labor market. Some Asian Indian businesspeople believe that self-employment provides the best opportunity at the present time in this society (Lessinger 1985; Khare 1980; Dutta 1982; Elkhanialy and Nicholas 1976). Citing adverse pressures from the local economy, Asian Indians have fought to gain minority group status in case after case. The National Association of Americans of Asian Indian Descent, at the behest of Asian Indian businessmen, petitioned for recognition as a socially disadvantaged minority in 1982 and obtained it from the U.S. Small Business Administration (Fornaro 1984: 30–31). This minority group status entitles Indians to some preferential awards but is controversial within the Asian Indian community—the Indian League of America and many individuals did not want minority or non-Caucasian status. Recent challenges to Affirmative Action programs at both state and federal levels may make it harder for South Asians to keep that status in any case.

A more positive explanation for the recent trend toward self-employment could be that overseas Indians engaged in business are simply extending their business acumen and kinship networks from India or elsewhere. Yet the Patels who dominate the motel business in California and elsewhere were not a business community back in their Indian state of Gujarat; they are not

Vaishyas and were agriculturalists. And the Sikhs who have done well in business both in India and overseas recently are also largely from agricultural backgrounds. However, other Gujarati-speakers who are in business in the United States are Vaishyas from merchant and banking communities in India. Moreover, there are transnational South Asian businesses expanding into the United States. And some older people, parents being brought by their adult children to the United States, are contributing their business experience, thereby helping to set the standards for restaurants and for the South Asian imported products being distributed throughout the country.

Certainly, family and community networks are important to many South Asian businesspeople. But countertendencies among small businesspeople see both partnerships and employer/employee relationships crossing religious and national boundaries. A preliminary survey of partnership arrangements among New York's South Asian immigrant businesses found that comparative strangers were financing and operating small businesses as partners, creating problems apparently not experienced in India. The lack of hierarchical structure and intimate knowledge of each other, such as that produced by joint family bonds, may lead Indian businesses here to fail more often than in India because of problems between partners (Lessinger 1985: 3).

The extent to which immigrant entrepreneurs benefit from employing family members or co-ethnics as workers is important. One might look for "intraethnic class exploitation" in terms of wages and hours, or indications that family labor is being abused (Lessinger 1985). Conversely, there might be offsetting advantages to being employed by co-ethnics, such as easier access to loans, flexible working hours, legal advice and protection, shares in the business, and perhaps sponsorship in setting up businesses. Where appropriate, South Asian small businesspeople employ Spanish-speakers (as do Korean, Chinese, Vietnamese, and other businesspeople). A study of Chinese-Vietnamese businesses points out that they may do this partly to exempt themselves from the paternalistic labor relations often expected by co-ethnics and to protect themselves from employees whose inside knowledge could be detrimental to the store owners (Gold 1989: 13). Women of the family can be employed instead of noncommunity members.

Ethnic networks are being mobilized by South Asian businesspeople to create new and wider clienteles that cross "traditional" linguistic, religious, and caste barriers. For example, in New York, some stores advertise for "Indo-Pak-Bangla" customers (Khandelwal 1995: 191). In Los Angeles, where South Asian Muslims are numerous, ethnic business owners deliberately appeal to wider regional or linguistic groupings. Thus, a Punjabi Hindu store prominently displays leaflets about Hajj trips (the pilgrimage to Mecca) and gives free food on *Id* (a Muslim holiday, a time of feasting after a long fast); it routinely advertises *mushairas* (recitations of Urdu poetry, associated with Muslim culture) along with *bharatnatyam* recitals (classical South Indian Hindu dance). Nearby, two Pakistani brothers named their grocery store and adjacent tailoring shop "Mah Bharat," a Sanskrit phrase meaning "Mother India" (this was partly to attract members of the nearby Hare Krishna temple, who were predominantly white Americans). Hossain (1982: 75) found that linguistic and religious affinities among immigrants were more important than country of origin. Similarly, Leonard and Tibrewal (1993) found that when seeking capital investment, businessowners turned to people of different religious and national backgrounds as well as to members of the same religious, national, or caste community. The new ways in which occupational and ethnic networks are being combined have implications for family and gender relationships.

MEN, WOMEN, AND WORK

For South Asian immigrants, the fact of women working in the United States has slightly different consequences than the fact of women working in the homelands, where immediate and extended family members and servants can share responsibilities within a broad support network. Perhaps the consequences are more far-reaching for those women who work in ethnic businesses, for an ethnic economy is almost by definition a gendered economy. Immigrant family businesses make use of women's labor as a cheap resource, keeping labor costs and wages low (Westwood and Bhachu 1988: 5). It is also a new resource for many South Asian immigrants, because "the woman who is running a grocery or restaurant in L.A. would not have done this back in India or Pakistan or Bangladesh" (Hossain 1982: 78).

But the changes go beyond bringing women into family businesses. In a study done in the Los Angeles area, not all the Indian women engaged in managing and working in ethnic business enterprises were doing so in their own family businesses. Also, the model was not that of a "mom and pop" store, where both husband and wife worked in the store with the man being clearly in charge (Leonard and Tibrewal 1993). Rather, the pattern most characteristic was that found for Vietnamese family businesses in California (Gold 1988: 421), with husbands holding other full-time jobs while their wives opened and ran groceries, restaurants, or boutiques. Indian grocery stores very often are managed by wives while the husbands work as engineers or in other specialized positions for American companies. Research on Gujarati motel owners found women taking important roles in the business (Jain 1989; Thakar 1982), whereas the men sometimes worked elsewhere. This marks a departure from employment patterns back in India, where private businesses, including family businesses, rarely employ women as managers and clerks. Most of the women working in ethnic businesses did not work at all, or did not work in such jobs, back in South Asia. In the case of the entrepreneurial Vietnamese women, Gold (1988) explained that in Vietnam women were always the money managers for the family, but this is not a tradition for South Asian women. It seems, rather, that the management of ethnic businesses by wives is a new strategy to maximize economic security and family income.

South Asian women in the United States are making desirable, often necessary, contributions to family earnings, thereby empowering themselves within the family. Women make more decisions about spending than do their mothers-in-law back home, and they make more decisions than do their visiting or even co-residing mothers-in-law in the United States. Parents now come to visit or live with their immigrant daughters as well as their sons (Thakar 1982: 68–73). The contribution of women to business efforts is publicly recognized in the ethnic press, too (e.g., in crediting the development of new dishes for a restaurant to one's wife, or having a woman make the presentation of blankets to the homeless on behalf of the business). Thus, even when the family histories of ethnic entrepreneurs show a continuity of entrepreneurial activity, important changes are occurring in gender roles within families.

Some South Asian women are taking up occupational options in the United States that have important implications for ideas about the homelands and South Asian ethnic identity. Women hold prominent positions in private businesses, and the ethnic newspapers feature articles about women entrepreneurs, from those dealing in clothes and snack products to those working in insurance and computer companies. The prominence of such women, and the highly visible roles of women managers and clerks in South Asian ethnic grocery stores and in motels owned by Gujarati families, gives an expanded idea of the capabilities of women and the range of economic roles available to them. Among Sri Lankans, many women run Montessori nursery schools. In fact, Montessori schools seem to have been pioneered in the United States by the Sri Lankan Leena Wichramaratne, who had studied with Maria Montessori in Sri Lanka (Montessori spent some time in South Asia, and other South Asian women also run such schools in the United States). Muslim women from India and Pakistan also run Islamic nursery schools; indeed, educational work by women is readily approved of among Muslims.

Immigrant women sometimes change careers in the United States. A dramatic example is Rupa Vyas of Houston, originally from India, who had trained and worked as a laboratory technician in Canada before coming with her husband to Houston in 1969. Finding that there was no grocery store in Houston serving the Indian community, she began ordering goods for herself and her friends and eventually got a bank loan and became a successful businesswoman (*Houston Chronicle*, Mar. 21, 1993: 18E).

It is South Asian women like Vyas, managers of ethnic grocery stores, who serve as cultural consultants for other immigrants and also for non–South Asian shoppers. They shape cultural tastes on a daily basis, helping diverse customers to formulate ideas about what is Indian, or Pakistani, or Sri Lankan, or Bangladeshi. The ethnic grocery stores provide many other goods and services: cookbooks along with the foodstuffs, audio and video cassettes, clothing, and even supplies for religious rituals. They stock ready-made and fast foods for other South Asian working wives and for the many students who have no time or ability to prepare meals for themselves (Dongre 1991: 41).

Food and its preparation are central to ethnic and national identity, and this domain is also strongly gendered. The Hispanic wives of the Punjabi pioneers had learned to prepare some Punjabi dishes, and this was central to their "Hindu" identity. Two restaurants run by Punjabi-Mexican sons from the Imperial Valley—El Ranchero in Yuba City and Pancho's in Selma—featured chicken curry and *roti* in addition to their full Mexican menus, and a "Spanish-Pakistani" cookbook was reportedly produced in Arizona after the partition of India in 1947. For the new immigrants as well, food is at the core of identity construction.

The entrepreneurial South Asian women in their grocery stores advise many customers not only about cooking but about a variety of cultural matters. An engaging article on the production of Indian cookbooks, particularly by and for the middle- and upper-class professional strata (and by and for Indians overseas), links cookbooks to the development of ideas about India and a national cuisine (Appadurai 1988). In ethnic grocery stores, the role of women managers and clerks has become even more important with the addition of fast food (or at least "fast snack") centers. Typically, snacks and sweets from several regional cuisines are sold side by side, the variety surpassing that available in almost any city in South Asia itself. There is variation, with Sri Lankan groceries featuring sauces for pork curries and many kinds of hoppers and dried fishes, and the Bangladeshi groceries serving fresh-cooked Bengali fish curries. Pakistani and Indian brands of *basmati* rice (a fragrant long-grained rice) compete for the customer's attention, and fresh hot *samosas* or spicy cool Punjabi snacks and mango milkshakes are served in most Indian and Pakistani stores.

South Asian women also shape ideas about their homelands as they prepare meals at home and dine out in restaurants. They play hostess to guests from different parts of their homelands and from other countries, so they adjust recipes and menus. They must also cater to their own children, who typically prefer more American foods than do their parents. (Thus, mothers are charged both with enculturation of their children in South Asian ways and with catering to their changing, Americanized tastes.) South Asian couples and families have begun to dine out, too, often in South Asian restaurants that have been long monopolized by non–South Asians. As a result, South Asian restaurants are adapting to the broadest possible clientele. For example, a Pathan restaurant offers "family day meals," one all-vegetarian buffet and one non-vegetarian buffet, although Afghans are not vegetarians (there are more examples of versatile restaurants in Chapter 5).

Just as the early Punjabi immigrants and their descendants redefined themselves, their families, and their work relationships, the newcomers from South Asia are defining and experiencing family and work relationships in new ways in the United States. First-generation women often play key roles in these changes. Charged with embodying and transmitting "tradition," women instead change it as they contribute to the material prosperity of the family. Indeed, South Asian women in the United States are active agents of change in public as well as private life.

As we mentioned in Chapter 1, women have achieved the very highest national political offices in four South Asian countries, and women's participation in public life is proceeding apace in most of the home countries. In the United States, this pattern may be more concentrated because of the fairly homogeneous nature of the new immigrant population from South Asia. Women participate prominently in South Asian associational activities, ranging from political groups addressing themselves to the South Asian and American governments to local vernacular and sectarian cultural and religious associations. Women are conspicuous promoters of cultural and recreational events, and these probably have the broadest impact on community life. South Asian women in the United States are doing many things beyond the family: providing support for battered South Asian women, educating women about physical and mental health issues, and working on legal issues related to marriage, divorce, and migration.

POLITICAL AND SOCIAL ORGANIZATIONS

Many writers remind us of the power relations embedded in the "politics of location," the local, regional, and national dimensions of "situatedness," and the ways in which "cultural location" produces new ethnicities and new political identities (Hall 1988; Keith and Pile 1993). South Asian ethnic, national, and transnational organizations are proliferating in the United States, and politics pervades their operations. Political organizations based on national origin, intended to influence the homeland or the United States or both, sometimes work at cross purposes to other organizing efforts. Thus, Pakistani and Indian Muslims may join together in Urdu literary activities but find themselves pressuring U.S. congressmen to take opposite sides on the Kashmir issue. In this section we will look at both social and explicitly political organizations and coalitions created by South Asians in the United States (we examine religious and cultural ones in the following chapters).

Despite the relatively high socioeconomic profile set for South Asians by the Asian-Indian majority, a 1992 compilation of social science surveys shows that Asian Indians are perceived by Americans to be relatively low in social standing. This national study made use of polls done over several years by seven national polling organizations comparing 33 ethnic and religious groups (and, in some tables, 58 groups). Of the 33 groups, Indians, who were highest in educational level and (in this survey) fifth in household income, were only 28th in social standing. When all 58 groups were ranked, Indians were 38th in social standing (*India-West*, Jan. 17, 1992). These findings are probably attributable to prejudice against immigrants from India (and South Asia generally), and political mobilization is one way to combat the prejudice.

Participation in American political life was a goal for the early Indian immigrants and has become one for most South Asian newcomers. After the Luce-Celler bill made them eligible for citizenship in 1946, the Punjabi pioneers helped elect Dalip Singh Saund from California's Imperial Valley in 1956, the first congressman from India (Saund 1960). After some hesitation (Minocha 1987: 364, refers to their political apathy) the new South Asian immigrants are becoming active in both Democratic and Republican Party political funding and campaigning.

Several competing national federations among the Indian Americans reflect U.S. regional differences and rivalry among leaders. The four leading national associations are the Association of Asian Indians in America (AIA), the National Federation of Indian Associations in America (NFIA), the Indian American Forum for Political Education (the Forum), and the National Association of Americans of Asian Indian Descent (NAAAID). AIA is the oldest, formed in the mid-1960s, and its members along with NAAAID spearheaded the move to rename and enumerate Asian Indians separately in the 1980 census. The NFIA was formed around 1971 on the East Coast and was reorganized and renamed over the years; today it is an umbrella federation of some 80 associations (with at least 300 others grouped under them). The

AIA and the NFIA undertake political, social, and cultural activities, whereas the Forum and the NAAAID are exclusively political. The latter represents only naturalized citizens of Indian descent and concentrates on fielding and funding candidates for political office. The Forum and the NFIA coordinated the efforts against a 1985 proposal to substantially cut Medicare funding to hospitals employing foreign medical graduates and against the 1986 immigration bill that proposed drastic reductions in family reunification quotas. In 1988, these groups joined with other Asian American organizations in a successful effort to keep smaller country-of-origin categories under the "Asian American" census heading (Basu c. 1986; Singh 1996).

Some association leaders claim that the more recent Asian Indian immigrants are relatively inactive politically, but recent immigrants protest that the longer-established immigrant associations make little effort to include or represent them (Basu c. 1986: 10). As Williams remarks, in many organizations there are tensions between the "doctors and engineers" who are already well established and the new immigrants who may be less successful and more traditional in their ways (1988: 285). Thus, some earlier and more prominent associational leaders may fight to retain family reunification preferences but at the same time may largely agree with proposed legislation that would limit immigration to the United States.

Political mobilization can be based on specific issues, such as crime or discrimination against South Asians. Crime impacts specific South Asian populations in specific places—for example, New York's cabdrivers and newsstand and gas station attendants, 40 percent of whom are from the subcontinent (*India Today*, Mar. 15, 1994). Another place known for discrimination and violence against South Asians is New Jersey, especially the towns where notorious "dot-buster" gangs have been active. (The name refers to the red dot, or beauty mark, worn on the forehead by many Indian American women.) Indians, particularly Gujarati Hindus, are heavily concentrated in Edison, Jersey City, and Iselin, and continuing problems range from local hooliganism to difficulties in getting municipal permits for the observation of the annual Navratri festival (a religious observance involving singing and dancing, typically attended by thousands of people).

Discrimination against people from the Indian subcontinent is a regular topic in the South Asian ethnic press. There are frequent reports about individual discrimination cases against employers, filed with the Equal Employment Opportunity Commission (EEOC) or in the courts (Joy Cherian, from India, was an EEOC appointee for many years). Sometimes South Asians turn to the National Association for the Advancement of Colored People for support and legal assistance. Reporters write about the "glass ceiling" in certain businesses, occupations, or federal agencies. In fact, the U.S. Department of Agriculture has been named as one in which Asian American career employees seem to have difficulty moving up the career ladder beyond a certain point (Sundaram 1996).

Several hopeful candidates of Indian American background have run for Congress, among them Neil Dhillon, Ram Uppuluri, Peter Mathews, Nimi McConigley, and Ramakrishnan Nagarajan, but to date Dalip Singh Saund stands as the only congressman from India. Bill Quraishi, an American of Pakistani background, has also been a congressional hopeful. Other South Asians are making their numbers and influence felt at the state level. In Ohio, where one in six doctors is Indian, the twelve-member State Medical Board had no Indian members, but after the 1990 elections the new governor asked for the names of qualified Indians for state jobs (Goel 1996: 9) and has since appointed an Indian American to head the Health Department.

Pakistani Americans, too, are becoming politically active in both major political parties. Like the Indians, they often have two or more competing associations. In Indianapolis, for example, there is the Pakistan Friendship Association founded in 1973 and the Pakistan Association founded in 1991 (*Pakistan Link*, June 25, 1993: 18). Pakistanis and Indians, the two largest communities, tend to mirror each other's associations. After the Pakistanis formed the Pakistan American Veterans Association, the Indians formed the Society of Indian Veterans of America (SIVA); these organizations celebrate Indian and Pakistani national and military holidays. They also sponsor cultural events and honor visiting polo players and former military officers from the home countries. Cricket teams in the United States are often based on South Asian national origin. The Sri Lankans have had a very high profile here (Sri Lanka was World Cup Champion in 1995).

South Asian businesses sometimes have trouble with municipalities, and the reverse is also true. In Chicago, Devon Avenue is the heart of the Indian and Pakistani business area (South Asian Muslims call it Diwan [prime minister, a Persian title from Mughal times] Avenue). The street has been unofficially renamed (but with city signs) Jinnah Road and Gandhi Marg—to the west and east of Western Avenue, respectively—in recognition of the Pakistani and Indian businesses there. However one refers to it, the street is known for being rather dirty. Businessowners charge the city with neglect of the area, and in 1994 the businesspeople and volunteers undertook a spring cleaning of the neighborhood. The city of Chicago donated paint, scrapers, and brushes to the goodwill effort (*India Tribune*, Apr. 30, 1994: 31).

Also in Chicago (and allegedly due to the long-standing feud between two Indian American groups that compete annually for permits to celebrate In-

Celebrating Pakistan's Independence Day, San Francisco, 1996. Courtesy of *Pakistan Link*.

dia's Independence Day), the city has instigated a high application fee ($35) for permits to hold public functions. The FIA (Federation of India Associations of Chicago, 33 organizations) held the parade annually from 1983, but in 1989 and 1990 the AMIA (Alliance of Midwest India Associations, 6 organizations) held a separate parade. The city has required the two organizations to draw for the right to hold the event from 1991 on, but the difficulty has persisted, with the FIA submitting an astonishing 324 applications in 1995 to hold the parade downtown. The FIA leader countercharged that the AMIA had put in 50 applications one year (Sundaram 1995).

In southern California, the Little India Chamber of Commerce in 1991 requested the city of Artesia to put up "Little India" signs there and on nearby freeways, but this was not granted. In fact, the mayor made some derogatory comments (for which he apologized later) about the local Indian businesses, which numbered between 50 and 75. Investigating the controversy, reporters (and the Indo-American Republicans of U.S.A., which tried to mediate) found that there were concerns on both sides. There was a feeling that the South Asians kept to themselves—neither an earlier short-lived Indian Merchants Association nor the existing Little India Chamber of Commerce interacted at all with Artesia's Chamber of Commerce. The city alleged

Shia Muslims celebrating Pakistan's Independence Day, San Francisco, 1996. Courtesy of *Pakistan Link.*

that some businesses were not paying sales taxes fully, and it complained that Indian businesses remained open on the Fourth of July while all other businesses were closed, showing a lack of respect to the "country of livelihood." Finally, there were almost annual problems within the FIA, and therefore with the city, over the permits for Indian Independence Day celebrations, as factions fought each other and the city even to the point of lawsuits (Potts 1991; Mathur 1991). Politics and religion back in India split the southern California FIA informally in 1994, with the formation of a "secular" FIA and competition between the two FIAs for Artesia Park, the favored venue for India's Independence Day celebrations (Potts 1994a). A formal split has taken place in 1996, and a Federation of Hindu Associations has been formed.

In presenting themselves to the wider society, people from the Indian subcontinent find that Americans often do not know much about their countries or the meaning of the term *South Asia.* Even within each immigrant population, there can be disagreement about the best term to designate the community. Having secured "Asian Indian" as a census category, Indian immigrants now think that "Indian American" or "Indo-American" might be better. There are regional preferences within the United States, with East Coast residents preferring the former and West Coast ones the latter (Anand 1994).

Indians and other South Asians are beginning to identify with larger categories. "Asian Americans" is the most obvious, and both Indian and Pakistani American groups are making this move. Among Asian Americans, "South Asians" (really "Asian Indians," the census category) has just become the third largest group. Only a few years ago, identifying as "Asian Americans" was a new idea (see *India-West,* Mar. 6, 1992, for a description of a special session on Indo-Americans and other "hidden Asians" at a conference on Asian and Pacific Americans in Higher Education), but it is catching on rapidly. In Orange County, California, in 1992, Pakistani Americans joined the Asian American Festival organized by the county Republican Party (*Pakistan Link,* Sept. 10–Oct. 3, 1992). Among South Asian second-generation students on American campuses, Asian American and Muslim American organizations are popular. In 1994, a major reorientation for business communities saw the Indo-American Hotel Owners Association joining with the Asian American Hotel Owners Association (AAHOA) under the AAHOA banner (Potts 1994b). (A step in the opposite direction, and perhaps a hypocritical one, came when the FIA in New York banned several groups with "South Asian" in their names, and allegedly for that reason, from participating in the annual India Day parade in the early 1990s. Coincidentally, these were groups for gay men and lesbians, against anti-Asian and anti-women violence, and for action on AIDS. In contrast, the FIAs in San Francisco, Los Angeles, and San Jose included such groups.)

Muslim American coalitions are also promising political options for some South Asians. Islam is or is about to be the second largest religion in the United States and has a strong indigenous minority membership. As we will see in Chapter 4, South Asian Muslims provide the intellectual and (to some extent) the political leadership for Muslim Americans; the potential of this linkage has yet to be fully realized. The smaller and newer immigrant groups from Sri Lanka, Bangladesh, Nepal, and Afghanistan have at present no political clout like that of the Indian and Pakistani immigrants.

The new South Asian immigrants have formed many linguistic groups, and these can draw as many as 5,000 or 8,000 people to annual conventions. Some cut across the national boundaries adhered to by the explicitly political associations. Just as the Punjabi language brought together Sikhs, Muslims, and Hindus among the early immigrants from India, the regional language associations bring together people in the United States from different religions, castes, and communities. An example is the Malayalees from Kerala, whose Federation of Kerala Associations in North America has Hindu, Christian, and Muslim members. In some cases, the linguistic associations link people from Pakistan and India (Urdu and Punjabi), India and Bangladesh

(Bengali), or India and Sri Lanka (Tamil). The Bangla Artists' Guild of Los Angeles proudly promotes Bengali-language artists and writers of all backgrounds—Bangladeshi, Indian, or American. Occasional confusion results. The inaugural celebration of a Los Angeles Urdu radio station called "Dil Dil Pakistan" (loosely translated, "Pakistan is my heart") was severely criticized, despite a performance by the lead singer from Vital Signs (a Pakistani rock band), for its heavy dose of Indian film songs and an Indian fashion show featuring a Hindu marriage vignette (*Pakistan Link*, July 7, 1995: 25).

In other cases, these linguistic associations are so large and so important that they have been riven by caste or other divisions. For example, the Telugu Association of North America is dominated by members of the Kamma caste, whereas their rivals in the countryside of Andhra Pradesh (the Telugu-speaking state in South India), members of the Reddy caste, have formed the American Telugu Association (*India-West*, Feb. 25, 1994, citing research by Rukmini Timmaraju). A Tamil organization in San Jose, California, has split into Brahmans and non-Brahmans; and an inclusive Kannada Kuta in Chicago could not preclude the formation of a separate organization by the Vokkaligas, a dominant caste in Karnataka (Rajagopal 1994: 38). It is not clear what will happen in the second generation, when both linguistic competence and caste consciousness have declined markedly.

Other associations are based on professional or educational affiliations. Again, some can attract thousands of members to banquets or conventions. There are strong alumni groups from the home countries: the Old Anthonians from Sri Lanka, the Karachi University Alumni Association from Pakistan, the Aligarh Muslim University Old Boys Association from India, the Mehbubia Girls' School from Hyderabad, India, and others too numerous to name. In contrast are the organizations formed in the United States: the Indian Lawyers Association of America, the Pakistan American Chamber of Commerce, the Urdu Journalists Association of America, and the Asian American Hotel Owners Association (now dominated by Gujarati Patels). Professional groups with special concerns about immigration and job-related policies have become powerful, and the huge American Physicians of Indian Origin has subgroups such as the Osmania Medical Graduates Association and so forth. These groups tend to invite leading U.S. politicians to their gatherings, whereas the language associations invite more politicians from the home countries to theirs.

Social service organizations aimed at women (e.g., the South Asian Helpline and Resource Association, or SAHARA, for abused women in southern California; the similar Sakhi (girlfriend) in New York; and many others across the nation) are strong and controversial. Groups have been started to help senior citizens, a relatively new part of the South Asian American population. These seniors can join the American Association of Retired Persons, but the national origin and linguistic associations are forming task forces for them as well.

There are other societies for age and marital categories. Parents anxious to have their youngsters socialize with others of similar background organize associations that are thinly disguised arenas for Indian youth to meet other Indian youth, or Pakistanis to meet Pakistanis, and so on. Somewhat surprisingly, second-generation Indian American college students are even joining fraternities and sororities, with their emphasis on coed social activities and dating. And there are organizations for older singles to meet each other: a Social Club for Indian Professional Singles; a Silicon Valley Indian Professional Association; a Pakistan Professionals, Engineers and Scientists Association. At least in the Indian-origin groups, a large minority of the members is female. These meetings are all advertised in the ethnic press. The singles organizations and the matrimonial advertisements featuring divorcees (and even widows) in South Asian periodicals published in the United States suggest that even though universal marriage continues to be the goal, the qualifications for marriage and the ways of finding marriage partners are changing.

The national, regional, and local ethnic newspapers and journals are important to the immigrant communities. They have developed rapidly over the last twenty or twenty-five years and often set high standards of journalism and production. Circulations vary from a few hundred to fifteen thousand or more. Another significant dimension of intellectual and political influence in the United States has been the establishment of small but high-profile groups and journals staffed primarily by academics of South Asian origin. Often these began as national-origin groups—the *Pakistan Progressive*, for example—but at least in title and increasingly in reality they reach out to the South Asian constituency. The *South Asia Bulletin*, the *Committee on South Asian Women*, the *South Asian Magazine for Action and Reflection*, and *South Asia Forum/Quarterly* lead in this category. It is these groups that tend to ally with Asian Americans and other minority populations in the United States (Basu and Anner 1991–1992).

The smaller groups of South Asian immigrants to the United States have not been studied in detail yet, or little has been published. Some groups are organizing and publishing their own newsletters, whereas others are too new, too large, and perhaps too internally divided to present a national profile. Two smaller groups, the Nepalese and the Parsis from India and Pakistan, have achieved a certain level of cooperation and coordination in North America.

Nepalese were not emigrants until the early 1950s, when India helped the king to return to power, and it was difficult for them to get passports and travel abroad. The first Nepalese to become a permanent resident of the United States did so in 1952 and the second in 1956; by 1990 there were 1,749 Nepalese residing in the United States (Shrestha 1995: 115). An immigrant to New York as late as 1971 found no countrymen there but had heard of a Nepali man in Florida, another in California, and a third in Ohio (Hada 1995: 141). U.S. development aid and educational connections drew those who came first; since then, family reunification and higher education have drawn more. The Nepalese may be few in number but they have some fifteen organizations in the United States and two in Canada, most founded in the 1970s. They have held national conventions amd recently formed a Nepalese American Council to coordinate activities and avoid duplication of efforts. The associations, some of them Nepali-American in composition and goals, celebrate Nepalese national, Hindu, and Buddhist festivals. Nepalese Hindus and Buddhists do not have separate temples but attend temples managed by other Buddhists and Indian Hindus. The Association of Nepalese in the Americas has recently acquired property in Maryland for a Nepal Educational and Cultural Center, where both Lord Pasupatinath and Lord Buddha can be worshipped. The community hopes to establish such centers in other sites soon. Members of the Nepalese second generation who grew up in the United States are marrying other Americans, sometimes Asian Americans, but those who came as young adults in their late teens or twenties are returning to Nepal for spouses (Joshi 1996).

Slightly more numerous than the Sri Lankans but much more homogeneous are the Parsis, who have joined with Zoroastrians or Zarthustis from Iran to build the Federation of Zoroastrian Associations of North America (FEZANA). Their journal, *Fezana*, estimates the combined population in both the United States and Canada at 3,000 (*Fezana* 1996: 13). Everywhere except in Los Angeles, the South Asians are the dominant group, and they see the community as declining in India and Pakistan but growing in America. Local groups began in various places, as early as 1929 in New York, and efforts at federation began in the 1960s and 1970s. FEZANA was founded in 1985, and a directory and census are almost complete. There are significant conflicts based on national origin and beliefs (e.g., the issue of whether conversion is possible is still debated), but this highly educated community has many resources and has already constructed several major religious and cultural centers in the United States.

Sri Lankans are another relatively small group—some 11,000 in the 1990 census. Tensions within the community reflect those at home, and although there are at least twenty-four Sri Lankan American or Sri Lankan associations

"Bhai Puja," or Worship of the Brothers, during the Nepali Festival of Lights, Los Angeles, California. Courtesy of Veda Joshi, Torrance, California.

in the United States (according to a list maintained by the Embassy), there is apparently no attempt to form an umbrella organization or a federation. Tensions between "authentic Sinhala" culture and Indian Tamil, Malaysian Muslim, Portuguese, and Dutch cultural variations in Sri Lanka sometimes come into play, and most Sri Lankan ethnic newspapers are noticeably pro-Sinhalese. Yet an infectious national spirit is often evident.

Sri Lankan associations arrange Christmas parties for the community at large, and Sri Lankan Muslims get together for Id Mubarak and other Islamic festivals. These events are publicized to the community at large (*Lanka Tribune,* May 1996: 19). Cultural heterogeneity is noticeable at Sri Lankan events, and the seductive *baila* dance music, accompanied by good food and drinking, draws many to festive evenings with a Portuguese flavor. The "fun-loving Sri Lankan medicos" have a North American medical association that holds an annual dinner dance. Held in New Jersey, the 1996 event featured the singing superstar from home, Sohan, and the X-periments. The popular "hopper," a form of the Sinhalese *appe* (a sort of crepe), is served at almost all Sri Lankan restaurants and catered events. Weddings nowadays, whether in Buddhist temples or American hotels, feature brides in white dresses and

The Sri Lanka America Association picnic, Los Angeles, 1996. Courtesy of Deeptha Leelarathna, *Sri Lanka Express.*

veils. However, the going-away outfit may still be the red *sari* traditionally worn by Sinhala Buddhist brides, and the wedding jewelery need not be brought from home but can be purchased from traveling Sri Lankan jewelers. Buddhist temples are being set up, first in rented buildings and then in new buildings where there are enough professionals in the community to fund them. (We discuss Sinhalese Buddhists further in Chapter 4.)

Afghans in the United States, at least twice as numerous as the Sri Lankans, were motivated to emigrate by the Marxist reforms initiated in 1978 and the 1979 Russian intervention in Afghanistan (see Appendix I). An early organization in the United States was the Afghan Community in America in New York, founded in 1979, which prepares information in English to educate and influence the American public and its political leaders. Afghan newsletters, however, are published in Pushto and Dari (Persian), the major languages of Afghanistan. Most Afghan immigrants reside in New York, Washington, D.C., California, Chicago, and Colorado. If there are enough to form an Afghan mosque, they may do so; in every mosque, the *imam* gives a talk or sermon on Fridays in the language of the congregation, which would be Pushto or Dari in this case. There are two Afghan mosques in Flushing, New York, and two in Los Angeles as well.

In the United States, a few Afghan men have American wives but most couples are Afghan. Their children are not able to visit Afghanistan and are losing the languages. The older military men and police officials who emigrated when the Marxist regime took power may not go back, but the young adults would like to go back and build up their country again. Kabul was a modern city and its women were well educated and fashionably European in their dress; many of the urban, educated women who have emigrated do not cover themselves with a head scarf or other *purdah* garment and hold themselves somewhat apart from Pakistani and Indian Muslims, whom they consider more traditional in dress and demeanor. Such Afghan women, when invited to Pakistani Muslim American homes, may wear sleeveless minidresses, smoke cigarettes, and generally set "bad examples" for the teenagers of the host family. Many Afghans in the United States had hoped that the king would return to Afghanistan and unite the many factions presently competing to rule the country. In 1996 there was still no clear winner in the struggles within the country, and the refugees despair of returning.

Becoming refugees and going to Pakistan, Italy, Germany, or India on their way to the United States was a shock for these refugees, who are an extremely diverse group. They do share an insistence that they are neither Middle Eastern nor South Asian but have their own culture. Those who are orthodox Muslims attend mosques (which include people from both categories), and the Afghan love of music, particularly *qawwali*, brings them often to South Asian gatherings. Many of these political refugees are well-educated professionals, but there are refugees of all socioeconomic backgrounds, including some young men escaping involvement in the fighting back home who are probably illegals. Many lack adequate education in English and depend on public assistance (Omidian 1996). Others have become small businessowners or workers. In the five boroughs of New York, there are about 300 Kentucky Fried Chicken franchises run by Afghans, and many Afghans are taxi drivers (a dangerous occupation, and one in which South Asians are disproportionately represented in New York).

The Bangladeshis are a very recent immigrant community and a rather polarized one, with elite professionals as well as many young men of lower qualifications, some of whom have probably come illegally. Most Bangladeshis reside in New York, California, and Florida. An interview with the president of the Los Angeles Bangladeshi Association serves well to introduce the community (Bacchu 1996).

At the end of a workday, I sat in Bacchu's office for one and a half hours listening to him juggle telephone calls in Bengali on his two phone lines. He is a travel agent, and many of the calls concerned tickets back and forth to South Asian countries; others concerned the acquisition of jobs and adjustment of visa statuses. The main concern for Bangladeshis, Bacchu told me in the ten minutes he could spare for me, is "getting legal." I had gotten his name on the street by asking people I thought to be Bangladeshi who their community leader was, and people knew Bacchu's telephone number by heart. During our interview, it was all too clear that people not only knew the number but used it! Finally I suggested going to a nearby Bangladeshi restaurant for coffee. "No, no," he said, "McDonald's would be better, no one will know me there and we can talk."

The Los Angeles Bangladeshi Association was founded in 1971, and there are elections for leadership every two years. When one party lost the election in 1984 it founded another Bangladeshi association, which is based in Orange County and consists largely of professional people. This association charges $20 dues annually to be a member, whereas the Los Angeles association has no membership dues and allows any Bangladeshi living in the greater Los Angeles area to vote. After the interview, I learned from another Bangladeshi that elections were fast approaching. (Perhaps this partly explains the volume of Bacchu's phone calls.)

Bacchu mentioned job referrals to convenience stores and Indian restaurants, and he also helps people with hospital referrals and funerals. He knows many lawyers and consulate officials, as well as many Bangladeshi university professors in the southern California region. He arranges cultural events, ranging from a visiting rock band from Bangladesh (Miles, with a very funky color poster) to two visiting theater artists at UCLA's summer Asian Pacific Performers Exchange (I had seen their comic performance there). Leaflets in his office documenting past cultural events show a freedom of dress and personal style for young Bangladeshi women, who do not generally wear any type of *purdah* covering except when going to the mosque; the older women wear *saris.* Most Bangladeshis marry other Bangladeshis (Angell forthcoming), but Bacchu sees many young men marrying Mexican, Guatemalan, Korean, Chinese, and other American women whom they meet in their downtown Los Angeles neighborhood. Of all the South Asian communities in Los Angeles, the Bangladeshis are the most residentially clustered, and in areas inhabited by many other immigrants.

A recently started Bengali newspaper and a cultural organization, the Bangla Artists Guild, complete the picture for the Los Angeles Bangladeshis. Both are intentionally promoting the Bengali language in America. There are two competing Bangladeshi conventions every year—one in Florida and one in New Jersey. In 1997 one or both are supposed to convene in Los Angeles, and community leaders are pushing for them to join forces.

Although the various South Asian immigrant populations are at different stages of social and political development in the United States, they share certain socioeconomic characteristics (which brought them as immigrants after 1965) and are undergoing similar changes as they become settled in the United States.

REFERENCES

Anand, Rajen S. 1994. "What Should We Call Ourselves: Let's Debate." *India-West*, Feb. 18.

Angell, Dorothy. Forthcoming. "Identity, Kinship and Community: Bangladeshis in the United States." In *The Expanding Landscape: South Asians and the Diaspora*, ed. Carla Petievich. Chicago: American Institute of Indian Studies.

Appadurai, Arjun. 1988. "How to Make a National Cuisine: Cookbooks in Contemporary India." *Comparative Studies in Society and History* 30:1, 3–33.

Appadurai, Arjun, and Carol Breckenridge. April 1986. "Asian Indians in the United States: A Transnational Culture in the Making." Paper presented at the Asia Society symposium, New York.

Assisi, Francis. 1989. "Overseas Indians." *India-West*, Aug. 18, 26.

Bacchu, Mominul Haque. 1996. Interview with author, Los Angeles, California.

Barkan, Elliott Robert. 1992. *Asian and Pacific Islander Migration to the United States: A Model of New Global Patterns*. Westport, Conn.: Greenwood Press.

Basu, Amrita. April 1986. "The Last Wave: Political Involvement of the Indian Community in the United States." Paper presented at the Asia Society symposium, New York.

Basu, Subham, and John Anner. 1991–1992. "South Asians in the U.S.: Just Another 'Model Minority'?" *Minority Trendsletter* 5:1, 11–14, 22.

Bhardwaj, Surinder M., and N. Madhusudana Rao. 1990. "Asian Indians in the United States: A Geographic Appraisal." In *South Asians Overseas: Migration and Ethnicity*, eds. Colin Clarke, Ceri Peach, and Steven Vertovec, 197–218. New York: Cambridge University Press.

Chan, Sucheng. 1991. *Asian Americans: An Interpretive History*. Boston: Twayne.

Clifford, James. 1989. "Notes on Theory and Travel." In *Traveling Theory, Traveling Theorists*, eds. James Clifford and Vivek Dhareshwar, 177–88. Santa Cruz: Center for Cultural Studies.

Desbarats, Jacqueline. 1979. "Thai Migration to Los Angeles." *Geographical Review* 69:3, 302–18.

Dongre, Archana. 1991. "Ready-Made Foods Thriving in Fast-Paced 90's." *India-West*, Feb. 8, 41, 56–57.

Dutta, Manoranjan. 1982. "Asian Indian Americans—Search for an Economic Profile." In *From India to America*, ed. S. Chandrasekhar, 76–85. La Jolla, Calif.: Population Review.

Elkhanialy, Hekmat, and Ralph W. Nicholas. 1976. *Immigrants from the Indian Subcontinent in the U.S.A: Problems and Prospects.* Chicago: India League of America.

Fezana. 1996. Publication of the Federation of Zoroastrian Associations of North America, 9:2. Hinsdale, Illinois.

Fornaro, Robert J. 1984. "Asian Indians in America: Acculturation and Minority Status." *Migration Today* 12: 28–32.

Goel, Vindu P. 1996. "The Rise of Asian Indians." *Sunday: The Plain Dealer,* July 28, 9–11, 15.

Gold, Stephen J. 1988. "Refugees and Small Business: The Case of Soviet Jews and Vietnamese." *Ethnic and Racial Studies* 11:4, 411–38.

———. 1989. "Chinese-Vietnamese Entrepreneurs in Southern California: An Enclave with Co-Ethnic Customers?" Paper prepared for the American Sociological Association, San Francisco.

Hada, Dibya. 1995. "Problems of the Nepalese Community in America." In *Nepalese American Perspectives,* 141–44. Cincinnati, Ohio: Association of Nepalese in North America.

Hall, Stuart. 1988. "New Ethnicities." In *Black Film British Cinema,* 27–31. London: Institute of Contemporary Arts.

Hing, Bill Ong. 1993. *Making and Remaking Asian America through Immigration Policy, 1850–1990.* Stanford: Stanford University Press.

Hossain, Mokerrom. 1982. "South Asians in Southern California: A Sociological Study of Immigrants from India, Pakistan, and Bangladesh." *South Asia Bulletin* 2:1, 74–82.

Houston Chronicle. 1993. Houston, Texas.

India Currents. 1993. San Jose, California.

India Today. 1994. Delhi, India, North American edition.

India Tribune. 1994. Chicago, Illinois.

India-West. 1988–1996. Los Angeles, California.

Jain, Usha R. 1989. *The Gujaratis of San Francisco.* New York: AMS Press.

Joshi, Veda. 1996. Interview with author, Torrance, California.

Keith, Michael, and Steve Pile, eds. 1993. *Place and the Politics of Identity.* London: Routledge.

Khandelwal, Madhulika. 1995. "Indian Immigrants in Queens, New York City: Patterns of Spatial Concentration and Distribution, 1965–1990." In *Nation and Migration: The Politics of Space in the South Asian Diaspora,* ed. Peter van der Veer. Philadelphia: University of Pennsylvania Press.

Khare, Brij B. 1980. "Cultural Identity and Problems of Acclimatization: Three Areas of Concern." In *Political Participation of Asian Americans: Problems and Strategies,* ed. Yung-Kwan Jo, 59–72. Chicago: Pacific/Asian American Mental Health Research Center.

Lanka Tribune. 1996. Los Angeles, California.

LEAP [Leadership Education for Asian Pacifics]. 1993. *The State of Asian Pacific*

America: Policy Issues to the Year 2020. Los Angeles: UCLA Asian American Studies Center and Asian Pacific American Public Policy Institute.

Leonard, Karen, and C. S. Tibrewal. 1993. "Asian Indians in Southern California." In *Comparative Immigration and Entrepreneurship: Culture, Capital and Ethnic Networks,* eds. Parminder Bhachu and Ivan Light, 141–72. New Brunswick, N.J.: Transaction.

Leonhard-Spark, Philip J., and Parmatma Saran. 1980. "The Indian Immigrant in America: A Demographic Profile." In *The New Ethnics: Asian Indians in the United States,* eds. Parmatma Saran and Edwin Eames. New York: Praeger Special Studies.

Lessinger, Johanna. 1985. "Painful Intimacy: The Establishment of Trust in Business Partnerships among New York's Indian Immigrants." Unpublished paper, University of Houston, Texas.

Los Angeles Times. 1991, 1996. Los Angeles, California.

Mathur, Raghu P. 1991. "Concerns, Suggestions for 'Little India' Controversy." *India-West,* Dec. 13, 2, 38.

Melwani, Lavina. 1994. "Dark Side of the Moon." *India Today,* Jan. 31, 60c-d-f.

Minocha, Urmilla. 1987. "South Asian Immigrants: Trends and Impacts on the Sending and Receiving Societies." In *Pacific Bridges: The New Immigration from Asia and the Pacific Islands,* eds. James T. Fawcett and Benjamin V. Carino, 347–74. New York: Center for Migration Studies.

Omidian, Patricia. 1996. *Aging and Family in an Afghan Refugee Community: Transitions and Transformations.* New York: Garland Publishing.

Pakistan Link. 1992–1995. Los Angeles, California.

Potts, Michel. 1991. "Whatever Happened to the Indian Merchants Assoc.?" *India-West,* Sept. 27, 51.

———. 1994a. "Dispute over FIA I-Day Fete in LA Resolved." *India-West,* July 29, A46.

———. 1994b. "Indian, Asian Hotel Owners Groups Join Forces at Meet." *India-West,* Dec. 16, C1, 60–61.

Rajagopal, Arvind. 1994. "Disarticulating Exilic Nationalism: Indian Immigrants in the U.S." Paper presented at the American Anthropological Association.

Safran, William. 1991. "Diasporas in Modern Societies: Myths of Homeland and Return." *Diaspora* 1:1, 83–99.

Saund, Dalip Singh. 1960. *Congressman from India.* New York: E. P. Dutton.

Schiller, Nina Glick, Linda Basch and Christina Blanc-Szanton, eds. 1992. *Towards a Transnational Perspective on Migration: Race, Class, Ethnicity, and Nationalism Reconsidered.* New York: The New York Academy of Sciences.

Sethi, Renuka. 1989. Interview with author, Bakersfield, California.

Shrestha, Mohan N. 1995. "Nepalese in America: A Historical Perspective." In *Nepalese American Perspectives,* 115–24. Cincinnati, Ohio: Association of Nepalese in America.

Singh, Inder. 1996. "NFIA: Mobilizing the Indian Community since 1980." *India-West,* Sept. 13, A5, 31.

Sundaram, Viji. 1995. "Chicago Levies Fees after Split over I-Day Parade." *India-West,* Jan. 20, A32.

———. 1996. "High USDA Posts Elude Most Asians." *India-West,* Jan. 12, A1, 30.

Thaker, Suvarna. 1982. "The Quality of Life of Asian Indian Women in the Motel Industry." *South Asia Bulletin* 2: 68–73.

Tilak, Visi R. 1996. "Boom in Business." *India Today,* Mar. 31, 48f–g.

Weiner, Myron. 1990. "The Indian Presence in America: What Difference Will It Make?" *Conflicting Images: India and the United States.* Sulochana Raghavan Glazer and Nathan Glazer, eds. New York: Riverdale.

Westwood, Sally, and Parminder Bhachu, eds. 1988. *Enterprising Women: Ethnicity, Economy and Gender Relations.* New York: Routledge.

Williams, Raymond Brady. 1988. *Religions of Immigrants from India and Pakistan: New Threads in the American Tapestry.* New York: Cambridge University Press.

4

South Asian Religions in America

ESTABLISHING THE RELIGIONS

South Asian religious traditions are becoming established in the United States. Hindu and Buddhist temples, Sikh *gurdwaras*, Islamic mosques, and Parsi fire temples are being built, and religious specialists and ritual items are being brought in from Asia. Some items are even being produced in the United States. Yet the "reproduction" of religions in the United States is a dynamic process, and a close look at the religious institutions, practices, and issues among South Asian immigrants shows that significant changes are occurring.

An analysis of several stages of development of South Asian religions in the United States (Williams 1992: 229–57) reveals that the early immigrants acted essentially on their own, either carrying out private religious acts or discarding their religions. Subsequently a "national" stage occurred during the 1970s as the immigrant population increased and people grouped themselves according to national origin, building Pakistani mosques and cultural associations, Hindu temples attended by all Indians, Sri Lankan Buddhist *viharas* or temples, and so forth. This was followed by an "ecumenical" stage, as temples and mosques became international in membership and united people in the United States of diverse national origins. Religious rituals and activities were combined in new ways and performed in new locations, including homes, temples, and community centers. As the immigrants continued to arrive, an "ethnic" stage developed, with Hindus and others dividing into subgroups and perhaps further subgroups. The last stage is an alternative structure, one of hierarchical loyalties to particular religious leaders extended abroad. Examples include the Hare Krishnas or, for Muslims, the Aga Khani Ismailis or Sufi orders. Length of residence, population density, and generational status determine family orientations, with longtime residents and members of the second generation moving to the ecumenical stage. Recent arrivals, however, particularly where populations are dense, seem to start with the ethnic or subdivision stage; perhaps they will move into the ecumenical stage following a longer period of residence.

As the numbers of immigrants have increased, South Asian religions have become more, not less, important to the immigrants, the United States, and, in some cases, to the homelands as well. In the view of many American historians, the United States has always been a fundamentally religious nation, and religious identity is an important and accepted way of being different and yet integrating into American society. Indeed, some South Asian Muslim immigrant educators and spokesmen argue that Muslim immigrants are closer in spirit to the founding fathers and the early years of America's national experience than are many other Americans today (Athar 1994: 7). A rather different view is that "Religion is a . . . resource for expressing difference while domesticating it at the same time, by evading issues of race and ethnicity," and that because South Asian religious practices are a kind of "reformulated Orientalism . . . religion . . . [is] a site of cultural rather than exclusively religious expression" (Rajagopal 1995: 5, 14). Thus, putting an emphasis on religious identity might be seen as a way of advantageously differentiating South Asians from other indigenous and immigrant minority groups.

Members of South Asian religious groups have had both positive and negative relationships with the pluralistic society in the United States as they try to maintain their religious faiths. Islam, Hinduism, Sikhism, and Buddhism have not only encountered prejudicial expressions and practices on the part of the dominant Christian religious culture, but have faced the incorporation of American converts to these faiths and the other immigrant members of these faiths. In the cases of Sikhism and Hinduism, there are the so-called white Sikhs, the Hare Krishnas, and others. For the Sri Lankan Buddhists, there are American followers as well as Buddhists from Taiwan, China, Japan, and Southeast Asia. Even Indian and Pakistani Parsis, who do not accept converts, meet "Zarthustis" from Iran (the ancestral group) in their fire temples in the United States. Nepalese Hindus mingle with Indians at temples, and Afghans mingle with Pakistani, Indian, and Bangladeshi Muslims at mosques. Relations with co-believers may be most challenging for the South Asian Muslims (Abdullah 1996: 6), because they are dealing not only with a very large group of Black American Muslims (probably the largest single component of American Islam) but with immigrant Muslims from all over the world, people whose backgrounds, beliefs, and practices vary widely.

Only the Christians, minorities in all the South Asian countries, find themselves part of the majority religion in their new home. Indian and Sri Lankan Christians, the largest immigrant groups, simply join the appropriate American churches (although Sri Lankans reportedly drop in regularly at Buddhist temples for the "homelike" cultural atmosphere). In another reversal of past patterns, Christian religious figures from South Asia now come to the United States. For example, the Catholic archbishop of Sri Lanka visited Los Angeles in 1996, delivered mass in a local church, and prayed for peace in Sri Lanka.

Even in the early twentieth century, the religious arena was an important site of change. The Indian pioneers met together in houses, rented halls, or buildings purchased and adapted for purposes of worship. Sikh, Muslim, and Hindu, they almost all adopted practices characteristic of American churches such as sitting on chairs, leaving one's shoes on, and seating men and women together as families. Now reversals are occurring as the newer and more numerous immigrants build traditionally designed religious institutions and introduce "more authentic" practices from South Asia. For example, the Punjabi pioneers had introduced chairs in their Stockton Sikh temple, and men and women sat together; but the new immigrants, disapproving of the mixed seating, have removed the chairs. One oldtimer, Mola Singh (Singh 1982), criticized this, saying to the newcomers: "That's all right, if you want to make a church, put the chairs back. Everybody should sit on a chair, the women and kids and everybody, they can be on chairs. A woman sits on the floor, doesn't it shame you? . . . Don't you change your mind? Today, yesterday, don't you see the world, people, all changing? . . . In this country, women and kids, they change their whole ways, you know."

Another early development was the arrival of charismatic South Asian teachers who recruited non-Asian Americans into their religious movements. Swami Vivekananda's appearance at the World Parliament of Religions in Chicago in 1893 inaugurated the Vedanta Society in the United States, although he did not stay to lead it; the Sri Lankan Theravada Buddhist Anagarika Dharmapala also spoke there. An early Muslim Sufi teacher and musician, Hazrat Inayat Khan from India, founded the Sufi order in the West in 1912 (Hermansen forthcoming). Also attracting American followers in the early decades of the twentieth century were Swami Paramahansa Yogananda, who taught Kriya Yoga and founded the Self Realization Fellowship in the 1920s, and Jiddu Krishnamurti, whose background in the theosophical movement led him to stress self-reliance and inner reflection in his spiritual teachings.

In the late 1960s, South Asian religious leaders could immigrate more easily and the American political and cultural climate made the "counter-culture generation" receptive to their teachings. Yogi Bhajan founded one of the major movements at that time with his Kundalini Yoga and Sikh Dharma in the West (Williams 1988: 144–51). Yogi Bhajan's Los Angeles Sikh temple helped transformed Sikhism from a Punjabi religion to a world religion by being the first to have western (i.e., non-Punjabi) Sikhs conduct the Sikh initiation ceremony (*Los Angeles Times* 1975). Another major development was the transcendental meditation (TM) movement founded by Maharishi Mahesh Yogi; there are now about one hundred TM centers in North America and a university in Iowa (Meer 1995). ISKCON, or the International Society for Krishna Consciousness (the Hare Krishnas), was founded in New York in 1966 by the Vaishnavite *sanyasi* Srila Prabhupada, who was sent from Calcutta to bring Krishna's message to the West (Williams 1988: 130–37). ISKCON has not only spread to India and founded temples there, but perhaps 50 percent of the U.S. followers are now of Indian origin. This may mean that local temples will realign themselves in accordance with the local Indian membership (in Houston, for example, the temple allegedly has become a Gujarati one: Sundaram 1996).

The Punjabi and other early immigrants carried out life-cycle rituals themselves, particularly those concerned with funerals. They found they could not simply cremate a body themselves but had to obtain a certificate from a doctor and use the facilities of a licensed crematorium. Thus, the funeral setting shifted from the family home and an outdoor cremation ground to an American-run funeral parlor. For the small group of Punjabi pioneers, the fact that their wives were not "Hindu" complicated the performance of death rituals and meant that the spouses could almost never be buried together. Most early wives were Catholic, and the Hindu and Sikh practice of cremation (then relatively rare in the United States) was unacceptable to them (the Catholic Church has subsequently changed its stance). Some Hispanic wives tried to bury their Sikh husbands' bodies in the Mexican Catholic sections of rural cemeteries—on one occasion Punjabi Sikhs kidnapped the body of their dead countryman from the grieving widow to prevent this. The Muslims from India's Punjab purchased cemetery plots for their burial, orienting the graves toward Mecca. Because all immigrants from India were considered "Hindus" in the early days, the resulting "Hindu plots" in Sacramento and the Imperial Valley had only Muslims buried in them!

The post-1965 immigrants from South Asia have also had to contend with different laws and procedures for funerals. They have changed their rituals in important ways, and American funeral homes have also changed to accommodate them (Leonard 1989). More facilities are available to them, and cremation has become popular. Hindus and Sikhs mail the ashes of the deceased to India or send the urns back with relatives so the ashes can be deposited in the Ganges or another holy river. Bottled Ganges water and certain spices and other supplies are imported and available for use in funeral rituals in the United States, and, as in the United Kingdom, some bodies of water in the United States are being designated as sacred repositories.

Changes in the death rituals often involve gender roles. These were quite distinct in Hindu funerals in India but have changed markedly in the new context. In India, women are not present at the most important ritual, the cremation; bodies are carried from the home to the cremation ground, and the cremation is held outside with only males present. In the United States, women attend the entire ceremony, including the cremation; the actual cremation takes place behind closed doors, but women are present when, typically, a son pushes the button that sends the coffin on its final journey (it was the sons who performed the final rituals in India). Men and women may sit on opposite sides of the central aisle, but other gender differences (e.g., the lighting of the pyres of women from the feet and of men from the head) are being eliminated by the new technology. Moreover, if it is a female relative who is traveling back to India, she will even be entrusted with taking ashes back and putting them in the appropriate river, something only men did in the past.

Religious specialists travel frequently, but when Hindu, Sikh, Muslim, and Buddhist preachers come to the United States now, they address themselves primarily to South Asian immigrant followers. Swami Chinmayananda, one of India's most popular spiritual leaders, died in 1993 in San Diego, California, on one of the extensive overseas lecturing tours he had undertaken in recent years; he had established missions and youth camps in the United States. Sikh congregations raise money to bring Punjabi preachers and hymn-singing groups for tours in North America, and Muslim groups also sponsor many visitors. All these relatively new religions in the United States sponsor the immigration of "religious workers" to staff their institutions. Although the Hindu and Buddhist priests, Sikh *granthis*, and Muslim *moulvis* are acceptable to first-generation congregation members, they are less satisfactory for the second generation because they often do not speak English well and are not at home in the American environment.

However, it is not the visiting gurus, teachers, and religious specialists who are changing the scene most dramatically. South Asians are building religious institutions of all sorts in the United States, and these are permanent additions to the religious landscape. Hindu and Buddhist temples, Sikh *gurdwaras*, and Muslim mosques in the United States may be older buildings taken over by immigrant congregations or they may be newly constructed. A few decades ago, people wanted the design to be inconspicuous so that the new structure would blend in (according to an architect originally from Pakistan who designs mosques in Canada and the United States), but in the 1990s people want to make a strong statement of pride and "authenticity" (Haider 1993). Now, if the congregations can afford it and local city councils permit it, South Asians try to faithfully reproduce South Asian structures in most exterior details (although Haider also indicates that second-generation members of the congregations have differing ideas about religious space and its use). Workers and building materials can be brought from South Asia, and the buildings are situated according to traditional preferences.

For example, Hindu temples should be placed near water and mountains so as to evoke home and recreate it in the new context at the same time. The Vaisnava Sri Venkateswara temple in Penn Hills, Pennsylvania, was built in a hilly area in 1976 (Narayanan 1992: 153), and similarly sited are two other Vaisnava temples: the Rama temple in Chicago, Illinois, in 1981 (Williams 1992: 228) and the Gujarati Swaminarayan temple in Independence Township, New Jersey, in the late 1980s (Williams 1988: 152). The first big Los Angeles Hindu temple was built in the Malibu hills near the ocean (Mazumdar 1995: 102–3). This temple is modeled after the Tirupati Vaisnava temple in Andhra Pradesh; craftsmen, materials, and continuing institutional ties help with its "reproduction" of the South Indian temple tradition. But the temple has recruited North Indian members by installing new images that appeal to them as well—this broadening of its appeal was partly inspired by the need to pay the mortgage.

Temple construction and operation in the United States show important innovations and adaptations. Conspicuous examples are a Hindu Unity temple in Dallas with eleven deities from different regional and sectarian traditions and a Shiva/Vishnu temple in Livermore (east of San Francisco) with both a *shikhara* and a *gopuram*, central towers typical of North and South Indian temples, respectively (Clothey 1983: 199; Rajagopal 1995: 14–15). Sometimes municipal governments force changes in design. A temple in Norwalk (in southern California) had to adopt a Spanish mission style of architecture before its congregation could obtain permission to build.

Temples and mosques present themselves to the public differently in the United States, often as part of "center" complexes or with enhanced roles as

The Malibu Hindu temple in southern California. Courtesy of Shampa Mazumdar, Irvine, California.

educational institutions, not just as places of worship. Thus, many mosques have shops with books and pamphlets about Islam. Again, some changes involve gender roles. At the Los Angeles Malibu Hindu temple, well-dressed South Indian women sit at the doorway and give out pamphlets to all visitors. It is they, not the three South Indian priests (brought from India and not well versed in English), who explain Hindu beliefs and rituals to casual visitors. On one visit I found these greeters amiably welcoming three generations of an immigrant family: the grandmother in traditional *sari*, the mother in Punjabi dress, and the teenage daughter in blue jeans. At this Malibu temple, women have filled a traditional role by preparing and distributing *prasad* (blessed food) and snacks during all the temple festivals since 1981, but in 1989 two women played a more innovative role by sponsoring the temple's anniversary on (American) Mother's Day (Hindu Temple Society 1990).

Hindu temples in the United States have become the sites of congregational worship and cultural as well as religious activities. In the Malibu temple basement, *bharatnatyam* (South Indian religious dance) performances are held, presenting young Indian American students of professional Indian female dance teachers for their *arangetrams*, or debuts. Temples in India were once the sites of *bharatnatyam*, and in the diaspora temples and *bharatnatyam* are being reunited. In an interesting turnabout, the Hindu temple in Pittsburgh actually had its origin in dance classes taught by a woman teacher in that city (Clothey 1983: 177–78). Though held in "traditional" temple settings, the social aspects of such dance performances in the United States can be enhanced by a meal served in the interval or afterward. In Atlanta, Georgia, the management committee of a new Indian cultural and religious center that serves in part as a temple is even allowing liquor and meat to be served on one floor (Fenton 1988: 184), and many temples are being designed with internal non-sacred spaces that encourage recreational activities.

Not only worship centers but religious schools, producers of textbooks and TV shows suited for youngsters in the United States, and institutes producing computer and Internet religious programs are springing up all over the country. There is a College of Buddhist Studies in Los Angeles and a Vedic University of America in San Diego, which is pioneering the teaching of Hindi and Hinduism on IBM and Macintosh computers. Sophisticated computerized teachings of Arabic, the Quran, and Islamic traditions are being produced and circulated in the United States. Islamic institutes and universities are numerous, and the TV program "Islam," initiated at the Islamic Center of Southern California, has national and international viewership (*Minaret*, Jan. 1996: 32–33). Teaching materials of all sorts are being produced, ranging from a Harvard project in which South Asian religions are being portrayed on CD-ROM (Eck 1997) to a visiting grandmother's book of collected hymns in both Hindi and Roman script meant for young Hindus being raised in the United States (*India-West*, Nov. 4, 1994).

A relatively new idea is community fund-raising to establish endowed chairs at American universities for South Asian studies. Because South Asian languages are taught in only a few universities, the Tamil Chair at the University of California, Berkeley, and the Bengali Chair at Arizona State University, Tempe, are two examples of community support for the study of South Asian regional cultures. More controversial, and not always so successful, have been attempts to establish endowed chairs for the study of Sikhism or other religions. At the University of Michigan, the successful Sikh Studies program provides Sikh Americans with instruction in their religious and cultural tradition and makes that tradition accessible to a wider non-Sikh audience.

DEBATING RELIGIOUS ISSUES

The religious issues posed in the contemporary immigrant communities include matters of doctrinal belief, social practice, and cultural tradition. To illustrate how South Asian Muslims, Hindus, Sikhs, Buddhists, and Parsis are working with their religions in the United States, I place them in context below and then describe aspects of the South Asian religious scene in Los Angeles in the mid-1990s. These descriptions illuminate both the American and transnational contexts of religious experience for recent South Asian immigrants, and they hint at the generational and gender tensions that will be addressed more directly in Chapter 5. Islam, then Hinduism, Sikhism, and Buddhism, will be considered in turn.

Estimates of the Muslim population in the United States today range from three to six to eight million, making Islam a very significant religion in the United States. All major groups—Sunnis, Shias, and Sufis—are represented, and there are smaller groups as well. About 40 percent of America's Muslims are African Americans, 25 percent are of South Asian descent, and 12 percent of Arab descent (Stammer 1996). South Asian Muslims are the most highly educated and are often the intellectual leaders of American Islam (Williams 1991), yet studies indicate that they (especially the Pakistanis) are the most conservative element in the immigrant Muslim community (Haddad and Lummis 1987). Many associations compete for leadership or reflect the diversity within Islam—the Islamic Society of North America, the American Federation of Muslims from India, the American Muslim Caucus, the American Muslim Alliance-PAC, the Naqshbandiya Foundation for Islamic Education (Sufis), the Fatima Islamic Societies (Shias), Muslim Students Association, and so on. These groups are brought together by American prejudices against Islam and specific political issues (e.g., the Gulf War, the bombing of the World Trade Center, the Bosnia catastrophe), and by common concerns about Islamic doctrine and practice.

Some concerns are being addressed organizationally through central, coordinating committees that resolve conflicts within the Muslim community. These bodies may set a single date for major observances such as the Ramadan *Id* (the breaking of the annual month-long fast), which has sometimes been set for several alternative days according to different Islamic lunar calendars and astrological systems. For example, there is an Islamic Shura Council in southern California and a Central Eid [Id] Committee in the Greater Chicago area. More explosive issues concern matters of individual or community practice that cannot be based clearly on the Quran but are strongly sanctioned by some South Asian Muslims, such as wearing of the *hijab* (a head scarf for women) and other gendered practices.

The following description of a single event evokes many of these issues. In the banquet room of a Los Angeles Pakistani restaurant in 1996, the featured speaker on the Quran, that most holy of Islamic texts, was a personable 75-year-old man, a retired general from the Pakistan army. His speech was sponsored by the local branch of the Pakistani American Veterans Association, which had "caught hold of him" on a break in his journey from his son's home in Massachusetts to his daughter's home in Sydney, Australia. Many in the audience knew him from his years of military service in Pakistan and his retirement years in Karachi. The issues he raised are those that trouble Muslims in many countries, and perhaps he was freer to raise them in the United States than in Pakistan. But it is also possible that being from an Islamic country, the retired general felt more able to explore and debate these issues than do many Muslims who have become "minorities" in the United States and other diasporic locations. At any rate, although it was midnight when he finished speaking, the questions put to him reflected a defensiveness and passion about religion that has become characteristic of many South Asian Muslims.

A central issue was that of religious authority. The general suggested that the Quran alone, studied in Arabic and without the need of supporting (and later) Hadith (traditional teachings and stories attributed to or about the prophet Muhammad), was authoritative. He also believed that *ijtehad*, or interpretation, had not been closed off centuries ago, but that Muslims had an obligation to interpret their faith in the light of changing historical conditions. Thus, he argued, Muslims no longer ride camels or dress the way Arabs did in the seventh century, nor should they be reluctant to look again at the way the prohibition on usury (i.e., the taking of interest) relates to modern economies or the ways in which their children make marriages.

As he talked about marriage and divorce, the general offended "orthodoxy" in several ways. The traditional Islamic position is that only Muslims, Jews, and Christians are "peoples of the book" (possessors of a divinely inspired text—this has been disputed from time to time) and that sons may marry non-Muslim peoples of the book but daughters must marry Muslims. In contrast, he argued that Buddhists, Hindus, and Parsis should also be considered peoples of the book and that not only sons but daughters as well should be allowed to marry within this expanded category. He stated that the traditional "triple talak," by which a man thrice pronounces divorce from his wife, is not Quranic; and he talked of marriage as a contract between consulting and consenting adults, made in the presence of witnesses, that can only be voided after consultation and again in the presence of witnesses. According to the general, the Quran suggested only, and did not mandate, that men "take the risks" in the outside world while women manage the household and children. He also spoke about Muhammad being the last of many prophets, who included Buddha and perhaps figures from Hinduism, and his being the last because God thought "humanity could then be on its own, like your 17- or 18-year-old." Along with his views that women's wearing of the *hijab* was not a Quranic injunction and that the modesty (i.e., nondisplay of women's "ornaments") enjoined in the Quran might mean different things in different times and places, these ideas gave far more freedom to young people and particularly to daughters than most South Asian Muslim leaders in the United States are currently advocating.

Invoking his almost sixty years of study of Arabic and the Quran, the general pressed on to argue that the holy day need not be on Friday (it could be, for example, on Sunday, or whenever Muslims chose to gather together), that the calendar could be solar and not lunar (therefore the month of fasting and the *hajj*, or pilgrimage, could be fixed conveniently according to favorable weather), and, finally, that the prohibition on taking interest could be reconsidered slightly in the context of inflation and the laws of the country in which a Muslim was currently residing.

Although he was a visitor the general's remarks indicate that he reflects the "ecumenical" stage mentioned earlier in this chapter, and his flexibility was altogether too much for many in his audience. The evening ended with one man bitterly accusing an organizer of endorsing the speaker's views by sponsoring the talk.

To further contextualize the general's views, one should note that some Muslims in the United States, particularly women of both the first and second generations, welcome views like his and talk about the heavy weight of centuries of male formulation and interpretation of Islam. Such women maintain that equality and respect for women characterized the early "pure" Islam of Muhammad's time, and they feel free to reinterpret and reform their religion (Ahmed 1992; Al-Marayati 1996).

The issue of gender (i.e., of differential treatment of men and women) is significant in all major religions and in all contemporary societies. Almost all Muslim women and men in the United States are angry about the widespread non-Muslim perception that Islam discriminates against women, despite the fact that Islam actually improved the situation for women in Saudi Arabia at its time of origin. Their anger can lead to attempts to reform South Asian Islam from within or to attempts to defend and justify its gendered beliefs and practices. Thus, putting on the *hijab* and advocating "family values" that place Muslim women firmly in the home can be a way of upholding positive and stable societal values, which immigrants feel are lacking or declining in the larger U.S. society. Many South Asian Muslims (and other South Asians, for that matter) feel that they can contribute in the United States by re-emphasizing religious and family values.

Islam's proclaimed universalism and the consequent desire of American

Muslims to present themselves as part of a worldwide community of believers sometimes leads to problems. An emphasis on the central beliefs obscures the different practices developed in specific places and times (and now evident in the United States, embodied in different immigrant groups). When learning about Muslim societies in the world today, for example, Muslim students may resist the diverse, local-level teaching materials (e.g., studies of Indonesia, Egypt, Sudan, Iran, Saudi Arabia, Turkey, and Pakistan will show somewhat different beliefs, practices, and systems of law). According to extremely orthodox Muslim students or leaders, because universal Islam is the same everywhere, "deviations from the ideal" are corrupt and wrong; teachers should present only the central texts—the Quran, the Hadith (traditions), and the Sharia (law)—and not material about actual conditions in Muslim societies today.

This ahistorical view, the nonrecognition of changes over time and of the differences among contemporary Muslim societies, can be a liability for American Muslims at times. Non-Muslim Americans generally know very little about Islam. Thus, when (rarely) terrorist activities carried out in the name of Islam take place, Muslims who have reinforced this ignorance by insisting that Islam is the same everywhere are put in an awkward position. They must then carefully differentiate between Muslims and Muslim nations in order to distance themselves from the few Muslims who carry out activities that are not at all approved by Islam. Similar tensions can arise in terms of the other South Asian religions brought to America by immigrants: consider the use of violence by some Sikhs who promote Khalistan, some Hindus who advocate a Hindu rather than a secular India, and some Sri Lankans, both Sinhalese Buddhists and Tamil separatists.

As South Asian American Muslims organize and reorganize their religious institutions in the United States, they are constructing new identities. Mosques, Islamic centers, and schools often reflect national or regional origins (Indian, Pakistani, Bangladeshi, and Afghan), but congregations and students come from American as well as diverse immigrant backgrounds. Sometimes language affiliations come into play (Urdu, perhaps Bengali, Punjabi, Sindhi, Pushto, Persian, and other vernaculars), but the second generation is turning to English. Mosque attendance and leadership is predominantly male, but as immigrants try to preserve and transmit religious identities from the homeland, the importance of women is increasingly recognized. In fact, African American Muslim women are very active and important in their congregations. Reinterpretation and change are inevitable in the new context.

Some religious reinterpretation is consciously and deliberately done. For example, in telephoning South Asian Muslims in the United States, one often hears the phone answered with "Asalam aleikum"; and if it is an answering machine, the message may be in Urdu (the home language of many North Indian Muslims and the national language of Pakistan). This is a conscious choice. It shows that the person expects to be telephoned only by other Muslims and/or Urdu-speakers; for these immigrants the social world has narrowed upon moving to a country with at least as many ethnic and religious groups as in South Asia. A more inclusive and secular greeting was "Adab arz," which means simply "respects," used in the old princely state of Hyderabad by members of all religions.

Although a telephone greeting may seem a minor example, other changes involve major reorientations. One Indian Muslim who had settled in California talked about purifying Islam, cleansing it of practices developed in India that reflected other religions. (This echoes a refrain often heard from South Asian Muslims working in the Middle East who consider Islam as practiced in the Gulf to be the "original" or "real" Islam.) This man maintained that Islam in India had somehow been "corrupted." He said, "Now, here in America, we have the opportunity to be real Muslims." He went on to talk about reforms to root out eclectic, non-Islamic customs. At weddings, for example, some of the joking rituals involving women are being eliminated, now considered "Hindu" and superstitious. As he told me this, his wife, who was also present, amplified, "Yes, we used to do that because we women got together so seldom; now we can see each other more, we all drive, we just get in the car and go." The husband looked at her with some surprise, not having thought about it in quite this way.

Transmitting religion and culture to the second generation also involves issues of language. Recognizing the declining competence of their children in South Asian languages, some South Asian Muslims are prepared to give up the Urdu (or other vernacular) literary heritage, saying that the religious heritage is more important and that English is adequate for the transmission of Islam. This question, of how much language and religion, or language and culture, are mutually implicated, is an important one—it is crucial in the teaching of religion and culture. Muslims do not use their mosques in the way the Hindus and Sikhs use their temples for language teaching, performances of music, poetry, and dance, and general socializing (Petievich 1994; Jha 1995). For Muslims, then, religion, language, and culture are more separate and perhaps less easily transmitted in the overseas context (although Sufi music and dance would be an exception to this generalization).

Another problem for the first-generation immigrants arises when they try to teach their children their religious and cultural heritage through membership in associations. Most associations are led by the older men, and (particularly in the case of South Asian Muslims) generational and gender factors prevent such associations from sponsoring the kinds of activities that even the leaders admit the youngsters would prefer to attend. That is, second-generation Muslim Americans might more easily be attracted by coeducational meetings featuring music and/or dancing, but this rarely finds approval among those who lead the associations. Also, many first-generation immigrant community leaders are reluctant to give up the Urdu (or other vernacular) language, even though they admit that the language is a barrier to the young people's understanding and full appreciation of the programs.

It is very difficult to disentangle culture, religion, and language, and the young people will do it on their own and in unexpected ways. Clothing and food have been among the strongest markers of distinctive ethnic, national, and religious identity in the diaspora. The *hijab* is a head covering for women that was developed and used in Iran in past centuries (Esposito 1988: 98–99), and South Asian Muslims may or may not wear variations of it depending on their regional, class, and family backgrounds. Far from donning the *hijab*, one young South Asian Muslim woman wanted to wear tank tops like all her friends. She argued with her mother that after all, a tank top was just like a *sari* blouse, which her mother wore, and *saris* were in any case un-Islamic (there was some attempt, in Pakistan after 1947, to discourage the wearing of *saris* because they were Indian). So why couldn't she wear a tank top?

For those South Asian Muslims who emphasize Islam as they build new identities in the United States, this means making alliances with other Muslims. Yet there are historical divisions between Indian, Pakistani, Bangladeshi, and Afghan Muslims (and within Sri Lankan Muslims, both Tamil and Malay), not to speak of Lebanese, Egyptians, Saudis, Iranians, African Americans, and so on. These divisions could be bridged in the diaspora as Muslim families meet and marry across boundaries, but in fact such marriages are unusual. More bridges could produce a "Muslim way of life" and "Muslim family values," and some propose that Muslim family values can make positive contributions to American life through greater care of the elderly and protection of women. Such assumptions need careful consideration, for there are bound to be misunderstandings and reinterpretations when values central to family life are involved. I remember the two Punjabi-Mexican daughters of a Punjabi Muslim who objected strongly to the way new Muslim immigrants conducted their father's funeral: "They didn't have any family values; they made the men and the women sit separately," they said.

LOCAL AND GLOBAL RELIGIOUS TRENDS

An *American Islam*—the very term is resisted by many—is being constituted. Islam as taught to the children of immigrants inevitably reflects its location in the United States. As a fairly new and a minority population, South Asian Muslims teach Islam here through texts. The texts are intended to convey universal teachings but often betray the relocation and reorientation of the teachers. Consider, for example, a textbook for Islamic education produced in Orange County, California, and authored by South Asian Muslim Americans. It explains *zakat* (charity) thus: "Some have a lot and some have none. We live in America, the richest country in the world. We live in big houses, drive good cars, wear good clothes and play with the best toys. . . . We should also look at the other people here or in other countries who have nothing" (Ali 1991: 67).

A fine example of a similarly recontextualized message, although not a solely religious one, is the simultaneously globalized and localized recorded message on the answering machine of an officer of a Los Angeles Pakistani association. The message begins with "Asalam aleikum," a distinctly Islamic greeting, goes on to give information about the association in Urdu, and ends in English with "and have an awesome day!" This message is definitely located in California, everyone agrees. Religious organizations, schools, and teaching materials cannot help but reflect such reorientations.

In Hindu circles, too, the pressures on immigrant communities in the United States and politics back in South Asia lead to the construction of stronger forms of religious identification. Hindu and Hindu-related associations are forming federations and coordinating religious, cultural, and political events. The Los Angeles Federation of Hindu Associations (FHA) includes 37 organizations—many of them linguistic or cultural, judging from their titles (Gune 1993). The Jains have a Federation of Jain Associations in North America, and the Bartlett Jain Temple in Chicago is the largest Jain temple outside India (Adalja 1995).

Hinduism has many sources of religious authority. First-generation Hindu immigrants generally accept numerous and diverse sources and follow a multiplicity of rituals and social practices. Any Indian newspaper or journal now reports on literally dozens of Hindu observances involving many different strands of Hinduism and groups of followers. Elaborate and "authentic" Vedic rituals are now being conducted in the United States, and annual Kali *pujas* (worship of the goddess) are carried out by purely Bengali congregations and also by American worshippers (some of the latter, in Laguna Hills, California, brought over the head priest of Sri Ramakrishna's home temple near Calcutta for one event). However, for second-generation Hindus being raised in the United States, such diversity and diffuseness are confusing.

Growing up in a predominantly Christian context and knowing little about the conflict and diversity that have characterized the history of Christianity, the children of Hindu immigrants look for a single unified tradition and a standard text or texts. The majority religion seems so monolithic and transparently simple that second-generation Hindus want to be presented with one easy set of beliefs, analogous to Christianity and Islam (or so they think). To achieve this, the immigrants tend to emphasize beliefs only, not socioreligious practices—not the caste system, not village society, not gendered practices or the daily interactions with fellow citizens of other religious backgrounds. Instead, they present to their children a static belief system floating through time, an ideal system unresponsive to changing economic, political, and social forces. Of course, such a religion does not exist, although many other believers view their respective religions in the same way. Thus, at a time when scholars are recognizing the constructed nature of "Hinduism," as well as the distortion and inaccuracy involved in treating it as an organized whole, Hindus themselves are constructing or reconstructing it in ways that simplify and unify it (Venkatachari 1992: 189). The many origins and levels of Hinduism, its decentralization, the complexity of its many teachings and practices—all this is too much for parents or teachers located in a non-Hindu country to convey adequately, or indeed to practice in the ways they practiced it at home.

A detailed study (Mazumdar 1995) shows how Hindus in the United States deal with the increased demands on their time and the loss of family priests and other religious specialists available in the Indian context, adaptations termed *pragmatic ritualism* by Clothey (1992: 127). Temples and temple priests have assumed increased importance, with temples often offering language and music classes. Hindu immigrants have found ways to continue the obligatory ritual performances (Mazumdar 1995: 178–79, 200–201). Daily rituals can be contracted, shortened on weekdays and lengthened on weekends; they can be combined, with both morning and evening rituals performed in the evenings. Rituals can be temporarily suspended, perhaps by students in dormitories, and resumed on return to the parental home. Ritual responsibility can be delegated to only one family member, perhaps an elderly mother, who performs religious observances on behalf of the entire family. Families can postpone all rituals to weekends, or they can rotate the observance of holiday rituals among a number of families, simplifying observances for any one family. Because the sacred fire altar cannot be used in many settings, incense or candles can be substituted. Hindus must make places in their American-designed homes for *puja* rooms or shrines, converting kitchen cupboards, closets, or studies into worship centers.

Beliefs as well as practices are being adapted to the new setting. Some forces in Hinduism are busy producing the kind of Hindu beliefs the second generation is seeking. One ambitious attempt is *Hinduism Today*, "The Hindu Family Newspaper Affirming the Dharma and Recording the Modern History of Nearly a Billion Members of a Global Religion in Renaissance," which moved to a magazine format in 1996. Published in Hawaii with a Shaivite orientation in line with Sankara's monistic or nondualistic teachings, its editors produce charts that standardize Hindu beliefs and practices and contrast them to those of other major religions.

Another effort to standardize and inculcate Hinduism abroad is being made by the VHP, or Vishwa Hindu Parishad (World Hindu Assembly) of America. In India, the parent organization is part of the militant Hindu political movement. Active in the United States since 1969, the VHP held a major conference in Washington, D.C., in 1993. This conference was ostensibly a centenary celebration of Vivekananda's 1893 address to Chicago's World Parliament of Religions, but it also celebrated the demolition by Hindus of the Babri Masjid (a mosque built in Mughal times) only a few months earlier in India and fueled the Hindu political right in America (Anand 1993). Yet Hindu parents in the United States have flocked to join the VHP, seeing it as a way to formalize religious classes for their children (Mazumdar 1995: 221). What the U.S. branch offers both first- and second-generation immigrants is an affirmation of their Hindu identity and Indianness.

The growth of the VHP in America is just one indication of the threat to the secular nature of the Indian state coming from Hindus in the United States. Both within India and transnationally, this contemporary insistance on the privileged position of Hinduism in Indian national culture is leading to a narrowed and more rigid view of Indian civilization. Thus, despite centuries of Muslim, Christian, Jewish, and Parsi presence in South Asia and many measures that show their deep and central integration into Indian civilization, these non-Hindu groups are being recast in the minds of some Hindu immigrants and their children as "alien" to India. Second-generation youth of Hindu background studying South Asia may ask why they have to learn about Islam and Muslims, whom they (or their parents) no longer see as important in Indian history. Add to this situation a new generation of young academics and writers from India or of Indian background (as well as Sri Lankans and Pakistanis, similar diasporic intellectuals) who are convinced of colonial and postcolonial misinterpretations of South Asian history and culture, and there is cause for a healthy ferment on American campuses today. The new South Asian generation of educators injects its fervently held (and by no means uniform) beliefs into community and academic politics, promoting brilliant and controversial new interpretations that have implications for politics and religion in the diaspora and in South Asia.

Other conflicts in South Asia affect the way immigrants practice their religions in the United States and the extent to which religion and politics are intertwined. For example, religious and political divisions within the immigrant Sri Lankan population reflect the bitter Tamil-Sinhala conflicts in the homeland; and elections in not only India but Sri Lanka, Bangladesh, Pakistan, and Nepal may be partially fought and funded in temples, mosques, and other arenas in the United States. The most conspicuous case is that of the Sikhs, who have intensified their religious identity abroad in interaction with politics in India.

The Sikh movement for a more autonomous or independent Khalistan ("land of the pure," a Sikh state) was very strong in the 1980s, particularly after Indira Gandhi's government sent the Indian army into Amritsar's Golden Temple to rout militant secessionists in 1984, damaging the holy shrine. Sikhs all over the world who had discarded the turban and beards adopted these outward markers again, enhancing their identity as Sikhs. The assassination of Indira Gandhi by two Sikh members of her bodyguard a few months later sent shock waves worldwide, with some outspoken Sikhs in America defending Gandhi's murder while several thousand Sikhs in India were being slaughtered by their fellow citizens in retaliation for it. Sikh *gurdwaras* all over the United States have seen takeovers or takeover attempts by Khalistani Sikhs, and the head of the governing body in Amritsar has been trying to extend his influence over Sikhs outside India. The Punjabi Sikhs are famous for rivalry and fighting in their *gurdwaras* outside India (and this is not at all unknown in Hindu temples in the United States, either), but now the American court system has become another arena for these contests. As Sikh militancy and orthodoxy has increased, use of external markers—the wearing of turbans or the carrying of *kirpans*, or swords—has sometimes been contested in American courts. (Can Sikhs wear turbans when a job requires safety helmets? Can Sikh youngsters carry *kirpans*, knives that are usually small and symbolic but have been known to inflict damage, on school playgrounds?) Sikhs have traditionally resisted outside authority from within or beyond their own community, but now they sometimes invoke outside authorities to achieve religious or political control over American Sikh congregations.

As Sikh identity in India and abroad has become politicized, writing and teaching in North America about Sikhism has come under heavy attack by a group of self-proclaimed orthodox Sikhs, also based in North America. The challenges have been particularly sharp to young Sikh scholars in North American universities. In the view of their critics, these young scholars have falsely stated that the Sikh religion has changed over time and that even the composition of its central text reflects change (Sundaram 1993). The leaders of the critics are concerned that their own children may discard elements of their ancestral religion, so they fiercely defend the most conservative version of that religion. Like other South Asian parents bringing up children in the United States, they are desperately looking for ways to keep their children faithful to their religious traditions.

Somewhat in contrast to the other South Asian religions, the Sri Lankan Buddhists seem to have moved directly into the ecumenical stage, although there are also ethnic congregations. Buddhists in the United States number between three million and four million. Most early congregations were from the Mahayana tradition that developed later in China and Japan. Theravada Buddhism in Sri Lanka has remained close to the Buddha's original teachings and uses the Pali canon, and it was a Sri Lankan Buddhist from that tradition who made a popular impact at the World Parliament of Religions in Chicago in 1893. However, the early growth of Buddhism in the United States came with Japanese and Chinese immigrants, in Hawaii and California, and then with the establishment of Dr. D. T. Suzuki as a Japanese Zen Buddhist teacher in New York.

In the early 1960s some Sri Lankan Buddhists began teaching in Washington, D.C., but the Theravada tradition is now more strongly based in southern California. Many Theravada monks, with their British colonial heritage, are well educated in English. This gives them an advantage over the recently arrived Mahayana Buddhist leaders who are less comfortable in English (in Los Angeles, these are Chinese, Koreans, and Vietnamese). Thus, even though the Theravada tradition is the minority, one might argue that here too the South Asians are the leaders in the wider Buddhist community.

There are some 4,000 to 5,000 Sri Lankan Buddhists and five temples in the Los Angeles area. The largest, the Dharma Vijaya Buddhist Vihara, has been strikingly innovative in its practices. It was established by young, university-educated monks brought from Sri Lanka in the late 1970s by laymen to serve another temple (the first Theravada temple in Los Angeles, founded in 1979). They broke away from that temple in 1980 and persuaded their elder and teacher from Sri Lanka, the Venerable Dr. Hvanpola Ratanasara, to come help the Venerable Abbott Walpola Piyananda lead in efforts at innovation. The laymen in the other temple had been opposed to making certain modifications. "When you go somewhere, you have to integrate there, or you will always be strangers," a spokesman said, mentioning certain gender issues that were central to the breakaway. In Sri Lankan tradition, a monk could not ride with a woman driver or shake hands with a woman, but women in the United States did not understand that and resented the prohibitions. The young monks also felt it unnecessary to have men and women sit separately or to have worshippers sit on the floor, calling all these things "very minor customs." Perhaps less minor, the laypeople also contested tradition—in this case the leadership of the congregation by the monks, trying themselves to control the temple and keep the membership Sri Lankan and the language Sinhalese. The newer *vihara* founded by the monks is open to all (some members are American, European, Thai, and Japanese) and uses English in its services and teachings. There is a Sunday school to teach Pali, Buddhism, and some music to the children, and there are meditation classes.

The leaders of this Dharma Vijaya *vihara*, finding no applicants for the long and difficult traditional training to become Buddhist monks, have developed a new category of lay minister, or *bodhicari*. A college degree and three years of guidance by a monk qualifies one to guide others in Buddhist meditation and teachings, and several *bodhicaris* now serve as chaplains on American college campuses. The same leaders were instrumental in forming the Buddhist Sangha Council of Southern California in 1980, the College of Buddhist Studies in 1983, and the national American Buddhist Congress in 1987. Stressing the Buddhist mission to bring peace, these monks downplay doctrinal differences among Buddhists as very minimal, talk about dialogues rather than disagreements, and state repeatedly that "customs and folkways" are minor matters.

The Parsis, clustered in North America's major cities, build Zoroastrian centers that include fire temples. Here a gas flame replaces the ever-burning sacred fire, which is prohibited by U.S. fire regulations. Funeral rituals are carried out fully, but there are no "towers of silence" on which to place the bodies for disposal by flesh-eating birds, so most Parsis choose cremation. The Parsis from India and Pakistan and the Zarthustis from Iran (the latter the majority in Los Angeles, with its large Iranian population) worship together but are conscious of national and linguistic differences. The male priests are mostly Indian-trained but, unlike priests in India, will perform marriage ceremonies for couples where only one partner is Parsi. Marital and religious ties are international, with the funders of the Westminster center/temple in southern California also funding temples in Chicago; Toronto, Canada; and Sydney, Australia. A North American journal, *Fezana* (pub-

Ordination of five Bodhicaris, a new category of lay ministers created by the Dharma Vijaya Buddhist Vihara, Los Angeles, 1995. Courtesy of the Venerable Abbot Walpola Piyananda, Los Angeles, California.

lished in the Chicago area), includes international news. The Parsis are concerned about their children's marriages, because the Parsi community in South Asia is declining, and a youth organization holds dances and cultural events at the center occasionally. The Parsis' status as an exiled minority is one long familiar to them, and their concern is for their youth.

We come back to a fundamental central point: despite the considerable development of South Asian religions in the United States, it is still primarily the family that must transmit religious and cultural beliefs and practices. Families from South Asia are more isolated here, forced to rely on themselves or on whatever texts are available. Religious institutions and communities may be steadily growing, but their context is an overwhelmingly American one.

Back in South Asia, the entire range of societal beliefs and practices is readily observable and provides a rich context for social, religious, and cultural learning. One can see how others practice their religions; how religions function in extended families, in subcastes and castes, in neighborhoods, cities, and nations. One can see how religions are implicated in social practices, economic systems, and political movements. But in the United States, immigrants initially lacked the most basic institutions (e.g., temples and

Minoo Netervala, a Parsi immigrant, and his Punjabi-Mexican wife at the *navjote* (confirmation) of their daughters Yasmin and Zarine, 1972. Courtesy of Amelia Singh Netervala, Los Angeles, California.

mosques) in which to worship and educate their children. The religious texts, the written words alone, present the beliefs, and one's own family is often the only context for the texts. This promotes the idea that there is only the one text or the one way—and too often this means that there is little knowledge of and respect for diversity.

In earlier decades, when there were fewer immigrants from any one country, greater community cohesion—the national stage—provided fuller contexts for socialization of the second generation. The early Indian immigrants, for example, included many kinds of Indians in their meetings and associations. In the case of the so-called Mexican Hindus in California, South Asian religious traditions may not have been transmitted in much detail, but there was recognition of religious differences and respect for them. Now, the many South Asian immigrants bring numerous and very specialized religious traditions, but these "ethnic" manifestations are not so meaningful to the second generation. On the other hand, the simplification, standardization, and shaping of these many strands into just a few major religous categories is taking place not only in an American context but in a politically charged global context. Children are growing up here with less knowledge and less tolerance of the religious differences their parents have brought from South Asia. Perhaps, however, participation in broader American and South Asian cultural activities is helping overcome the new kinds of differences.

REFERENCES

Abdullah, Aslam. 1996. "Ethnic Diversity and Islamic Identity." *Minaret*, 18: 4, 6.

Adalja, Archana. 1995. "Mid-Western Meets Promote Heritage." *India-West*, July 14, C1, 14.

Ahmed, Leila. 1992. *Women and Gender in Islam: Historical Roots of a Modern Debate.* New Haven, Conn.: Yale University Press.

Al-Marayati, Laila. 1996. "Perspective." *Minaret*, 18:6, 36–37.

Ali, Faiz-u-Nisa A. 1991. *The Path of Islam, Book 3*, 3rd ed. Tustin, Calif.: International Islamic Educational Institute.

Anand, Tania. 1993. "Gift-Wrapping Hindutva." *India Today*, Aug. 31, 48c-d.

Athar, Shahid. 1994. *Reflections of an American Muslim.* Chicago: QAZI.

Clothey, Fred W. 1983. *Rhythm and Intent.* Madras: Blackie and Sons.

———. 1992. "Ritual and Reinterpretation: South Indians in Southeast Asia." In *A Sacred Thread: Modern Transmission of Hindu Traditions in India and Abroad*, ed. Raymond Brady Williams, 127–46. Chambersburg, Pa.: Anima.

Eck, Diana, ed. 1997. *On Common Ground: World Religions in America.* CD-ROM. New York: Columbia University Press.

Esposito, John L. 1988. *Islam: The Straight Path.* New York: Oxford University Press.

Fenton, John Y. 1988. *Transplanting Religious Traditions: Asian Indians in America.* New York: Praeger.

Gune, Ramesh. 1993. "Federation of Hindu Associations Formed in LA." *India-West*, Apr. 9, 78.

Haddad, Yvonne Yazbeck, and Adair T. Lummis. 1987. *Islamic Values in the United States: A Comparative Study.* New York: Oxford University Press.

Haider, Gulzar. 1993. Comments at conference on The Expanding Landscape, Columbia University, New York.

Hermansen, Marcia. Forthcoming. "Hybrid Identity Formations in Muslim America: The Case of American Sufi Movements." In *Muslims on the Americanization Path,* eds. Yvonne Y. Haddad and John L. Esposito.

Hindu Temple Society of Southern California Newsletter (n.d., n.pl., n.p. [1990, Malibu, California]).

India-West. 1994. Los Angeles, California.

Jha, Alok K. 1995. "Not for God's Sake Alone." *India Today,* Apr. 30, 64b–c.

Leonard, Karen. 1989. "Mourning in a New Land: Changing Asian Practices in Southern California." *Journal of Orange County Studies* 34: 62–69.

Los Angeles Times. 1975. Apr. 14, 1:11.

Mazumdar, Shampa. 1995. "Sacred Spaces: Socio-Spatial Adaptations of Hindu Migrants." Ph.D. dissertation, Boston: Northeastern University.

Meer, Aziza K. 1995. "Flocking to Alien Gods." *India Today,* Aug. 15, 60h–i.

Minaret. 1996. Los Angeles, California.

Narayanan, Vasudha. 1992. "Creating the South Indian 'Hindu' Experience in the United States." In *A Sacred Thread,* ed. Raymond Brady Williams, 147–75. Chambersburg, Pa.: Anima.

Petievich, Carla. 1994. "Intertwining Religion and Ethnicity: South Asian Cultural Performance in the Diaspora." Paper presented at University of Iowa, Iowa City.

Rajagopal, Arvind. 1995. "Disarticulating Exilic Nationalism: Indian Immigrants in the U.S." Paper presented at the American Ethnological Society, Austin.

Singh, Mola. 1982. Interview with author, Selma, California.

Stammer, Larry B. 1996. "Muslims Call for Unity at International L.A. Summit." *Los Angeles Times,* Aug. 3, B4.

Sundaram, Viji. 1993. "A Thesis of Discord." *India Today,* Aug. 31, 48h.

———. 1996. "Krishna's Children," *India-West,* Aug. 30, B1, 16.

Venkatachari, K. K. A. 1992. "Transmission and Transformation of Rituals." In *A Sacred Thread: Modern Transmission of Hindu Traditions in India and Abroad,* ed. Raymond Brady Williams, 177–90. Chambersburg, Pa.: Anima.

Williams, Raymond Brady. 1988. *Religions of Immigrants from India and Pakistan: New Threads in the American Tapestry.* New York: Cambridge University Press.

———1991. "Asian Indian Muslims in the United States." In *Indian Muslims in North America,* ed. Omar Khalidi. Watertown, Mass.: South Asia Press.

———. 1992. "Sacred Threads of Several Textures." In *A Sacred Thread: Modern Transmission of Hindu Traditions in India and Abroad,* ed. Raymond Brady Williams, 228–57. Chambersburg, Pa.: Anima.

5

Cultural Traditions: Continuity and Change

The presence and vibrancy of South Asian culture in the United States has increased dramatically, providing many resources for the construction of immigrant identities and strongly influencing the host society as well. In earlier decades, "Hindu" recreational activities were few: visiting with other Punjabi-fathered families, or going to the Stockton *gurdwara* and to wrestling matches and political speeches. The pioneer Punjabi farmers had to persuade Indian students from colleges in nearby cities to give amateur performances in the small farm towns of California and Arizona in the 1950s, putting the students up in their own homes. Hindi movies from India began to be screened soon after 1965, in movie theaters that became central to new South Asian immigrants, but with the coming of VCRs around 1980 the moviegoers retreated to home settings. Now, the new South Asian immigrants sponsor and attend cultural performances and other popular recreational activities that are almost as accessible as those in the homelands. A broad range of South Asian cultural performances takes place in the United States, of a quality to satisfy the most demanding of "purists," and there is also a range of "fusion" or crossover arts and activities.

MUSIC, DANCE, AND POETRY

In most U.S. cities it is possible to attend South Asian festival and cultural performances throughout the year, their timings often adjusted to coincide with American holidays. They are sponsored by established organizations (e.g., a Carnatic Music Circle, a Pakistani American Arts Council, or a Sri

Lankan American Association) or by private entrepreneurs (e.g., ethnic grocery store owners or other business owners). Events can be scheduled far in advance or announced suddenly, taking advantage of someone's visiting father, mother, or grandparent who is a famous artist. Events are advertised in the South Asian ethnic newspapers and by flyers distributed in grocery stores and religious centers.

When a really big name performer comes to town—such as Ravi Shankar, India's player of the classical *sitar* (stringed instrument); Nusrat Fateh Ali Khan, Pakistan's *qawwali* singer (of Sufi devotional poetry in Persian or Urdu); or Sri Lanka's Desmond De Silva, singer of the *baila* (Portuguese-style dance music)—the mainstream press may also give advance notice and review the performance. Depending on the sponsor and audience, these performances may run on "Indian" or "Pakistani" time (starting late—and later than scheduled—and continuing far into the night), or they may be more attuned to American timings (starting when scheduled and ending at a "sensible" hour). One problem related to scheduling is the correlation of particular Indian *ragas* (classical music compositions) not only with certain seasons but with certain times of day or night. Indian morning *ragas* should only be performed in the morning and thus are rarely heard in the United States, because it is easier to schedule performances at regular concert hall hours and at times when more people can attend. Some societies that strive for cultural authenticity and variation try to schedule occasional performances of morning *ragas*.

All over the United States there are South Asian organizations that sponsor concerts by local and visiting artists. A high point for the Music Circle of southern California was an eleven-hour concert in honor of Ravi Shankar's 75th birthday in 1995, held in a Los Angeles college auditorium and featuring outstanding instrumentalists and vocalists. An Indian restaurant provided tea and food during the breaks. Ravi Shankar now maintains a home in southern California and frequently appears in the area, and this celebration drew a majority of non–South Asians. In contrast, an event more narrowly publicized and attended largely by Urdu-speakers was hosted by the Pakistani American Arts Council: an evening of *geet* (songs, classical *ragas*) and *ghazals* (Urdu love songs) in a college auditorium. The featured artists were Salamat Ali Khan, a well-known vocalist from Pakistan; two of his sons, who are apparently based in San Francisco; and Sattar Khan "Taree," a noted *tabla* (drum) player from Pakistan who now resides in New Jersey. Scheduled for 8 P.M., the program began at 9:30 and the first break came at midnight; catered food was available, and enthusiasm was high.

The South Asian cultural scene is strikingly transnational, in ways that

Pakistani *ghazal* singer Mehdi Hassan inaugurates a travel office branch, 1992. Courtesy of Rasheed Ul Haq, Torrance, California.

either invoke or revoke earlier political boundaries. For example, the Sabri Brothers or Nusrat Fateh Ali Khan, Sufi *qawwali* singers from Pakistan, can be enjoyed by Indians and Bangladeshis when they perform in the United States. *Qawwali* is impassioned and explicitly religious poetry, whereas *ghazals*, erotic love songs, are performed at both formal and lighter, more popular occasions. *Ghazal* singers too are in demand, in the photo above to cut the ribbon opening a travel agency branch. Here the famous *ghazal* singer is from Pakistan, but local guests included the heads of both Pakistan's and India's national airlines. The president of the southern California Hyderabad Deccan Association was also there. Sure enough, this particular travel agent's ancestral home was in Hyderabad, India, before his family migrated to Pakistan after partition. In the United States, previous migrations can be rolled back and reconnections made to relatives, friends, and countries (*India-West*, Jan. 24, 1992: 67).

A *mushaira*, a formal evening of Urdu poetry, typically features both local and visiting international poets. An excellent command of the language is needed to appreciate these compositions, and many associations have been formed to sponsor *mushairas* in the United States. Sometimes these are branches of Indian, Pakistani, or international associations, such as Bazm-i-Urdu, Aiwan-i-Urdu, or Urdu Markaz International. The events often start late and last far into the night. A local society in the northern California area, Awaan-e-Faiz, commemorates the late great Pakistani Urdu poet Faiz Ahmed Faiz. That society held a *mushaira* at Berkeley in 1994; in addition to poems on traditional themes, poems entitled "Flowers of Harlem" and "Ozone Layer" were recited. Urdu poetry might reduce hostility between India and Pakistan—or so one poet hoped at this gathering (*Pakistan Link*, Dec. 9, 1994: 24). The poetry societies and events do bring together not only Indians and Pakistanis but also Afghans, Bangladeshis, and others who may speak and appreciate Urdu.

The transnational visitor scene is only the icing on the cake, for there are permanently settled South Asians who provide instruction in music, dance, and other arts all over the United States. Many have become trainers of non–South Asian performers as well, but they are not true "fusion" institutions because they are teaching mostly traditional arts in mostly traditional ways. An outstanding example is Ali Akbar Khan, master of the *sarod* (a stringed instrument), whose northern California Ali Akbar College of Music has become a Bay Area institution that is well integrated into the dominant culture. Ali Akbar Khan has been in the United States for many decades, and his 1994 summer concert of *kathak* (North Indian classical dance) featured five dancers who were, judging from their photographs and names, all Euro-Americans (*India-West*, Aug. 12, 1994). Claiming ancestors from the lineage founded by Tansen, the renowned court musician of the Mughal emperor Akbar, Ali Akbar Khan believes that sixteenth-century North Indian classical music can now be learned better in the United States than in India (*India Today*, Dec. 31, 1994: 64c).

Vocal and instrumental South Indian or Carnatic music is developing equally well in the United States. Cleveland, Ohio, hosts an annual Easter weekend of Carnatic music that is the largest assemblage of Carnatic musicians outside of India. This is the Thyagaraja festival, celebrating the great composer of the eighteenth century. Begun in 1977 by a small group in a church basement, the festival has grown to a four-day event with an audience of over 3,000, and it is now officially recognized by the state of Ohio. More than 100 musicians perform, some 15 or 20 from India and of national stature there. Half the audience may be drawn from Cleveland's Indian population of about 5,000, and an equal number come from outside (Shanker 1994; Hansen forthcoming). There are many other centers of Carnatic music activity, where great teaching and performing lineages from India are continuing in the United States. For example, Viji Krishnan, daughter of the violin and vocal music maestro T. N. Krishnan, teaches in Cerritos, California. Young Indian American Carnatic vocalists and instrumentalists can trace their ancestries back to famous disciples of Thyagaraja in India, and some of them now tour in India (Balagopal 1994).

Although the American public may be somewhat more familiar with North Indian Mughlai music (Ravi Shankar on *sitar*, Ali Akbar Khan on *sarod*, and Zakir Hussain on *tabla*) than the Carnatic or South Indian music, it is the South Indian *bharatnatyam* dance that has become best known in the United States. Originally practiced in South India by girls given to temples for dancing and perhaps for prostitution, *bharatnatyam* has become highly respected and remains strongly connected to Carnatic music and devotional Hindu themes. Outstanding schools established in the United States trace their lineages to India, such as the Kalanjali school run by K. P. and Katherine Kunhiraman in northern California and that of Padmini, a former Indian movie star, in New Jersey. Indian Americans who want to explore their roots study classical Indian dance in the United States, but so do Chinese, Japanese, European, and Hispanic Americans (Sundaram 1994; Tilak 1994). American museums and funding agencies are now sources of support for Indian dance.

The first southern California issue of *India Currents* (April 1990)—initially a northern California magazine of Indian arts, entertainment, and dining—included an editorial entitled "The American Bouquet." It praised the pluralistic society in the United States and quoted the *kathak* master Chitresh Das, who teaches Indian classical dance in America because he wants to "add an Indian flower to the American bouquet." Some maintain that traditional Indian dance is being better preserved in the United States than in India (Yodh 1989; Thakkar 1993), and indeed there are many signs of its integration into the American cultural landscape.

For those Indian American daughters who study Indian classical dance with female professional teachers in the United States, the controlled sensuality and formal beauty of the performances convey new meanings in America. One study of Indian classical dance performances in the New York area analyzes the *bharatnatyam* performance as "a marker of ethnic and feminine identity" and an opportunity for lavish public display of eligible daughters in an Indian cultural, even spiritual, setting. At the same time, Indian classical dance significantly changes ethnic boundaries as it preserves or "transfers" ethnicity from India to North America. New York students of *bharatnatyam* include South Asian Christians and Muslims as well as Hindus, and girls from South Africa, Sri Lanka, and the Caribbean as well as South Asia, "a veritable collapsing of categories" (Abramovitch 1988). Perhaps South Asians from different subcultures and regions can be unified through participation in Indian classical dance. One scholar expects the classical dance to move South Asian culture into the North American mainstream through the host culture's respect for this high form of artistic endeavor, and he sees the female dance teachers leading this achievement (Thakkar 1993).

Dance traditions from North India also can be seen in the United States—not only the *kathak* dance patronized by the Mughals but the slightly less respectable (more erotic) *mujra* dance associated with courtesans and old-style weddings of the nobility. At the Mughal Darbar restaurant in Anaheim, California, the owners recreated a "Mujra Night" featuring the style of courtesans from the Nawab of Lucknow's court. Although they initially billed it as a "men only" night, protests forced them to invite women as well. Five professional *mujra* dancers came from India, and the restaurant was redecorated to recall the dance setting in the classic Indian movie of the 1950s, *Mughal-e-Azam* (the Great Mughal, that is, Akbar). The guests reclined on sumptuous cushions on the floor and were served a 21-course meal (*India-West*, Nov. 17, 1995: C16). Perhaps inspired by that Nawabi Lucknavi evening, when a very special visitor came to Los Angeles from Hyderabad (a woman who runs a catering business and cooking school), emigrant members of the Nizam of Hyderabad's old Muslim and Hindu nobility seized the opportunity to enjoy a Nawabi Hyderabadi night of fine food and wines (*India Journal*, June 28, 1996: B8).

Not only classical and courtly art forms but folk art forms as well are being taught and celebrated in the United States. On this more popular level, the cultural performances typical of Indian celebrations and festivals have been analyzed by a second-generation Indian American scholar of dance in southern California, Kiren Ghei (1989). She points to the crucial role of women in training and costuming the performers and in sponsoring these performances. The performances inculcate proper South Asian female behavior, but they also express the sexuality of daughters and expand the parameters for permitted behavior in public for young Indian women. Teenage Indian American girls dance in public in alluring costumes, and the Hindi film dances are erotic and provocative. Indian American girls do not simply reproduce the film dances as they see them on video; rather, they reinterpret them. Their solo presentations are choreographed for live performance, not for a film stage, and the girls compete with other daughters of the community through their presentations. These dances are acceptable displays of adolescent beauty and skill in a coeducational setting. Parents approve of the performances because they are Indian, "ethnic," and "traditional." In her interviews with the teenage girls who perform film dances, Ghei found that they are "evocative of a distant India" but are also thought of as "local and contemporary" art forms (Ghei 1988: 13).

There are also more exuberant popular folk dances, especially Punjabi and Gujarati ones, which similarly evidence an expanded public role for South Asian women in community events in the United States. Second-generation Punjabi girls are performing the *bhangra*, the more flamboyant male form of Punjabi dance, rather than the tamer *giddha*, which is traditionally danced by women. And in southern California a married couple performs dances at the Gujarati Garba Raas (autumn festival) programs, an uncommon practice in India; but "the emigres celebrate their festivals better than do people in India," a drummer at Garba festivals stated. There are other adaptations: locally eminent musicians might have to make their music part-time while managing a grocery store, and the festivals are held at basketball courts or school and college facilities as often as at temples, but they usually draw several thousand people (*India-West*, Oct. 6, 1989: 52).

Where there are enough Afghans, Sri Lankans, or Bangladeshis to support an association and a radio or TV station, special cultural programs may be mounted regularly. Sri Lankans produce dramatic performances and musical evenings. In Los Angeles, a midnight TV program hosted by an Afghan woman features Persian and Pushto songs and poetry every Saturday night. Bangladeshis can attend Indian Bengali association events, and the Tamil Sri Lankans often join Indian Tamil activities.

South Asian language theater is one of the least visible arts activities in the United States, but Gujaratis, again, are numerous enough to support even transnational productions. Amateur and professional artists are settled in the United States and support visiting groups from India, bringing Gujarati plays to New York, New Jersey, Chicago, Houston, and Atlanta. Some Gujarati directors and playwrights travel back and forth between Bombay, California, London, and New York (*India Today*, Feb. 15, 1995: 64e). Sri Lankans also mount dramatic productions in the United States—in some cases these include plays by local immigrant authors and under local associational sponsorship (*Sri Lanka Express*, Aug. 9, 1996).

FOOD, FASHION, AND YOGA

We have already discussed ethnic groceries and markets selling snacks and meals, but there is also a growing market for South Asian restaurant food among both Americans and South Asian immigrants. More Americans than South Asians patronize these establishments during the week, but there is a more evenly balanced clientele on weekends. Many South Asian restaurants aim for affluent customers and offer Mughlai court cuisine, but some are moderately priced and many have gone into the catering business. Fancy hotels now may seek convention business by advertising catered South Asian food. Mughlai cuisine is most common, but a few South Indian and vegetarian restaurants are springing up. Sri Lankan, Bangladeshi, Afghan, and Nepali restaurants remain unusual.

Transnationalism is evident in the restaurant trade, as great restaurant chains from India or Pakistan come to the United States. This might happen when an owner migrates. For example, Kapal Dev Kapoor, the man who founded Delhi's Embassy restaurant in 1948 and began the first automated ice-cream plant in India in 1957 (Kwality ice cream), came to Los Angeles in 1977, introduced excellent Mughlai and *tandoori* (baked in a clay oven) cuisine to southern California by taking over the Akbar in Marina del Rey, and eventually died here (*India-West*, Oct. 18, 1991). Dasaprakash, a South Indian vegetarian restaurant chain, has branches in southern California that help set the standard for such food in the United States. Bundoo Khan of Los Angeles is thought to be a branch of the famous parent chain in Pakistan and serves *halal* (the Islamic equivalent of *kosher*) meat Pakistani-style.

For the Sri Lankans, Bangladeshis, and Afghans, ethnic groceries and restaurants now play the central role they did earlier for the Indians and Pakistanis. Sri Lankan groceries and restaurants offer the unique specialities beloved of Sri Lankans, Sinhalese and Tamil alike, such as hoppers and pork curry. Bangladeshi shops and restaurants reflect their primarily working-class clientele, with Bengali-style fish being the favorite offering. Afghans shop at Irani markets but offer hot kebabs and Kabuli *nan*, or bread, at restaurants frequently named Kabul or The Khyber Pass.

In terms of South Asian clothing, the United States is now a major market for producers in South Asia. Exhibitions and sales of Pakistani and Indian women's clothing are held in hotels or private homes, and the styles available in Little India shopping centers around the United States often come straight from Bombay or Karachi. Famous boutiques from South Asia's biggest cities send annual displays to northern and southern California, Austin and Dallas, Chicago, New York, and Indianapolis. *Sari* stores from India are even opening outlets in the United States, and they usually carry the Punjabi outfits, *salwar-kameez*, as well. Jewelery stores are very big business, and other accessories are available; the buyers of all these goods include many non–South Asian Americans.

The topics of food and clothing suggest the need for exercise, and yoga needs no definition. Originally imported as a South Asian religious practice to accompany meditation, yoga has become popular among Americans as a means of physical conditioning. There are many schools of yoga and yoga teachers from even more backgrounds in the United States today. This should be classified as a "fusion" or crossover activity, but it seems relevant to mention it here.

FINE ARTS, ENTERTAINMENT, AND LITERATURE

South Asian Americans pioneering in many arenas draw on their cultural heritage. Their training, knowledge, and cultural references may be originally South Asian, but they use this background in new ways and for American (or international) audiences. There are many artists of South Asian origin (most are painters and most live in New York) and a few well-known curators and scholars of South Asian art (e.g., Ananda Coomaraswamy from Sri Lanka who was formerly at the Boston Museum, Pratapaditya Pal from India at the Los Angeles County Museum of Art). There are world-famous cultural figures who maintain residences in the United States or travel and work here frequently: Zubin Mehta and his father Mehli Mehta, conductors originally from Bombay; Ismail Merchant, an independent filmmaker, also from Bombay; and Shabana Azmi, an Indian actress and political activist. The movie stars Kabir Bedi and Persis Khambatta act in both Hollywood and "Bollywood" (Bombay) films, and Kavi Raj acted regularly on TV's "St. Elsewhere."

Moving more into the area of conscious and sweeping cultural change, serious use is being made of bicultural heritages by many younger South Asian immigrants and members of the second generation who are working into the mainstream of American culture. In the entertainment and media industries, these include older filmmakers such as Amin Chaudhri, Krishna Shah, Ashok Amritraj, and Jagmohan Mundhra, and younger women such as Mira Nair, Radha Bharadwaj, and Deepa Mehta. The women's films are being distributed by major Hollywood studios, and each draws substantially on her South Asian background. Less-established directors of Indian ancestry are showing their works in film festivals and museum series. Among them are Kavery Kaul, Vivek Ranjen Bald, Erika Anderson, Indu Krishnan, Ritu Sarin, Hima B., Madhavi Rangachar, David Rathod, Prem Kalliat, Michelle Taghioff, and Ashraf Meer (Melwani 1994). From Bangladesh, the filmmakers Shams Choudhury and Mohammed Jaimy Hossain are producing for American television. There are news reporters and anchors, too. Perhaps the best example is the New York cable newsman Karim Hajee, an Indian Muslim; when the World Trade Center was bombed in 1993, Hajee was able to go into mosques and interview a chief suspect. On the lighter side, the Bangladeshi workers Sirajul and Mujibur are often featured on the "David Letterman Show," and the character Apu, an Indian grocer, appears on "The Simpsons." These media figures come from very different backgrounds, but all are working with bicultural perspectives in one way or another.

Even as authors, South Asian Americans are highlighting cultural or multicultural themes. The long list includes many award winners and book club nominees. The best known include Bharati Mukherjee, from India, Canada, and now the United States; and Bapsi Sidhwa, from Pakistan and the United States. Others from India and Pakistan whose names are likely to be known are Agha Shahid Ali, Meena Alexander, Dr. Deepak Chopra, Dr. Mantosh Singh Devji, Chitra Divakaruni, Amitav Ghosh, Zulfiqar Ghose, Gita Mehta, Ved Mehta, A. K. Ramanujan, Raja Rao, and Dr. Abraham Verghese.

CULTURAL FUSION

Beyond the mixture of cultural elements within a production or performance are the genuinely new hybrid cultural productions, termed *fusion.* The concept is most often applied to music or food, where new combinations of instruments, rhythms, ingredients, and methods lead to innovative sounds or tastes. I use it here rather loosely to talk about the purposeful combination of cultural elements from different traditions. The Beatles in Britain would be an early example of fusion, in a postcolonial case of "the empire strikes back."

Often the fusion producers are second-generation South Asian immigrants, but not always—they can be first-generation immigrants, or they can be American businesspeople. For example, Indian American leaders may send out party invitations featuring a couple in tuxedo and swishy dress. American telephone companies have begun seeking long-distance subscribers with ads featuring an Islamic-style geometric design or Akbar and his Hindu prime minister speaking in a Hindi-like script (depending on whether the ads are running in the Pakistani or Indian ethnic press). Dalip Singh Saund, the first South Asian American to become a congressman in 1956, was a member of the Toastmasters Club—joining that group is recommended for those who want to speak well in public. To paraphrase Murarka, who cited Saund's example, "who will ask you to be the CEO if you enter the boardroom in Indian clothing and speak with a *desi* [country] accent?" (Murarka 1991).

Dance, music, food, and restaurants are the main areas where fusion occurs, as the new products attract followers and customers in the United States. Indian dance academies offer not only classical *bharatnatyam* but regional folk dances and dances from popular Hindi movies. The Ghungroo Dance Academy in northern California offers a popular combination of *bhangra, giddha,* theme and film song dances, and hip-hop *bhangra* for teenagers and children (*India-West,* May 6, 1994). Indian dance is also inspiring American dance leaders, lending its instrumental music, vocals, and costumes. In some cases, such companies will perform in New York and then tour in India. This is happening not only with the classical *bharatnatyam* and *kathak,* but with film songs as well. For example, a Korean American choreographer has written a seven-dancer performance of the bawdy Hindi film song "Choli ke peechhe," or "What's behind the *sari* blouse?" (Melwani 1996).

Examples of "high culture" fusion music in the United States include Carnatic violin virtuosos L. Subramaniam and L. Shankar playing with Western musicians, or *ragas* and *ghazals* combining saxophone and voice (e.g., that of Shafqat Ali Khan, son of the Pakistani vocalist Salamat Ali Khan). These experiments are often truly transnational. Another striking example involves the late *qawwali* singer Nusrat Fateh Ali Khan doing the sound track on the Hollywood films *The Last Temptation of Christ* and *Dead Man Walking.*

Popular among the younger crowd (and taking the lead from the Punjabi British hit singer Apache Indian) is *bhangra* rock or reggae. This loud, vibrant dance music combines Punjabi peasant stock with Caribbean reggae, British rock, and Black American rap. Dance parties throb to this music, which now incorporates elements of hip-hop, chutney, and jungle. In the United Kingdom *bhangra* is performed live, whereas in the United States it is offered mostly by deejays—but it will be home-grown soon and features live tours already. Weddings are occasions where the boisterous *bhangra* promotes cultural mixture. If the wedding guests include friends from Pakistan or India's Punjab, they may insist on dancing the *bhangra* even at the most dignified of South Asian weddings. Even American rock music may be played by the end of the wedding festivities on the demand of young people.

Fusion cuisine is another new trend, being pioneered in New York. Chutney Mary, a restaurant in Manhattan, mixes *desi* flavors with Mexican, Italian, and Thai cuisine; the restaurant once catered Mexican food with an Indian touch for 30,000 Indians, mostly vegetarian Gujaratis, attending a festival in New Jersey (Melwani 1995). Vegetarian burritos, tacos, quesadillas, and nachos are natural candidates for such crossover cuisine (I was served vegetarian burritos in India some fifteen years ago by a daring Gujarati daughter-in-law who had been in the United States and was trying to persuade her family to accept this strange food). Another standout is in Memphis, Tennessee, where Raji Jallepalli from Hyderabad runs a fusion restaurant. In Indian restaurants,

An American sitarist, David Garza, with a Pakistani *tabla* player opening a South Asian cultural evening in Los Angeles, 1996. Courtesy of Atiya Niazi, Los Angeles, California.

the trend is to use less oil and fewer spices. There is a spate of Indian cookbooks tailored to American tastes, including popular ones by Ismail Merchant, Bharti Kirchner, Julie Sahni, Yamuni Devi, and Madhur Jaffrey.

Restaurants are offering amazing combinations of food, cultural performances, and ambience. (Similar changes are occurring in South Asia, too; but with American clientele being a major factor in the United States, the changes are made more rapidly and are partly attuned to non–South Asian tastes.) One well-established South Indian restaurant, Pasand Madras in Berkeley, offers both live Indian classical music and live jazz, a sweets counter, and full bar service. Advertisements in the mid-1990s in the South Asian ethnic press tout Chinese Islamic restaurants run by Chinese and Taiwanese Muslims, as well as Thai Islamic restaurants, where all meats are *halal* (slaughtered according to Islamic law). There are also *halal* Mexican restaurants and an Indian restaurant with Hindi karaoke. Another Indian restaurant featured a Super Bowl party in January 1995. The Westin Bonaventure, perhaps the most prestigious hotel in Los Angeles, now offers banquet facilities with

Indian cuisine (i.e., full-service catering by two of the finest local Pakistani and Indian restaurants). At a recent Islamic conference there, the four food choices, all *halal* preparations, were Arab, Pakistani, Irani, and Kentucky Fried Chicken.

Fusion can occur between recent immigrant cultures, too. One example is the joint production of the Ramayana, India's great epic story of Ram and Sita, by Indian and Indonesian artists. Two northern California groups, Abhinaya (an Indian dance company) and Gamelan Sekar Jaya (a Balinese orchestra), are producing a version of the Ramayana entitled "Asian Variations" (*India Today*, Apr. 30, 1996: 721). Other examples of fusion come directly from the homelands to immigrant audiences and are reminiscent of earlier fusions: the famous Pakistani star of theater, film, and TV, Zia Mohyeddin, presented a program in Los Angeles in 1996, alternating Urdu verses from Ghalib and Faiz with English recitations from Shakespeare.

Probably not entirely representative of fusion but nonetheless reflecting a mix of cultural traditions is a miscellaneous collection of enthusiasms and practices. This would include (1) South Asian entrants to beauty pageants—not only young women of the second generation or of mixed parentage (e.g., Miss Paramsothy, Irish Sri Lankan American and Miss New York of 1996) but older women who compete in pageants honoring married women (e.g., the Mrs. New Jersey pageant). Here the "showcasing of daughters" and "transfer of ethnicity" analyses applied to *bharatnatyam* seem relevant, and the prize monies can be used for higher education ("for medical school," one can hear the daughters telling their parents). (2) An Indian entrepreneur in Anaheim sells Hallmark Diwali cards, some 98 designs for that Indian festival (*India-West*, Nov. 12, 1993). (3) Certain florists will send flowers to one's mother in any of 87 cities and towns in India for a Mother's Day surprise. (4) The annual Himalayan Fair in Berkeley brings together Nepalese and Bhutanese and mountain-climbers and tourists of many nationalities to sample food and buy handicrafts and clothes from the Himalayas. (5) An innovative entrepreneur has established a company named Wash Wali ("the wash person," in English/Hindi). The company converts one's toilet into a bidet, thus approximating the South Asian splashing-with-water cleaning habit—a conversion that would be particularly useful if one's elderly parents were coming to visit. (6) However, Freddie Singh Bidasha, the "Turban Cowboy" from Yuba City and the first Indian to become a country western singer, is not really a fusion musician; he is a second-generation Punjabi-Mexican-American farmer.

REFERENCES

Abramovitch, Ilana. 1988. "Flushing Bharata-Natyam: Indian Dancers in Queens, N.Y." Conference on South Asia, University of Wisconsin, Madison, Wis.

Balagopal, Sudha Sethu. 1994. "Sound of Music." *India Today*, Dec. 31, 64k.

Ghei, Kiren. 1988. "Hindi Popular Cinema and the Indian American Teenage Dance Experience." Conference on South Asia, University of Wisconsin, Madison, Wis.

———. 1989. "From Bhangra to Kuchipudi: Movement Dimensions of Indian Public Events in Los Angeles." Paper presented at Western Conference of the Association for Asian Studies, California State University, Long Beach, Calif.

Hansen, Kathryn. Forthcoming. "Singing for the Sadguru: Tyagaraja Festivals in North America." In *The Expanding Landscape: South Asians and the Diaspora*, ed. Carla Petievich. Chicago: American Institute of Indian Studies.

India Journal. 1996. Los Angeles, California.

India Today. 1994–1996. Delhi, India, North American edition.

India-West. 1989–1995. Fremont, California.

Melwani, Lavina. 1994. "Migratory Montage." *India Today*, Dec. 15, 60d–f.

———. 1995. "United Tastes of America." *India Today*, Oct. 31, 68b–c.

———. 1996. "Cultural Crossings." *India Today*, July 31, 60b–c.

Murarka, Ramesh. 1991. "On Desi Accents." *India-West*, Sept. 13, 4.

Pakistan Link. 1994. Los Angeles, California.

Shanker, Meenakshi. 1994. "The Annual Pilgrimage." *India Today*, Apr. 30, 44i.

Sri Lanka Express. 1996. Los Angeles, California.

Sundaram, Viji. 1994. "Nurturing Their Passion of Bharatnatyam in the West." *India-West*, July 15, C-49, 68.

Thakkar, Ramesh. 1993. "Transfer of Culture through Arts: The South Asian Experience in North America." In *Ethnicity, Identity, Migration: The South Asian Context*, eds. Milton Israel and N. K. Wagle, 217–37. Toronto: Center for South Asian Studies, University of Toronto.

Tilak, Visi R. 1994. "Route to Roots." *India Today*, Dec. 31, 64c–f.

Yodh, Medha. 1989. "Dance as Communication: Bharata Natyam in Los Angeles." Paper presented at Western Conference of the Association for Asian Studies, California State University, Long Beach, Calif.

6

Keeping the Family Together

FAMILY ISSUES

The owner of a Bangladeshi grocery store leaned over the counter, his face serious. "Here," he said, "100 percent of Bangladeshis get divorced, not like at home." No, of course he didn't mean himself and his wife. "I am not here," he said. "What I mean is, we've only been here five years; we may go back at any time. Those others, who've been here longer or who mean to stay, they're the ones who get divorced." Like him, many South Asian immigrants feel the negative aspects of American life looming so large that they do not really see themselves as "here."

The perception that being in the United States heightens family problems for South Asian immigrants is a common one. At a 1996 International Islamic Unity conference in Los Angeles, a workshop on "Binding the Muslim Family in the West" addressed other ways of dealing with the problems. A woman speaker was especially instructive and provoked a lively discussion. The daughter of an immigrant father, a medical practitioner and an outstanding leader of Islamic women's activities in southern California, she spoke of the need to give serious consideration to marriage, the need for premarital consultation between the partners to ensure compatibility, and the need to write a good marriage contract for both husband and wife, because such contracts are legally binding in U.S. courts. She spoke movingly of two principles to create and preserve a strong Muslim family: respect and flexibility. She said children should be wanted and should always be listened to and shown respect, disciplined firmly but not physically. When young, they need boundaries. Later they need to be given loving autonomy, so they can make choices and take the consequences as they become adults in the United States. Flexibility might be needed with respect to sex roles in the family and society, she said, pointing out that modern educational and occupational patterns, combined with the uncertainties of the larger economy, could mean new roles. Women might play a major economic role; men should be able to accept that and help with domestic chores and childcare. She spoke also about problems of domestic violence and abuse, teenage drug use, sex, and violence, and the need for community support and resources to deal with such problems. Do not deny those who are struggling, she appealed; embrace them—create extended families here by drawing on friends and neighbors. Finally, she said, if problems between husband and wife are damaging the family, there is an Islamic process of arbitration and of peaceful divorce.

A South Asian man in the audience stood up and gave different advice, presenting himself and his wife as successful role models. He exemplifies those first-generation immigrants who think that their family can stand apart, unaffected by the context in which it lives. Be sure to breastfeed your children, he urged; do not neglect this in the name of going out to work. Give your children books and education, plenty of love, and prayers led by the father. Take them back to their home country often. And when you give them orders, tell them this comes from God, not from you, so they must obey. His view was reinforced by pointed questions from a young man to the woman speaker. "Would you spell out what you meant by 'old roles' and how your 'new roles' differ," he asked, "and also tell us clearly what you see as the source of family problems here, internal or external causes?"

The discussion pursued these alternatives vigorously, as American Black Muslim women and others in the audience urged linkages with broader community services as well as mobilization of women, or women and men, within Islamic communities. Again and again the question was raised of relationships between men and women within Muslim families and communities. Should women and men meet separately for conflict resolution and mutual support, or should they meet together, perhaps at a later point in the process? Can mosques be utilized to publicize women's support groups and as meeting places for groups dealing with domestic violence, or are some of them hostile to such activities, too conservative and paternalistic to acknowledge these problems? One woman cited bitterly the recent case of a man known to have beaten his wife unconscious who was nevertheless honored in the local mosque—the brothers should shame such people, not honor them, she said. Can these problems be labeled American and blamed on the wider society, or have they existed within South Asian families but been denied and repressed? Is it not true that the divorce rate is rising in South Asia, too?

These issues are especially sensitive when they concern gender relations within families and communities. Indeed, the issue of divorce is far more controversial among Hindus than among Muslims. Lingering religious ideals discourage divorce and remarriage among Hindus, but these practices have been legal in India for many decades and are steadily rising there. Furthermore, among Hindus there is no tradition of women's consent to marriage or marriage contracts to protect women's interests, as in the Muslim tradition. Issues of divorce and remarriage are made more complicated by appeals to different legal systems and the exercise of legal rights across national borders (e.g., a marriage made in India can be unmade in the United States, perhaps even before the bride is brought over). The complexities and injustices can be overwhelming. The ethnic press has devoted space to domestic abuse, divorce, fraudulent marriage, long-distance divorce, the children of divorce, and single mothers (*India-West*, Mar. 13, 1993, Dec. 9, 1994, Mar. 3, 1995; *India Currents*, June 1993; *India Today*, June 15, 1993; *India Tribune*, June 25, 1994, July 1, 1995).

Such discussions take place in all sorts of meetings held by South Asian immigrants. A young Hindu woman who convened a 1994 conference on South Asian women announced that when she had approached potential funders for the conference, one had refused to give money because there was to be a panel on domestic abuse and violence, which he did not consider a problem among South Asians. Another woman, a Sikh who writes for the ethnic press, recalled her article in the early 1980s on domestic violence and the need for women's shelters. Of all her articles, this drew the biggest response, mostly from South Asian men who denied that there was a problem.

Other family issues relate to the care and disciplining of children, and these too are explosive. Many South Asians argue that their cultures express tenderness and love, as well as discipline, in more physical terms than does American culture. In at least two recent cases, a father's alleged fondling of his child's genitals brought outside intervention, and in one of case Muslim children were taken away and placed in a Christian foster home. (Authorities protested that there were no Muslim families on the foster family rolls. At least one Muslim women's group has recognized this as a problem and is recruiting Muslim families for fostering.)

Most first-generation South Asian immigrants probably do not agree fully with prevailing U.S. definitions of domestic violence or child abuse, and they certainly do not think that society should intervene in family life to the extent of overseeing and regulating expressions of love and punishment. The fact that physical disciplining of children or parental drinking or abuse might result in the children's removal from the family is an unfamiliar and troubling idea for them. Horror stories of such occurences are featured in the South Asian ethnic press in the United States and are related abroad among those contemplating migration.

Another perceived threat to family life in the United States is the more open sexuality. South Asians generally place great emphasis on women's virginity at marriage, a goal achieved by arranged marriage for brides and grooms at fairly young ages in South Asia but achieved more recently by prevention or control of dating. Sexual experience before marriage and the open expression of physical affection between men and women are not condoned. An extreme statement is the donning of the *hijab*, or head scarf, by some young Muslim girls. Many young girls of South Asian parentage do not take up sports that require wearing shorts, feel shy about bathing nude in the girls' locker room, and avoid any kind of physical contact with young men. A father who is proud of his daughter's social success with American classmates will nevertheless be shocked if he sees her sit down briefly on a boy's lap, even in play, and he will probably forbid her to go out with boys unless it is a group activity and he knows the young people.

Homosexuality is another area of concern. Not unknown in South Asian cultures and even sanctioned in specified arenas, homosexuality is nonetheless viewed as a danger to family life by most immigrants and sometimes is opposed on religious grounds. Growing American acceptance of homosexual preferences as a matter of biological fact is resisted, although some South Asian youth have "come out" and become leaders of the gay and lesbian movement at local and national levels. Most South Asian parents view homosexuality as a chosen life-style, an undesirable indulgence of individual freedom in the United States. That view is reflected in the annual battles over whether or not the Federation of Indian Associations should include the South Asian Lesbian and Gays Association, which marches in the New York City Gay Pride Parade but has been denied a place in the India Day parade there (*India Today*, Aug. 15, 1995: 60p).

Similarly, South Asian parents may see "Western women's liberation" as a threat to the family. Leaving aside the seemingly unlikely possibility of one's own daughter voluntarily engaging in premarital sexual behavior, some parents analyze the feminist movement as encouraging criminal acts against women. One father earnestly explained, "Walking about, dating, going in the dark, this leads to rape and worse." On the subject of feminism, he said, "But don't you believe that a woman is by nature delicate, a flower, not to be opened to the public?" Parents want their daughters to be well educated, and many encourage them to pursue careers, but particularly among Muslims there may be ambivalence about unrestrained mixing with men, even for purposes of the job. Among most immigrants, modesty is enjoined for daughters; and among Muslims, daughters might put on the *hijab*, or head scarf, when they become teenagers.

The *hijab* is worn by some Muslim women but not by most, because it is not Quranic in origin but a later cultural imposition in some Muslim countries (principally in Iran). Yet South Asian leaders of some mosques and Islamic centers are teaching that the *hijab* is mandatory, perhaps as a defense against conditions in the United States that they see as threatening to their young women. When they encourage or mandate Islamic attire, it applies to women; there is no agreement on what Islamic attire for men might be, other than modest.

Another aspect of American family values that troubles many South Asian immigrants is the apparent isolation of small nuclear families and a related "neglect of the elderly." In talk and in articles in the ethnic press, immigrants express harsh judgments about American family life, comparing the "Western nuclear family" and the "Eastern extended family" and exhorting fellow community members to maintain traditional South Asian family values. Misunderstandings abound in this as in other areas of family life. There is an unmistakable correlation between material progress in societies and expanding opportunities for individuals (for women, this can mean divorce). Despite this, and despite state policies that affect households in the United States differently than those in South Asia, the married-couple household is the norm and roughly 70 percent of all children in the United States live in families with two parents (*Economist*, Sept. 9, 1995: 19). Moreover, there is some nostalgia in the West for the extended family—although family is easily confused with the extended household, which was hard to achieve before the demographic increase in numbers of parents and siblings surviving to old age and adulthood. The same empirical reality characterizes the Asian past. In India, too, the extended family was the ideal; but most households were actually of about the same size—just over five persons—as those in England in the past (Laslett 1966; Anderson 1971; Kolenda 1968). Now, as Asian nations undergo a demographic transition and young career people experience the occupational and residential mobility that has scattered members of American extended families far from each other, initial impressions of sharp East-West contrasts should be adjusted.

I, writing as an anthropologist brought up in American culture, would argue that in the United States, too, families still emphasize love and support, although they may show this differently than South Asian families do. For example, close friends and neighbors may be incorporated into the places filled by members of an extended family in former days. Again, South Asian immigrant families are not slow in turning to friends and neighbors if they find themselves far from relatives in the United States; and if there are no Hyderabadi Muslims nearby, Gujarati Hindus will do, or even Euro-American Jews!

In terms of respect for the elderly, there are some real differences. In the United States one is taught to respect parents and older people, but part of that respect means honoring their wishes about where they want to live out the end of their lives. American core values that guide people's actions include autonomy and individualism, and these values operate throughout the life cycle. People teach their children to be self-reliant, and the children grow up and move out, establishing households of their own. Parents remain independent as long as possible, not wanting to become "burdens" to their children but also, more important, wanting to retain a sense of themselves as competent and autonomous. Contrary to some South Asian immigrant assumptions, many elderly people in the United States prefer living on their own. Some adult children may spend years urging a widowed mother to move in with them, but the widow resists giving up her own life, her friends and activities, to become a diminished, dependent person. Even nursing homes and senior citizens' homes might be preferred to the homes of children as opportunities to have "a life of one's own."

At a workshop sponsored in 1996 by the Sikh community in Ann Arbor, Michigan, an American woman married to a Sikh described how she presented her widowed mother's situation to her American and Sikh friends. In American culture, she said, the independence of the elderly is the ideal, whereas in Sikh (South Asian) culture it is expected that the elderly will be dependent on their children. When this woman's father died, her mother came to live in her own apartment a mile away from her. She found herself explaining to Indian friends that her mother was within a mile, that she shopped for her and did other things for and with her, that they were very close and talked on a daily basis. To her American friends, she found herself emphasizing that her mother was a mile away, fully self-sufficient with many friends and a full round of activities of her own, and not really dependent on her. This was one and the same mother! The woman's awareness of difference allowed her to stress the positive aspects of the situation as each group would see it.

The "problem" of elderly parents is facing South Asian immigrant families on a global scale, as adult children recognize that they are settled "here" and must either bring their parents over or arrange for their care at a distance. Some elderly parents from South Asia may even develop sympathy for the American point of view after being brought to the United States and settling with one or another child in an American suburb. Sometimes an older parent enjoys taking up childcare and household duties, which harried sons and daughters and their spouses have cut back on in their race for individual fulfillment and material prosperity in the United States. More often, one senses that elderly parents brought to the United States have little choice but to spend their time as babysitters, cooks, and the like, with their own friends and activities left far behind in South Asia or unreachable because of lack of transportation.

The location of love and the balance of commitments within and beyond the family is what concerns South Asian immigrants. They are troubled by the American emphasis on individualism, on marriage based on romantic love, on love between the married couple and for immediate family members rather than on love between parents and children and for extended family members. The more broadly distributed love that has sustained South Asian families across generations and many sets of cousins and "uncles and aunties" seems diminished by the narrower emphases described above. Certainly the American focus on individualism, the freedom to make mistakes and correct them, explains many of the differing values and behaviors (e.g., those centered on divorce) between American society and that desired by recent South Asian immigrants. But instead of constructing stereotypes about "Western" and "Eastern" societies that hinder understanding and mutual appreciation, one needs to see those differences in historical perspective and recognize that the second generation of South Asian immigrants is bridging them.

SECOND-GENERATION IDENTITIES

The children of South Asians being raised in the United States (referred to here as the second generation) are not just Indians, Pakistanis, Nepalese, Sri Lankans, Bangladeshis, and so on. Their parents may think of them in that way, as heirs to an identity that is an extension in space and time of "a prior natural identity rooted in locality and community" (Ferguson and Gupta 1997), but culture proves not to be bounded and portable. Of course, some elements of South Asian culture are now abundantly available in the United States. But these importations or reproductions are rooted in an American context, and the young people, even if they are consumers of South Asian culture in the diaspora, are themselves situated outside of South Asia. They do not share the physical spaces or the sociocultural landscapes romanticized by their parents, and few of them are able to read and write their parents' native languages.

The young people are likely to be citizens of the United States. Given that South Asians generally do not cluster residentially, the youngsters have neighborhood and school friends who link them to the majority culture. They may feel ethnically or racially different from the Euro-American majority, or they may feel less different than other, more racialized minorities. The children locate themselves in the American social landscape, and they are engaged in building new conceptions of personal, ethnic, and national identities in the United States.

For first-generation immigrants from South Asia, "the youth problem" looms large. Many conference sessions, public talks, and private conversations are devoted to issues about the children of South Asian descent being raised in the United States. Parental ambitions for the economic success of their offspring are extremely high. Young people are encouraged to undertake higher education and professional training, particularly in medicine and engineering. (This is an Asian American trend, not just South Asian American: Asian American applications to U.S. medical schools are 18% of the total applications, whereas Asian Americans represented only 2.9% of the population in the United States in the 1990 census [*India-West*, May 28, 1993: 36]). Material security seems to be critical when careers are being considered, and parental expectations and pressures for high achievement can bear heavily on the children.

Parents also stress the retention and transmission of South Asian culture, and first-generation immigrants make many efforts to provide cultural support to their children. In some areas Hindi or Punjabi are offered in school systems at the lower levels. Some communities raise funds to provide language and cultural instruction at universities: the Sikh Studies Chairs at the University of Michigan and at Columbia, the Tamil Chair at the University of California, Berkeley, and the Bengali Chair at Arizona State are examples. Hindu temples have begun holding Graduation Day celebrations (often combined with Father's Day if the dates coincide), and many linguistic and cultural associations make special efforts to attract young people. Gujarati Americans are initiating a boarding school in Gujarat for quality multicultural education of the children of NRIs (Non Resident Indians), and there are other similar projects.

Thus, although they have brought their children to the United States, most South Asian parents have reservations about their children "becoming American." This puts the children in a difficult position, because they are inevitably products of the American cultural context and are comfortable in that context in ways that their parents are not. As one article title indicates, "It Ain't Where You're From, It's Where You're At" (Gilroy 1987), and both parents and youngsters are quite aware of this. One Hindu grandmother from Hyderabad, India, when asked if her grandchildren being brought up in Texas are in any way Hyderabadi, replied despairingly, "Hyderabadi? They're not even Indian," and then cried as she told how her granddaughter asked her to wear some other clothing—specifically not a *sari*—when accompanying her to school. Children at a Sri Lankan fundraising picnic elected to start a baseball game rather than join the cricket game organized by their elders, and a potluck dinner arranged by South Asian Muslim parents included pizzas for the children. An adult son whose elderly parents were visiting from Karachi made a clear statement about his identity by seating his parents and their visitor in a smaller room while he watched the Super Bowl in the main living room. The parents explained that they had sent him to the United States at an early age for schooling, so his manners were not good.

Identities are constructed comparatively in terms of sameness and difference with other individuals and groups in the larger population. In the preceding examples, clothing, sports, and food are marks of difference for the young people. Their own preferences differ from those of their parents. In every family, such expressions of difference signal historical ruptures within the "same" community (Radhakrishnan 1994: 223)—ruptures of personal, ethnic, and national identity between generations. Even as these ruptures are unwelcome, they are recognized. For example, a life insurance ad in an ethnic newspaper appeals for future planning for a pictured family: the traditional parents stand in front, the father in a formal suit, with white hair and spectacles, the mother in a *sari* with a *bindi* (decorative dot) on her forehead and her hair neatly rolled up in a bun; behind them are a son and daughter, the boy informally attired and holding a basketball, the girl, her hair loose, in a blouse and long skirt and holding a small dog on a leash.

The second generation's difference, its participation in American culture in all its contemporary diversity and intensity, is borne out in many ways. A young lawyer whose father worked only in partnership with co-ethnics may himself have a Vietnamese American law partner. At the 1995 (10th) annual Diwali celebration of Indian dealers in gemstones, one small boy impersonated Judge Lance Ito, and others dressed as Lord Krishna or Jawaharlal Nehru. Young women of the second generation are moving beyond the South Asian ethnic beauty contests to compete in more general ones, from Miss Asian America to Miss Iowa and Miss Teen America; Pasadena's Rose Queen in 1994 was the daughter of a Pakistani immigrant. In Chicago, 8- and 10-year-old Indian Muslim girls earned Black Belts in Tae Kwon Do in 1994 (encouraged by a father who is himself a 9th Degree Black Belt and noted teacher). South Asian youth conferences in the 1990s include discussions on Interracial Marriage, South Asians and Hip Hop Culture, Homosexuality, Premarital Sex, and Violence against Women, as well as on Identity Formation, Discrimination in Corporate America, and Racism. At least one newspaper ad for an Indian youth event included a dress code specifying that no jeans, sneakers, or jackets with gang symbols would be allowed. South Asian gangs are now undeniably part of the scene in the United States (*India Today*, May 15, 1996: 60b–c; *India-West*, Sept. 15, 1995: A2, A35–36).

There is a marked contrast, one should note, between the presentation and discussion of generational differences in the Indian and Pakistani ethnic presses. Pakistani Muslim American papers and journals such as *Pakistan Link* and *The Minaret* have columns on Children and the Family, Career Counseling, and occasional special features on the second generation, but these are limited in the range of subject matter and in writings by young people compared to *India Today, India-West, India Tribune, India Currents*, and many others. In the latter publications, Youth Pages or spotlights on youth regularly feature young people writing about dating, homosexuality, marriage out of community, and even living together before marriage. There are humorous observations about first-generation parents and relatives back in India, whereas a typical second-generation quote from the Pakistani press is: "We associate closely with our family traditions rather than the country we're in" (*Pakistan Link*, July 1, 1994: 32).

Actual behavioral patterns among Indians and Pakistanis may not be as different as the preceding examples suggest, but there are no good comparative data. Among the smaller groups, the second generation is still young and less information is available. The Sri Lankan ethnic press is less developed and tends to focus on sports and the conflict in Sri Lanka, whereas the Bangladeshi immigrant press is in Bengali and the Afghan newsletters are in Dari (Persian) and Pushto. Young people in these groups, along with Nepali and Parsi young people, may or may not be encouraged to observe "orthodox" dress and behavior, and the reasons undoubtedly vary from group to group.

Collective expressions of identity can be very different for the members of the first and second generations. Furthermore, the cultural pluralism in the United States offers young South Asians several ways to place themselves. Most South Asian immigrants and their children locate themselves as "white" in America (in Great Britain, they might be engaged in "black" politics), but a minority does see itself as allied with African Americans. The youngsters, even if born in Pakistan or Sri Lanka, can position themselves within the history and culture of the United States and engage in the construction of pan-ethnic groups, building new conceptions of ethnic and national identities in the United States. The term *South Asian American* is itself a new construct, and the formation of such groups is a tentative but growing trend among members of the second generation (the umbrella group "Indus" at the University of California, Berkeley, is an example). South Asian university students may look to the growing Asian American movement for involvement, although their status there is somewhat unclear both to them and to the East and Southeast Asians who constitute most of the members. Muslim American, Buddhist, and Christian associations and coalitions also attract some young South Asians.

At the international level, some organizing efforts reach back to India (e.g., the neo-Hindu movements) or across the world (e.g., the Tamil and Telugu world conferences, Islamic unity conferences). Such movements are dominated by first-generation immigrants, but when the children of immigrants become active in them, they operate in these arenas as Americans. They may have emotional allegiances to their ancestral identities, but their knowledge of those histories and cultures is often comparable to the knowledge of non–South Asian Americans. Ethnic identities become symbolic or situational, just as they have for many Euro-Americans (Waters 1990).

ADOLESCENCE

Growing up in America has not been a uniform experience for youngsters of South Asian descent, but most seem to go through a cycle of early identification with American culture and then, later, identification with South Asian culture. One writer has called this a "second migration" in late adolescence or young adulthood, an emotional return to the ancestral country (Maira 1995: 10). Even after they become more interested in their heritage, these young people do not necessarily regard themselves as part of a larger community of South Asian Americans, and they may identify with a different segment than that of their parents. In one instance, young girls of Pakistani background are studying *bharatnatyam*, the classical dance of Indian and Hindu origin.

However, one writer asserts that what these second-generation South Asians do have in common is "parents who are overinvolved, overworried, overprotective. Parents who have an opinion on every minor life decision, who make demands, impose guilt, withhold approval." She goes on: "We entered the world the axis around which our parents' lives revolved, their source of fulfillment, their contract with the future. . . . As children of immigrants, the promise we fulfill is our parents' own promise, long deferred and transmuted now into the stuff of American dreams (and nightmares). So we must become respectable, make money, buy a house, bear children. . . . My parents' love supports me and enfolds me, but sometimes also weighs me down. . . . Still I carry the burden of their unhappiness." This writer became interested in her Indian heritage, but "as this Indian fire flickered and grew—it shed light on my American self, too. . . . I see that I am in love with the complexity of the American culture I grew up in, and cherish my easy familiarity with it . . . that I love to defend it against detractors, revel in its excesses . . . that after attending many Indian dinner parties . . . I long to be with American friends, because with them I relax and return to myself" (Bhat 1992: 1–6).

It is the young women of South Asian background, not the young men, who are of most concern to their parents. One young Indian Muslim woman wrote, "in my culture, it's O.K. for a man to marry outside our Muslim community, go away to college, stay out at night, do whatever he pleases. A girl, on the other hand, must learn to cook, not say what's on her mind, and repress sexual desires. . . . Moslem boys brought up in America integrate much faster into American society than Muslim girls" (Saba 1992: 8). In a Focus on Youth feature in an ethnic newspaper, a young Hindu woman cited a father who stated that because daughters can get pregnant they are controlled much more strictly than sons, since it is they who can damage the family's reputation. This writer asserted that it was time to face up to the issue of sex in her Indo-American generation, and she quoted a Hindu woman doctor who said that 40 percent of her Indo-American adolescent patients were sexually active. The writer and the doctor both termed the refusal of parents to accept this possibility as "extreme denial" (*India-West* July 30, 1993: 62). Sexuality is a major theme in a powerful new anthology of writings by predominantly young women of South Asian descent in America; the collection treats not only heterosexual feelings and activities but lesbian ones as well (Women of South Asian Descent Collective 1993). Intergenerational conflict and anger are evident in these short stories, poems, and analytical essays, and in recent conferences on South Asian women that address issues such as sexuality, divorce, lesbianism, and physical and verbal abuse of women.

Both the dangers of raising girls in America and the double standard are constantly emphasized in the South Asian ethnic press. During Women's History Month in 1993, a series in *India-West* focused on this (Melwani: 57–58). A young woman said that "one of the healthy aspects of living in America is that you are taught to question and you are taught to think. In

India you don't question your parents, while in the American culture you do."

An illuminating panel on parent-youth dialogue took place in 1996 at a Sikh Studies conference at the University of Michigan, Ann Arbor. This kind of panel occurs all around the United States—a participating parent reported that one had taken place between Pakistani parents and youth in Indianapolis just a week earlier, and the same issues had surfaced. The Sikh youth went first, introducing themselves as Indians and as Sikhs speaking as individuals about their experiences in North America. They carefully explained that their skit involved role playing, that they were not representing their real selves, and that they did not mean to accuse or blame their parents or "uncles and aunties" in the audience. Their goal was to have a dialogue, to open the lines of communication and raise the adults' awareness of the problems as the youth saw them.

The skit was skillfully done and brought out many important issues. One centered on a perceived lack of respect for young adults living at home: parents continued to set curfews and monitor friendships (e.g., reacting negatively when friends of the opposite sex showed up as visitors); the privacy of phone conversations was sometimes violated; parents continued to supervise (i.e., nag about) the daily routines of eating and so forth as though the young adult was still 6 years old. Another issue involved academic achievement and career goals: parents pushed children toward certain professions (medicine and engineering), forcing them into double majors and extra work so that they could study what they were really interested in; parents competed with others in the community, announcing grade point averages and achievements in the local *gurdwara* or other sites almost before the young people knew the results themselves. "There is more to me than grades," one said, "and I work really hard doing the major that makes them happy and the one that makes me happy." They resented the way some parents spoiled their teenagers with gifts of cars and other material items, thereby setting an inappropriate standard, and the way some parents did all the daily tasks for their children, preventing them from learning simple survival tasks such as warming up food in a microwave!

With respect to Punjabi culture and Sikh religion, the young people felt that expectations were too high and parental teachings were inadequate. Although parents want their children to know the Punjabi language and use it on occasion (e.g., quoting poetry at public events), Punjabi often is not spoken in the home. And when questioned about Sikh beliefs and practices, parents are usually unable to explain the reasoning behind them; parents merely insist on their acceptance. The young people want to know the background not just for themselves but so they can explain their religion to others, and they would rather hear their parents say "I don't know" and then make a mutual attempt to find the answers.

The most difficult issues involved dating and marriage. The young people asked for permission to date on several grounds. First, virtually all their friends are allowed to date, and parental prohibition makes them feel different and "backward." Second, parents are needlessly afraid of dating, thinking it means indulgence in sex; parents should recognize a "redefinition" of dating as a range of activities, and they should trust the sense of morality the young people have developed. Dating can involve either couples or groups, and it provides experiences that help people learn about themselves as well as how to interact with members of the opposite sex. A young woman made an eloquent argument that more experience with dating might prevent the divorces they saw among those making "semi-arranged" marriages. She thought the divorces were happening because the husband and wife were inexperienced, got scared, and gave up trying to make the marriage work. "We don't have that mentality to just stay in a marriage regardless, so we leave."

There was some discussion of arranged marriage, and the youngsters insisted that the definition was changing or should change. They were open to arranged marriages because to them it meant not just the exchange of photos and biodata, but initial introductions and then the freedom to get to know the person for some time before making a decision. They indicated that it was hard to meet eligible Sikh youth—the pool was smaller than for Hindus or others. In addition to the Sikh youth camps set up by elders, the youth were setting up university associations and national conferences themselves. "We set up events organized around feminism or whatever, but parents don't let their kids go to these events," one youth said.

The youth on the panel also thought that parental pressure to marry another Sikh complicated dating even when it was allowed. One young man, criticized by an elder for taking a white girl to his prom, replied, "Well, you have a daughter the right age, would you have let me take her?" The parental equation of dating with intended marriage also made it difficult to do things with Sikh friends of the opposite sex, because "uncles" would immediately be calling from India to inquire when they should be planning a trip to the wedding! And even when a young woman had parental support for casual friendships or dates with young Sikh men, if such relationships did not result in marriage, the girl's reputation was sullied in the wider community through the gossip of local "uncles and aunties." Similarly, a divorced woman was not respected in the community, although the end of the marriage may not have been her fault. A plea was made for gender equality and for the extension of real respect and equal opportunity to young women in the Sikh community. The general themes of respect, open communication, and trust dominated all the discussions.

A representative response from the parental point of view appears in the official newsletter of the Association of Nepalis in the Americas, where a mother responded to a charge in an earlier issue that parents were being "overprotective." She said:

> It just shows that we parents care a lot for your welfare and your future. Our definition of love is not just "oh honey I love you" and letting you do whatever you feel like doing. Yes, it might make you happy, but is it good and safe for you? Hey, remember teenagers, America is a land of opportunity, so this is why we chose to raise you here, so that you can realize your individual potentials. But America is also the most violent country in the world. According to one Oprah Winfrey show, every fifteen minutes a teenager is raped or killed. This is why we so-called "protective parents" are extra concerned about the freedom that you all desire. (Khanal 1995: 5)

MAKING MARRIAGES

The generational clash is strongest on the issue of marriage. Some concern comes from religious leaders and organizations, both Hindu and Muslim. This concern is ostensibly about the continuity of family, caste, and community religious traditions; but just as clearly it is about sexuality and marriage, in particular about parental arrangement of marriages and parental control of family life. In a North American edition of *Hinduism Today*, the publisher discussed the threat to Hindu families represented by marriages not arranged by the parents, perhaps marriages with non-Hindus in the United States. Stating (probably overstating) that 80 percent of the young Hindu women in Texas are marrying "outside of Indian tradition," he blamed parents for not arranging marriages early enough, for permitting their children to pursue personal fulfillment rather than fulfillment of duty (Subramuniyaswami 1993). In the *Pakistan Link* a medical doctor presented an Islamic perspective on dating, opposing it on the grounds that it inevitably leads to having sex or to date rape (Athar 1994: 44). This echoes the South Asian parental view of dating as inevitably involving sex, a view that prevailed in a survey of post-1965 Indian immigrants conducted in 1990 (Agarwal 1991: 48–49).

Given the general opposition of South Asian immigrant parents to dating and "love-marriages," it is not surprising that a recent survey of Indian Americans reports that dating and dating preferences are major sources of conflict and stress between young people and their parents (*India-West*, May 24, 1996: B12). Nondisclosure, (i.e., not telling one's parents about dating or other activities) is one way of avoiding or postponing generational conflict. In a book dealing with social issues for second-generation Indian Americans, a young man talks about going with a girl for four years without telling his parents anything about the relationship; in fact, more than half the young people surveyed for that book preferred to date without telling their parents (Agarwal 1991: 50–59, 48–49). Interviewed about the pressures for an arranged marriage, one young woman commented: "A lot of kids just do things and [do] not tell their parents" (*India-West*, Mar. 26, 1993: 57–58). A young man, while saying that guys have it easier than girls, cited a male friend of his who had not told his parents about a girlfriend of three years' standing. "If he tells his parents, his relationship is basically over. Yet, on the other hand, going against his parents is something he does not want to do. It goes against everything he believes in." In the same column, a young woman testified that although most of her friends date, "their parents do not come into play until the relationship is serious. . . . Indian parents have difficulty grasping the concept of a boyfriend-girlfriend relationship. . . . Many Indian parents tend to overanalyze or underestimate the seriousness of their daughters' relationships. . . . I must give credit to Indian parents for being so concerned with their daughters' well being. However, there is a limit. I don't believe in overprotective parenting." She advocated simply bringing a boyfriend into the home and confronting one's parents with the fact of an existing relationship (*India-West*, Sept. 23, 1994: 55).

The management of desire, of sexuality and marriage, is an area of crucial negotiation for second-generation South Asians. As some of the preceding quotes show, they do not want to break with their parents, but they control and limit what their parents learn of their feelings and activities. Trusting themselves, boys and girls both sometimes choose to date secretly, even to marry and keep the marriage secret. A 1994 conference on marriage and family relationships brought sharp exchanges between parents and young people. One father said, "Kids, 99 percent of you lie," and the young people answered by saying they were afraid of parental reactions. The same father talked about "rights and duties" but was answered by "We have a duty to be true to ourselves." Youngsters feel that parents freeze up, stop learning when they migrate, and are often mistaken about conditions that are changing even in South Asia. At this same panel in 1994 the final comment was,

A Pakistani American bride and her newly Muslim American groom with their families, Los Angeles, 1996. Courtesy of Atiya Niazi and Maheen Anderson, Los Angeles, California.

"Kids don't need to be educated. Parents need to be educated" (*India-West*, Oct. 14, 1994: C57).

South Asian young people seem to be saying that parental love is legitimate and should be honored, but that parental power is not—parental power is to be resisted; exercising one's own power is more legitimate. But disclosing one's exercise of power is problematic. In one extreme case, a young South Asian woman has kept the fact of her marriage secret from her own parents for three years now, although she visits them almost every weekend (and this despite her American husband's conversion to Islam). A number of recent films about and by South Asian young people, most notably Gurinder Chadha's acclaimed *Bhaji on the Beach*, also feature love relationships kept secret from parents.

Generally, however, marriages were and are arranged by one's elders, even in the diaspora, and marriages were and are major events in family and community life. In the United States, arrangements made by parents bridge national boundaries to continue family, caste, or religious preferences. In matrimonial advertisements in all the ethnic newspapers, caste, religion, sect, and regional origin are usually specified or implied. Preferences for particular professions or for possession of a green card or U.S. citizenship are often included. Matrimonial ads are placed for Hindus, Muslims, Sikhs, Christians, and Buddhists; and sometimes caste preferences are included for the latter three "casteless" religions. Characteristically, it is parents or older siblings who place these ads, although some men (especially divorced or widowed men) place their own ads. An exchange of information and photographs

Two Pakistani American doctors marry each other, with three American doctors as groomsmen, Los Angeles, California, 1996. Courtesy of Dr. Hameed Khan, Los Angeles, California.

follows. Matrimonial services are springing up within the United States, as stricter regulations and changing immigration laws make it harder to import brides and grooms from South Asia. Sometimes the desired attribute is occupation (there are many couples where both husband and wife are doctors) or "ethnicity" (this may mean nationality, as in Indian or Pakistani, or language, as in Punjabi- or Gujarati- or Sinhala-speakers).

The arranged marriages reflect family strategies, emphasizing the parents' dominance and wisdom and the malleability and dependence of members of the second generation. Although there are now sufficient numbers of South Asian immigrants abroad for marriages to be arranged entirely within the immigrant communities (except perhaps for the Nepalese), often the marriages continue to be arranged with partners back in South Asia. (In the worst such cases, arranged marriages are strategies to assist individuals who want to migrate to the United States, but few families risk their children's happiness to this extent.)

Making transnational marriages does pose problems for marriage-arrangers and potential brides and grooms. People are conscious of the different context in which second-generation South Asians are being raised in the United States. They recognize that those raised here and back in South Asia will have differently contextualized identities and that this brings certain risks to the marriage. Marriages between cousins (practiced primarily by Muslims), essentially within family cultures, can overcome these differences, some say.

Others stress that girls raised in the South Asian countries can adjust. One person said that "American-raised wives are a disaster, they won't sacrifice to those men the way an Indian-brought-up woman will do"; another claimed that "girls brought up in Pakistan in a modern way will adjust themselves anywhere." One man referred to sending U.S.-raised girls back to India as "not a relocation, but a rehabilitation"! The preference is to bring brides from South Asia, but then the girls worry about marrying boys raised in the Western countries. Boys raised in the United States may already have girlfriends, and every young woman knows of friends who have married, migrated, and then found themselves in second place. (The British Punjabi singer Apache Indian remarks on this in his song "Arranged Marriage.") To guard against the possibility of divorce, relatives may serve either as potential spouses or as go-betweens who have the family interest at heart; yet even this does not prevent tragedies.

Perceptions of social distance and national difference engage those who manage the transnational marriage networks. For example, Indians say that it is easier to make marriages between India and Great Britain than between India and the United States. This is because the standard of living in England is lower and South Asians are more segregated there, so it is more like India, whereas in the United States the higher standard of living and greater integration with Americans means a wider gulf between the two ways of life. Also, the U.S. second-generation is said to be Americanizing more rapidly than the second generation in Britain is becoming British, so marriages between India and Britain have a seemingly better chance of success.

Even though the marriage networks have expanded worldwide, parents still want to keep the networks narrow with respect to potential partners. Indeed, according to some young people, immigrant parents are more conservative than those back home. While cousins and girlfriends in India or Sri Lanka are being allowed to date (and even within widening social circles), second-generation young people in the United States may still be marrying within the community according to parental arrangement and in carefully reproduced traditional marriage ceremonies.

WEDDINGS

Most members of the second generation in the United States do seem to be entering arranged marriages, despite complaints to each other and in conference settings. They also play little part in making the actual wedding arrangements. Parents know how many guests they can afford, and it is they who control the guest lists. Many South Asian relatives and friends expect to be invited, and there are usually at least two evenings of festivities including full dinners. The parents pay a great deal for the marriage, from the bride's dowry (yes, even among Muslims now, and even in the United States) to the rituals and dinners. The ideal marriage is a large, lavish, and very public display of the two families and their resources. The dowry may include not only clothing and jewelery but a house, a car, major home furnishings, and even a young man's continuing educational expenses. The guests may number from 300 to 1,300, some of them flown in from South Asia and put up in local hotels. Weddings represent substantial parental investments.

The central, public, and highly celebratory nature of South Asian weddings helps reconcile young people to some degree of marriage arrangement. Often young people get to meet the proposed spouse or spouses and exercise a veto power or choice. And if one does not go along with the choice of spouse made by one's parents, or if one marries against one's parents' wishes, there will be no wonderful wedding, no beautiful photo album, no four- or six-hour video—basically, no parental approval of or investment in the marriage. And that is something no one willingly forfeits. Alternatively, young people are quite aware of problems that can arise after the arranged marriage has been carried out, after the money has been spent on dowry and wedding and honeymoon and house. They know that all marriages do not work out, and they know that divorce is an option. If the child has trusted the parents and gone through with a recommended marriage, in exchange the parents may now support the child; their love for the child may triumph over the lifelong commitment to a badly made marriage that would have been endured in South Asia. Nonetheless, these hard decisions cause pain and suffering in South Asian immigrant families when they must be made.

A somewhat fuller description of South Asian weddings will give a better sense of the gender and generational balances of power in these diasporic communities. The weddings of Hindus and Muslims take several days and include rituals and dinners at both homes and public wedding halls, gardens, or hotels. Many types of traditional clothing, foods, decorations, flowers, and other paraphernalia are involved. Until quite recently, the preferred locations for marriages were back in the South Asian cities, partly because they were major sources of brides for the transnational marriage networks and partly because many relatives and friends still resided there. Also, weddings were held in South Asia because of the availability of necessary supplies and the relatively low cost of holding weddings there. Although it is more costly and difficult to hold Indian, Pakistani, and other weddings in the United States than in, say, Delhi or Karachi, the balance is now tipping toward holding weddings in the United States. A South Asian wedding economy has developed in the last few years in North America, so that weddings can be carried out in, say, Newark, Cleveland, or Houston quite adequately. Families may need to master various national regulations about visas for fiancees, spouses, and wedding guests, but for those with means (and many South Asians have them) almost anything is possible.

Pandits, moulvis, granthis, and priests are available in the United States to perform the various Hindu, Muslim, Sikh, Buddhist, and Christian ceremonies. The marriage ceremonies themselves usually last one or two hours but are preceded and followed by other rituals and festivities. Despite astrological forecasts in some cases, they are scheduled on weekends just prior to a noon or evening meal, for the convenience of guests. Some marriages now make use of English language texts, complete with explanations of text and rituals, whereas others reproduce the ceremonies of the homeland as closely as possible.

Providers of goods and services for weddings are springing up all over. In fact, an annual Indo-Pak Bridal Expo is held in Buena Park, California. Like the first one in 1989, billed as showing "everything needed for an authentic wedding," this Expo is complete with fashion shows and the displays of more than thirty merchants. Ads for horoscope matching ("Astro Scan USA"), wedding *puja* (Hindu worship) items, wedding catering, flower decorations for weddings, Indian-style disposable plates for weddings, wedding jewelry, and the like have joined other ads in the pages of the ethnic newspapers. Weddings provide many opportunities for new ethnic businesses or for the expansion of existing ones, because they give immigrants a chance to demonstrate their success and status in the United States. One very lavish wedding in Malibu, California, was an all-day affair at which food and entertainment were provided for some fifteen hundred guests—the groom came on horseback, champagne was flowing, and a *bhangra* group was brought over from India!

Weddings held in the United States do present some problems, particularly for those who practice forms of gender segregation. The spatial arrangements in American hotels, community halls, or other hired meeting places where weddings are often held are not gendered. In the "function halls" of India or the outdoor tented pavilions of Pakistan, built-in *purdah* arrangements are typical. In the United States, *purdah* must be enforced by those attending, and South Asian immigrant men sometimes try to manage the space. Women had their own spaces and their own ceremonies in South Asia, but they are making space for themselves at weddings in the West. For example, at an Indian Muslim wedding in a Los Angeles hotel, men designated a rear section of the large room (a raised area with a railing around it), as the women's place to sit. However, the women were not satisfied to be so far from the platform where the *nikah* (the actual marriage ceremony, the signing of the contract) was to take place, and they immediately filtered down into the general seating area, taking over the very front rows. Later, as the wedding guests entered the banquet room on another floor, Mexican-American waiters tried to seat all the women on one side of the room and all the men on the other, as they had been ordered to do. But one of the first parties to enter was led by a young wife who had been brought up in the United States. She insisted on sitting at a central table "as a family, family style," and this example was followed by many of the other guests. Thus, a member of the second generation successfully posed "family values" against gender segregation, suggesting a fruitful avenue for negotiation of traditions.

Because many diasporic networks are transnational, weddings are now being scheduled all over the world, and the multicultural considerations become mind-boggling. For example, a young Indian Muslim man who had settled in Phoenix, Arizona, wanted to marry in Kuwait, where the bride and her family were living; but it was too difficult to secure visas for all the guests, so the wedding was held in Karachi, Pakistan, where both families had relatives. In another case the bride and her family were in India, but the groom's family wanted to hold the wedding in Ohio, where most of the relatives on both sides had settled. In this case the Immigration and Naturalization Service, which anxiously checks to be sure a bride and groom know each other well before granting visas to prospective spouses, had to be persuaded to let the fiancee, who "naturally" had not met her intended, come into the country for her wedding! (It was the custom in that family for intended spouses not to meet at all before their weddings.) Rich parents may fly guests over from Bangladesh and put them up for days, whereas those of more modest means settle for holding a reception back in Dhaka, sending just the bride and groom there to be honored by relatives and friends.

There is a strong level of commitment to weddings among those who can afford it, involving numerous instances of travel from California to Toronto, from New Delhi to New Jersey, from Kathmandu to Seattle, from London to Karachi, and so forth, for the weddings of relatives or of the children of friends. In fact, even old childhood friends from the home country are now bridging religious and national boundaries to attend the weddings of each others' children, and the United States is often the site of these reunions. Indian Hindu guests are traveling to Pakistan, and Pakistani and Bangladeshi Muslim ones to India (some for the first time since leaving it), although they do seem to meet most often in a city in the United States, making numerous visits to relatives and friends around the world en route.

In the making and unmaking of marriages for and by members of the second generation of South Asians in the United States, issues of generation, gender, and power come into play in conjunction with migration. Many issues relating to marriage remain to be worked out. Just as second-generation South Asian women in Britain (children of earlier migrations) have emerged as powerful actors, working to constitute and control their own dowries and acting in locally based British patterns of consumption and cultural innovation (Bhachu 1996), South Asian young people in the United States are slowly but surely forging new identities for themselves and envisioning new kinds of marriages and families.

A recent photograph in *India-West*, a South Asian newspaper published in California, stands out: one looks directly into the eyes of a happy young bride. Her address is a California one, and she is seated next to the groom with a dazzling smile on her face (Mar. 18, 1994: 84). Back in South Asia, however, almost all brides—whether in person, on video, or in photo albums—look down modestly and are covered with a veil. The contrast found explicit and amusing confirmation in an account given by an Asian Indian American of her trip to India for her Indian cousin's wedding:

> I had a blast like everyone else, except maybe the bride . . . [who] wore a very distressed look throughout. . . . During the obligatory picture-taking sessions with the 700-plus guests, she did not look up or smile once. I had to bribe her with a 5-Star chocolate to smile when taking a picture with us. Afterwards, she whispered that I would get her in trouble. . . . Even though she was happy about the beginning of her new life, [she] had to act, at the least, modest. But wouldn't it be really neat if Indian women weren't made to feel they had to act in such a way and actually enjoy the most important day of their lives with some overt tranquility and merriment . . . just like the bridegroom? (Singh 1995: 59)

South Asian girls who are born or brought up in the United States are not like the women of their mothers' generation, and they say so in body language and in words. What they do and say is generally positive. However, one second-generation woman trying to understand the first generation's view wrote: "[South Asian] Society is clearly worried about the conduct of women not strictly confined within limited boundaries. It is to perpetuate these boundaries that the arranged marriage system is still strongly encouraged for

Sikh bride and groom in Los Angeles, California, 1988. Courtesy of Dr. and Mrs. Hakam Singh, Bradbury, California.

. . . even Indo-Americans. The concept of a father deciding on a spouse for his daughter with no input from her is *deplorable* [emphasis added]" (Gupta 1994). Taking such negative reactions seriously, many South Asian parents are listening and trying to find a middle ground, helping their children to meet with others of similar background and encouraging them to talk to potential spouses at length about family issues before deciding to marry. They are not ready to trust love-marriages, noting the high rate of divorce in the United States and attributing it to the American way; but they are ready to take the best elements from both systems, balancing attraction, sensibilities, and family guidance, to strengthen their families in the West. The speaker at the Islamic Unity conference cited at the beginning of this chapter proposed such a middle ground, with her emphasis on respect and flexibility in family relationships, and her thoughts were echoed by the Sikh youth in their parent-youth dialogue.

CONCLUSION

We have come full circle. It is time to remember the experiences of the Punjabi pioneers and their Punjabi-Mexican families—experiences that emphasize the flexibility of ethnic identity and respect for diverse cultures. For the new immigrants from South Asia as well, the historical construction of identity is taking place in several social contexts and on several levels, although they connect and overlap. Now the South Asian components of identity are constituted differently than in the past, and the international or transglobal level is far more important. Individuals and families can retain strong connections between old and new homelands, which earlier immigrants found difficult to retain. They can also make reconnections with homelands and relatives from whom they were severed some fifty years ago in 1947, reconstituting a South Asian landscape overseas that the pioneer Punjabis and others experienced as a unified one in the Indian homeland.

Time and place are important components of identity, and both are subject to change. Changes in the historical context have powerful consequences for individual, family, and community identity. The turnabouts in U.S. citizenship and immigration policies in the 1940s and 1960s had dramatic consequences for Punjabi-Mexican family life in California, and the changing global economy and society are having dramatic consequences for the much larger and more diverse population of South Asian immigrants in the United States today. "South Asian" henceforward will have very different meanings in the many places South Asians are now living, and for older and younger South Asians. South Asian culture and identity in the United States must be seen as flexible and be respected in its many incarnations; no constructions or voices should be judged as "inauthentic." Just as identities and communities have been constituted and reconstituted over time in the South Asian homelands, new concepts of identity and community are being produced in the United States by South Asian immigrants and their descendants, and some of these will have consequences back in South Asia.

REFERENCES

Agarwal, Priya. 1991. *Passage from India: Post 1965 Indian Immigrants and Their Children.* Palos Verdes, Calif.: Yuvati Publications.

Anderson, Michael. 1971. *Family Structure in Nineteenth Century Lancashire.* Cambridge: Cambridge University Press.

Athar, Shahid. 1994. "Social Concerns for Muslims in North America." *Pakistan Link*, May 20, 44.

Bhachu, Parminder. 1996. "Multiple Migrants and Multiple Diasporas." In *Explorations in Punjabi Identity*, eds. Pritam Singh and Shinder S. Thandi. Coventry, U.K.: Association for Punjab Studies.

Bhat, Gauri. 1992. "Tending the Flame: Thoughts on Being Indian-American." *COSAW* [Committee on South Asian Women] *Bulletin* 7:3–4, 1–6.

Economist. 1995. Sept. 9, 19.

Ferguson, James, and Akhil Gupta. 1997. "Introduction." In *Culture, Power, Place: Explorations in Critical Anthropology*. Durham, N.C.: Duke University Press.

Gilroy, Paul. 1987. "It Ain't Where You're From, It's Where You're At: The Dialectics of Diasporic Identification." *Third Text* 13: 3–16.

Gupta, Sangeeta. 1994. "Indo-American Women and Divorce." Paper presented at South Asian Women's Conference, Los Angeles, California.

India Currents. 1993. San Jose, California.

India Today. 1993–1996. Delhi, India, North American edition.

India Tribune. 1994–1995. New York, New York.

India-West. 1993–1996. Fremont, California.

Khanal, Jayashree. 1995. "Growing Up in USA—Revisited." *Official Newsletter of the Association of Nepalis in the Americas*, Dec., 5.

Kolenda, Pauline. 1968. "Region, Caste and Family Structure: A Comparative Study of the Indian Joint Family." In *Structure and Change in Indian Society*, eds. Milton Singer and Bernard Cohn, 339–96. Chicago: Aldine Publishing.

Laslett, Peter. 1966. *The World We Have Lost*. New York: Scribner.

Maira, Sunaina. 1995. "Making Room for a Hybrid Space: Reconsidering Second-Generation Ethnic Identity." *Sanskriti, a Bimonthly Publication of Progressive South Asian Politics* 6:1, 6, 10–11.

Melwani, Lavina. 1993. "Voices of a New Generation." *India-West*, Mar. 26, 49, 57–58.

Minaret. 1994–1996. Los Angeles, California.

Pakistan Link. 1994–1996. Los Angeles, California.

Radhakrishnan, R. 1994. "Is the Ethnic 'Authentic' in the Diaspora?" In *The State of Asian America*, ed. Karin Aguilar-San Juan, 219–23. Boston: South End Press.

Saba. 1992. "Reflections of a Young Feminist." *COSAW Bulletin* 7:3–4, 8.

Singh, Mona. 1995. "Oh Darling, Yeh Hai India." *India-West*, Feb. 3, 59.

Subramuniyaswami, Satguru Sivaya. 1993. "When It Is Too Late to Say, 'No.' " *Hinduism Today*, June.

Waters, Mary C. 1990. *Ethnic Options: Choosing Identities in America*. Berkeley: University of California Press.

Women of South Asian Descent Collective, eds. 1993. *Our Feet Walk the Sky: Women of the South Asian Diaspora*. San Francisco: Aunt Lute Books.

Appendix I: Migration Statistics

Year of Admission to United States	India	Pakistan	Bangladesh	Sri Lanka	Afghanistan
1946–1964	6,319	1,310[a]			
1965	582	187			
1966	2,458	347			
1967	4,642	646			
1968	4,682	673			
1969	5,963	851			
1970	10,114	1,528		242	
1971	14,317	2,125		180	
1972	16,929	2,480		306	
1973	13,128	2,525	154	455	
1974	12,795	2,570	147	379	
1975	15,785	2,620	404	432	
1976	17,500	2,888	590	411	
1977[b]	23,208	3,931	762	475	
1978	20,772	3,876	716	375	180
1979	19,717	3,967	549	397	353
1980	22,607	4,265	532	397	722
1981	21,522	5,288	756	448	1,881

Year of Admission to United States	India	Pakistan	Bangladesh	Sri Lanka	Afghanistan
1982	21,738	4,536	639	505	1,569
1983	25,451	4,807	787	472	2,566
1984	24,964	5,509	823	554	3,222
1985	26,026	5,744	1,146	553	2,794
1986	26,277	5,994	1,634	596	2,831
1987	27,803	6,319	1,649	630	2,424
1988	26,268	5,438	1,325	634	2,873
1989	31,175	8,000	2,180	757	3,232
1990	30,667	9,729	4,252	976	3,187
1991	45,064	20,355	10,676	1,377	2,879
1992	36,755	10,214	3,740	1,081	2,685
1993	40,121	8,927	3,291	1,109	2,964
1994	34,921	8,698	3,434	989	2,344

[a]Data for 1954–1964 only.

[b]Data for 1977 include the transition quarter (July 1, 1976–September 30, 1976) and therefore cover the fifteen months ending on September 30, 1977.

Sources: Adapted from Urmila Minocha, "South Asian Immigrants: Trends and Impacts on the Sending and Receiving Societies," in *Pacific Bridges: The New Immigration from Asia and the Pacific Islands*, eds. James T. Fawcett and Benjamin V. Carino (New York: Center for Migration Studies, 1987), p. 348; and *Statistical Yearbooks of the INS*, 1988 and 1994 (Washington, D.C.: U.S. Government Printing Office, 1989 and 1995, respectively).

Appendix II: Census Statistics

	Countries of Origin*			
Year of Census	**Bangladesh**	**India**	**Pakistan**	**Sri Lanka**
1980	1,314	387,223	15,792	2,923
1990	11,838	815,447	81,371	10,970

*Afghanistan, Bhutan, and Nepal are not listed. Before 1970, Bangladesh and Pakistan were counted together; before 1947, they were counted with India. For statistics on Asian Indians in earlier censuses, see Table 3.1.

Source: U.S. Bureau of the Census, *1990 Census of the Population, General Population Characteristics of the U.S.*, Vol. 1 (Washington, D.C.: U.S. Government Printing Office, 1992), p. 3.

Appendix III: Noted South Asian Americans

Chandrasekhar, Subrahmanyan (Oct. 19, 1910–Aug. 21, 1995). An Indian-born astrophysicist and educator, Chandrasekhar became a U.S. citizen in 1953. He had come to the University of Chicago in 1936–1937 after spending seven years at Cambridge in the United Kingdom. He won the Nobel Prize in Physics in 1983 for his stellar research, particularly his study of white dwarfs that laid the groundwork for the discovery of black holes. Some of his many books on astronomy and physics are used today as basic college texts.

Chopra, Deepak (ca. 1947–). Born in Delhi, India, and a graduate of the All-India Institute of Medical Sciences there, Chopra came to the United States in 1970 and became chief of staff of a Boston-area hospital. He resigned in 1985 to promote Ayurveda, an Indian system of holistic healing. His many books (including *Creating Health, Quantum Healing,* and *Perfect Health*) on the mind/body connection have found a wide audience.

Khan, Ali Akbar (Apr. 14, 1922–). Born in Bengal, India, the son of the noted musician Allauddin Khan, Ali Akbar Khan is most noted as a player of the *sarod,* a stringed instrument. Following a prestigious career in India, he took a faculty position at McGill University, Canada, from 1959 to 1961 and then moved to the United States. In 1967 he founded the Ali Akbar College of Music in Marin County, California, where students are trained in Indian music and dance.

Khan, Fazlur Rahman (Apr. 3, 1929–Mar. 27, 1982). Born in Dhaka (now Bangladesh), Khan came to the United States on a Fulbright scholarship to the University of Illinois and became a structural engineer and architect. He designed the famous Sears Tower in Chicago.

Khorana, Har Gobind (Jan. 9, 1922–). Born in India, Khorana studied in the Punjab, Liverpool, Zurich, and Cambridge; then moved to Vancouver, Canada, in 1952; to the University of Wisconsin in 1960; and to the Massachusetts Institute of Technology in 1971. A molecular chemist, he synthesized the first gene in 1970, building on his work on nucleotide synthesis. Khorana shared the Nobel Prize in Medicine in 1968, and in 1987 he was awarded the U.S. National Medal of Science.

Mehta, Ved Parkash (Mar. 21, 1934–). Born in Lahore, India (now Pakistan), Mehta became a U.S. citizen in 1975. Blinded by meningitis at age 4, he studied at the Arkansas School for the Blind in Little Rock, Arkansas, and went on to Pomona College, California; Balliol College in Oxford, England; and Harvard University. He has been a staff writer for the *New Yorker* magazine since 1961 and has written many books, of which the autobiographical *Face to Face* and *Daddyji* are perhaps best known. His film *Chachaji, My Poor Relation* is also widely known. Winner of a John D. and Catherine T. MacArthur Foundation fellowship from 1982 to 1987, he has held many other grants, awards, and visiting professorships as well.

Menon, Vijaya Bhaskar (May 29, 1934–). A recording and entertainment company executive, Menon was born in Trivandrum, Kerala, India. After earning an M.A. at Oxford, England, in 1956, he became an executive in London and then in the United States, serving as chairman and chief executive of Capitol Records and EMI Music Worldwide from 1971 to 1990. From his home in California, he continues to exercise influence on the satellite communications industry as it develops transnationally.

Mukherjee, Bharati (July 27, 1940–). Calcutta-born, Mukherjee came to the United States by way of Canada (1968–1978), having gone in 1948 to the United Kingdom and then to the Writer's Workshop at the University of Iowa in 1961. In 1980 she became a naturalized U.S. citizen. She is now on the faculty at the University of California, Berkeley. Her writing has won many awards; among the best known of her novels are *Wife* and *Jasmine.*

Ponnamperuma, Cyril (Oct. 16, 1923–Dec. 20, 1994). Born in Ceylon, he received degrees from the University of Madras, the University of London, and the University of California, Berkeley (the latter a Ph.D. in chemistry in 1962). A professor of chemistry at the University of Maryland for most of his career, he analyzed soils from the moon landing in the U.S. Apollo program and received many national and international awards.

Qureshey, Safi U. (Feb. 15, 1951–). Born in Karachi, Pakistan, Qureshey came to the University of Texas, Austin, and earned a degree in electrical engineering in 1975. He went on to found AST Research Inc. with Thomas Yuen and Albert Wong, from Hong Kong, in 1980. This high-technology consulting firm was a leader in the production of computer products and computers, one of many electronic engineering success stories in which South Asians have been involved.

Ramanujan, Attipat Krishnaswami (Mar. 16, 1929–July 13, 1993). Born in Mysore, India, Ramanujan came to Indiana University for his Ph.D. and served as a professor of linguistics and Dravidian studies at the University of Chicago from 1962 until his death. An author, translator, and poet in Kannada, Tamil, and English, he published books including *The Striders, Speaking of Siva*, and *Hymns for the Drowning.*

Saund, Dalip Singh (1899–Apr. 22, 1973). Born in India's Punjab province, Saund was the first Asian American elected to Congress. With a B.A. from the University of the Punjab in 1919, Saund earned a Ph.D. in mathematics at the University of California, Berkeley, in 1924. He went into farming in southern California and was active in his Westmoreland community Toastmasters Club, the Imperial Valley Democratic Central Committee, and others. He became a citizen in 1949, was elected justice of the peace for Westmoreland Township, and then congressman from the 29th District, House of Representatives, in 1956 from Imperial and Riverside Counties, California. He served in Congress from 1957 to 1963.

Sidhwa, Bapsi N. (Aug. 4, 1938–). A Parsi from Lahore, Pakistan, Sidhwa received her B.A. from Kinnaird College for Women, Lahore, in 1956. She subsequently became a naturalized citizen of the United States, where she has been a visiting literature professor at Columbia University, Rice University, the University of Houston, and Mount Holyoke College. Among her four novels are *The Bride* and *Cracking India.* She has received awards for her writing from the United States, Pakistan, and Germany.

Singh, Inder (Oct. 1, 1935–). Born in India's Punjab province, Singh came to the United States in 1968 and received an M.S. in management science; he became a U.S. citizen in 1976 and now is a computer software company executive. A political leader within the Indian community, he currently chairs the Board of Trustees of the National Federation of Indian American Associations (from 1992). He served for many years as officer of the Indian American Forum for Political Education and Indian Associations of Southern California; he has also been nationally prominent as an Asian American leader for the Republican Party.

Spivak, Gayatri Chakravorti (Feb. 24, 1942–). Calcutta-born, Spivak came to Cornell University and earned an M.A. and a Ph.D. in comparative literature in 1967; she is now a professor at Columbia University. She is an authority on Yeats and a translater of Jacques Derrida. Her writings on French poststructuralism, modernism, and French and international feminism have made her one of the most influential critics and educators in the interdisciplinary field of cultural studies.

Vaid, Urvashi Vaid (1958–). Having immigrated from India with her parents at the age of 7 or 8, Vaid graduated from Vassar and Northeastern University Law School in Boston, worked for the American Civil Liberties Union, and then became media director for the National Gay and Lesbian Task Force (NGLTF). She served as executive director of the NGLTF from the late 1980s to the early 1990s. Selected by *Time* magazine in December 1994 as one of 100 young people changing the history of our generation, she is now a writer in Massachusetts. Her book *Virtual Equality: The Mainstreaming of Gay and Lesbian Liberation* was published in 1995.

Glossary

ahimsa Sanskrit for non-violence, concept from Hinduism and Jainism developed by Gandhi in India's nationalist movement against British rule

arangetram debut dance recital of a bharatnatyam classical South Indian dancer

Aryan linguistic term for the speakers of Indo-Iranian languages, those Indo-European languages based in central Asia and eastern Europe

atman Sanskrit for individual soul or self

avatar Sanskrit for form or incarnation

baila Sri Lankan dance music of Spanish/Portuguese origin

Bhagavad Gita poem in the Mahabharata epic, a dialogue between Krishna and Arjuna written between 200 B.C.E. and 200 C.E.; early bhakti or devotional text in Hinduism

bhakti devotion; the path of devotion, love, and faith in Hinduism, in contrast to those of jnana (knowledge) and karma (works or actions)

bhangra vigorous traditionally male Punjabi peasant folk dance

bharatnatyam classical South Indian Hindu dance

bindi decorative dot or beauty mark worn by South Asian women on the forehead

bodhicari student or lay minister in Buddhist tradition

Brahman name of the highest caste category (varna) of priests in Hinduism; also the name of the universal soul or supreme godhead

Carnatic South Indian, stemming from the region around Madras (now renamed Chennai)

darshan sacred sight or blessing, bestowed by an image or living guru

desi Hindustani for "country" or "rustic," as in ABCDs (American-born confused desis) for second-generation Indian Americans

dharma one's obligations or duties in life; in Hinduism, determined by one's status in the varna or caste system

Diwan Persian term for Prime Minister, in Mughal Empire and later

dowry gifts, often including money, given with the bride to the groom in many South Asian marriage systems

Dravidian the family of the four South Indian languages: Telugu, Tamil, Kannada, and Malayalam

endogamy marriage within, for example within one's caste or village; opposed to exogamy, or marriage outside a given boundary

Granth Sahib Sikh sacred scriptures, written in Gurumukhi script

granthi Sikh religious specialist, teacher, or singer of hymns

gurdwara Sikh term for place of worship, temple

hajj pilgrimage to Mecca, sacred center of Islam

halal ritually pure food for Muslims, i.e., meat slaughtered according to Islamic law

Harijan children of god, Hindi term for Untouchables developed by Gandhi during India's nationalist movement against British rule

hijab head scarf worn by some Muslim women as a form of purdah; not indigenous to South Asia

Hindi Hindustani, an Indo-Aryan north Indian language written in Sanskrit script; the national language of India

Hindu earlier, a person from India, from Hindustan; follower of the Hindu religion

Hinduism inclusive term for the diverse religious beliefs and practices evolving in India based upon the Sanskrit Vedas, later Brahmanical writings, and many indigenous traditions

Hindustani North Indian, stemming from Mughlai or Indo-Muslim culture

Id observance of the end of fasting in Islam, particularly of the annual month-long Ramadan fast

Indo-Aryan a linguistic term, branch of the Indo-European language family from which Sanskrit and the North Indian languages are derived

jati Hindustani word derived from Portuguese for caste or endogamous group

jizya a tax supposed to be collected by Islamic rulers from non-Muslims, seldom enforced by Mughal rulers in India

jnana knowledge; the path of knowledge in Hinduism in contrast to those of karma (ritual actions) or bhakti (devotion)

karma actions that carry out one's dharma or duty in life and that determine one's status in the next life; the path of discipline or actions, in contrast to those of bhakti (devotion) and jnana (knowledge)

kathak style of North Indian classical dance

kirpan small knife carried by initiated Sikhs; symbolic sword, not to be used as a weapon

Krishna major god in Hinduism, an avatar or form of Vishnu; favorite forms are the baby Krishna and the lover Krishna

moksha Sanskritic or Hindu term for release from samsara or the cycle of reincarnation

moulvi Islamic clergyman, religious teacher

Mughlai the synthesis of court and popular culture developed under the Mughal emperors of India; also, Hindustani or Indo-Muslim

muhajir exile, refugee, or outsider; term used in Pakistan for those who migrated from India after 1947

mujra North Indian dance style associated with professional dancing girls or prostitutes

mukti Sanskritic or Hindu term for release from samsara, the cycle of reincarnation

mushaira recitation of Urdu or Persian poetry, associated with Mughlai culture in India

nikah the offical wedding ceremony in Islam, the signing of the marriage contract

nirvana Sanskritic or Buddhist term for release from samsara, the cycle of reincarnation

Pali Indo-Aryan language in which earliest Buddhist texts of Sri Lanka are written

pandit Hindu temple or domestic priest

polyandry marriage of one woman and more than one man

polygyny marriage of one man and more than one woman

prasad food that has been blessed by a form of divinity, distributed to worshippers in Hindu and Sikh temples and gurdwaras

puja worship of an image in a home, temple, or shrine, characteristic of devotional or later Hinduism

Punjab area where Punjabi is spoken, centered on the Indus river valley; "five waters" or rivers, from *panch* (Hindi) or *panj* (Punjabi) *ab* (Persian)

purdah the segregation of men and women in both Hinduism and Islam, usually accomplished by the seclusion or covering of women by a head scarf or fuller garment

qawwali musical performance of Sufi mystical poetry, usually by a band of qawwali singers

Quran the holy book of Islam, Arabic poetry; Allah's revelation to the Prophet Muhammad

raga scale or melody form, each with a particular compositional theme or mood, in Indian classical music (both Hindustani and Carnatic)

Ramayana Hindu epic centered upon the king, Rama; his wife, Sita; and his brother, Lakshman; source of popular values concerning marriage, family, and citizenship

roti North Indian bread

salwar-kameez shirt and trouser outfit for women, of Punjabi origin

samsara cycle of reincarnation, of life, death, and rebirth; transmigration of the soul from one life to another

Sanskrit Indo-Aryan language in which the oldest texts of Hinduism are written, such as the Vedas and the Upanishads

sanyasi the fourth stage of life in Hinduism, that of the religious mendicant, the seeker of salvation

sari traditional Indian women's clothing, six or eight yard cloth length

sarod stringed instrument in Indian classical music

sati Sanskrit for virtuous woman or wife; the (rare) Hindu practice of burning a widow on her husband's funeral pyre

satyagraha Sanskrit for grasping the truth or truth force, developed by Gandhi in India's nationalist movement against British rule

sepoy Indian term for soldier trained in the European manner; the sepoy mutiny or first war of independence in 1857 began as a soldier's revolt against British rule

Shakti female divine energy or power; major goddesses in Hinduism such as Devi, Durga, Saraswati,and Parvati

Shia a major branch of Islam, supporters of the Prophet's son-in-law Ali as Muhammad's true successor and their first Imam (leader); division stemming from the battle of Karbala, Iraq, in 682 C.E.

Shiva a major god and consort of the powerful goddesses in Hinduism, often represented as an ascetic or engaged in the dance of destruction; followers of Shiva are termed Shaivas

Sikhism religion evolving from about 1500 C.E. from bhakti and Sufi teachings in India's Punjab during Mughal times under ten successive Sikh gurus

Sinhala Indo-Aryan language of Sri Lanka or Ceylon

sitar long-necked stringed instrument in Indian classical music

Sufi mystical branch within Sunni Islam, stressing devotional teachings, poetry, and music

Sunni dominant branch of Islam, followers of the Sunna or traditions; supporters of the historical Caliphs or political leaders of the Muslim community from the time of the Prophet

swaraj Sanskrit for self-rule, developed by Gandhi in India's nationalist movement against British rule

tabla pair of small drums played by hand in Indian classical music

Upanishads Sanskrit texts of speculative Hindu philosophy

Urdu Hindustani in Perso-Arabic script, an Indo-Aryan language developed in the Deccan and North India; the national language of Pakistan

varna Sanskrit for caste category: the four traditional Hindu varnas are Brahman (priest), Kshatriya (warrior/ruler), Vaisya (merchant/trader), and Sudra (artisan/peasant); the Untouchables are a fifth varna

Vedas the oldest texts of Brahmanical Hinduism, Sanskrit verses to accompany the performance of sacrifices by Brahman priests

vihara Buddhist term for place of worship, temple

Vishnu a major god in Hinduism, whose many forms include Rama and Krishna; followers of Vishnu are termed Vaishnavas

Bibliography of Recommended Reading

CHAPTER 1

Agarwal, Bina. 1994. *A Field of One's Own: Gender and Land Rights in South Asia.* Cambridge: Cambridge University Press.

Ahmad, Aziz. 1964. *Studies in Islamic Culture in the Indian Environment.* Oxford: Clarendon Press.

Arasanayagam, Jean. 1995. *All Is Burning.* New Delhi: Penguin Books India.

Basham, Arthur Llewellyn. 1963. *The Wonder That Was India: A Survey of the Culture of the Indian Subcontinent before the Coming of the Muslims.* London: Sidgwick & Jackson.

Bayly, C. A. 1983. *Rulers, Townsmen, and Bazaars: North Indian Society in the Age of British Expansion, 1770–1870.* New York: Cambridge University Press.

Boserup, Ester. 1970. *Women and World Development.* New York: St. Martin's Press.

Chand, Tara. 1963. *Influence of Islam on Indian Culture.* Allahabad: Indian Press.

Chatterjee, Partha. 1986. *Nationalist Thought and the Colonial World: A Derivative Discourse.* London: Zed Books.

———. 1993. *The Nation and Its Fragments: Colonial and Post Colonial Histories.* Princeton: Princeton University Press.

Cohn, Bernard S. 1996. *Colonialism and Its Forms of Knowledge: The British in India.* Princeton: Princeton University Press.

de Bary, William Theodore, ed. 1958. *Sources of Indian Tradition.* New York: Columbia University Press.

Duncan, Emma. 1988. *Breaking the Curfew.* London: Michael Joseph.

Eaton, Richard Maxwell. 1993. *The Rise of Islam and the Bengal Frontier, 1204–1760.* Berkeley: University of California Press.

Eck, Diana. 1981. *Darshan: Seeing the Divine in India.* Chambersburg, Pa.: Anima Press.

Gandhi, Mohandas Karamchand. 1959. *An Autobiography, or the Story of My Experiments with Truth.* Ahmedabad: Navajivan Publishing House.

Guha Ranajit, ed. 1994. *Subaltern Studies I: Writings on South Asian History and Society.* Delhi: Oxford University Press.

Jalal, Ayesha. 1995. *Democracy and Authoritarianism in South Asia: A Comparative Perspective.* New York: Cambridge University Press.

Kolenda, Pauline. 1978. *Caste in Contemporary India: Beyond Organic Solidarity.* Menlo Park, Calif.: Benjamin Cummings.

Lamb, Christine. 1991. *Waiting for Allah: Pakistan's Struggle for Democracy.* Calcutta: Viking.

Nandy, Ashis. 1983. *The Intimate Enemy: Loss and Recovery of Self under Colonialism.* Delhi: Oxford University Press.

Oberoi, Harjot. 1994. *The Construction of Religious Boundaries: Culture, Identity, and Diversity.* Oxford: Oxford University Press.

Rao, Raja. 1963. *Kanthapura.* New York: New Directions.

Roy, Asim. 1996. *Islam in South Asia: A Regional Perspective.* New Delhi: South Asian Publishing.

Said, Edward. 1993. *Culture and Imperialism.* New York: Knopf.

Sangari, Kumkum, and Sudesh Vaid. 1990. *Recasting Women: Essays in Indian Colonial History.* New Brunswick, N.J.: Rutgers University Press.

Schwartzberg, Joseph E., ed. 1978. *A Historical Atlas of South Asia.* Chicago: University of Chicago Press.

Singh, Khushwant. 1975. *Train to Pakistan.* Westport, Conn.: Greenwood Press.

Suleri, Sara. 1992. *The Rhetoric of English India.* Chicago: University of Chicago Press.

Van Buitenen, J. A. B. 1959. *Tales of Ancient India.* Chicago: University of Chicago Press.

CHAPTER 2

Chan, Sucheng. 1986. *This Bittersweet Soil: The Chinese in California Agriculture, 1860–1910.* Berkeley: University of California Press.

———. 1991. *Asian Americans: An Interpretive History.* Boston: Twayne.

Jensen, Joan M. 1988. *Passage from India: Asian Indian Immigrants in North America.* New Haven: Yale University Press.

La Brack, Bruce. 1988. *The Sikhs of Northern California, 1904–1975: A Socio-Historical Study.* New York: AMS Press.

Leonard, Karen Isaksen. 1992. *Making Ethnic Choices: California's Punjabi Mexican Americans.* Philadelphia: Temple University Press.

Oberoi, Harjot. 1994. *The Construction of Religious Boundaries: Culture, Identity, and Diversity.* Oxford: Oxford University Press.

Puri, Harish. c. 1983. *Ghadar Movement: Ideology, Organization and Strategy.* Amritsar: Guru Nanak Dev University Press.

Singh, Jane, ed. 1988. *South Asians in North America: An Annotated and Selected Bibliography.* Occasional Paper No. 14. Berkeley: Center for South and Southeast Asia Studies.

CHAPTER 3

Appadurai, Arjun. 1988. "How to Make a National Cuisine: Cookbooks in Contemporary India." *Comparative Studies in Society and History* 30:1, 3–33.

Fisher, M. P. 1980. *The Indians of New York City.* New Delhi: Heritage Publishers.

Gardner, Robert W., Bryant Robey, and Peter C. Smith. 1985. "Asian Americans: Growth, Change and Diversity." *Population Bulletin* 40:4. Washington, D.C.: Population Reference Bureau.

Helweg, A. Wesley, and Usha M. Helweg. 1990. *An Immigrant Success Story: East Indians in America.* Philadelphia: University of Pennsylvania Press.

Hing, Bill Ong. 1993. *Making and Remaking Asian America through Immigration Policy, 1850–1990.* Stanford: Stanford University Press.

Kitano, Harry H. L., and Roger Daniels. 1988. *Asian Americans: Emerging Minorities.* Englewood Cliffs, N.J.: Prentice-Hall.

Saund, Dalip Singh. 1960. *Congressman from India.* New York: E. P. Dutton.

Van der Veer, Peter, ed. 1995. *Nation and Migration: The Politics of Space in the South Asian Diaspora.* Philadelphia: University of Pennsylvania Press.

CHAPTER 4

Ahmed, Leila. 1992. *Women and Gender in Islam: Historical Roots of a Modern Debate.* New Haven, Conn.: Yale University Press.

Eck, Diana, ed. 1997. *On Common Ground: World Religions in America.* CD-ROM. New York: Columbia University Press.

Esposito, John L. 1988. *Islam: The Straight Path.* New York: Oxford University Press.

Fenton, John Y. 1988. *Transplanting Religious Traditions: Asian Indians in America.* New York: Praeger.

———. 1995. *South Asian Religions in the Americas: An Annotated Bibliography of Immigrant Religious Traditions.* Westport, Conn.: Greenwood Press.

Goodwin, Jan. 1995. *Price of Honor: Muslim Women Lift the Veil of Silence on the Islamic World,* 2nd ed. New York: Plume.

Haddad, Yvonne, and Jane Idleman Smith, eds. 1994. *Muslim Communities in North America.* Albany: SUNY Press.

Haddad, Yvonne Yazbeck, and Adair T. Lummis. 1987. *Islamic Values in the United States: A Comparative Study.* New York: Oxford University Press.

Melton, J. Gordon, and Michael Koszegi, eds. 1992. *Islam in North America: A Sourcebook.* New York: Garland.

Richardson, E. Allen. 1985. *East Comes West: Asian Religions and Cultures in North America.* New York: Pilgrim Press.

Williams, Raymond Brady. 1988. *Religions of Immigrants from India and Pakistan: New Threads in the American Tapestry.* New York: Cambridge University Press.

———. 1991. "Asian Indian Muslims in the United States." In *Indian Muslims in North America,* ed. Omar Khalidi. Watertown, Mass.: South Asia Press.

———. 1992. "Sacred Threads of Several Textures." In *A Sacred Thread: Modern Transmission of Hindu Traditions in India and Abroad,* ed. Raymond Brady Williams, 228–57. Chambersburg, Pa.: Anima.

CHAPTER 5

Petievich, Carla, ed. Forthcoming. *The Expanding Landscape: South Asians in the Diaspora.* Chicago: American Institute of Indian Studies.

Rustomji-Kerns, Roshni. 1995. *Living in America: Poetry and Fiction by South Asian American Writers.* San Francisco: Westview Press.

CHAPTER 6

Agarwal, Priya. 1991. *Passage from India: Post 1965 Indian Immigrants and Their Children.* Palos Verdes, Calif.: Yuvati Publications.

Lessinger, Johanna. 1996. *From the Ganges to the Hudson: Indian Immigrants in New York City.* Boston: Allyn and Bacon.

Radhakrishnan, R. 1994. "Is the Ethnic 'Authentic' in the Diaspora?" In *The State of Asian America,* ed. Karin Aguilar-San Juan, 219–23. Boston: South End Press.

Women of South Asian Descent Collective, eds. 1993. *Our Feet Walk the Sky: Women of the South Asian Diaspora.* San Francisco: Aunt Lute Books.

Index

About the Author

KAREN ISAKSEN LEONARD is Professor of Anthropology at the University of California, Irvine, where she specializes in South Asian and Asian American history and culture. She is the author of *Making Ethnic Choices: California's Punjabi Mexican Americans* (1992) and *Social History of an Indian Caste: The Kayasths of Hyderabad* (1978).